AMERICAN POTTERS
AND POTTERY

"Blue Rockingham" and White
Granite, Wm. Brunt, Jr., East
Liverpool, Ohio (1866-1878)
(*center*), Brownware, opaque
cream slip, brown glaze markings
(Mogadore, Ohio, c.1870).

(*Left*) Redware, modeled by
hand, probably Bell Pottery,
Waynesboro, 1833-1880; Redware, Solomon Bell, Winchester,
Va., c.1830; Brownware, Ohio,
c.1870.

(*Right*) Brownware hounds, modeled by hand, unglazed, painted,
Tuscarawas County, Ohio,
c.1860; Brownware, buff glaze,
Eastern Ohio, c.1870-80. (Author's Collection.)

AMERICAN
POTTERS
and
POTTERY

by
JOHN RAMSAY

ILLUSTRATED

TUDOR PUBLISHING CO.
NEW YORK

PRINTED IN THE UNITED STATES OF AMERICA
BY THE COLONIAL PRESS INC., CLINTON, MASS.

FOR

HOMER EATON KEYES

MY ACKNOWLEDGMENT OF THE DEBT
DUE HIM FROM
ALL STUDENTS OF AMERICAN CRAFTS

INTRODUCTION

WRITING this book has been a very pleasant experience. Difficulties of all sorts have been met, and the arrangement of so much heterogeneous material into a clear and readable study brought on several headaches. But it has been, on the whole, interesting work, although the final result is hardly as complete and comprehensive as I would like. The mere listing of twelve hundred makers of pottery, and of a hundred types and variations of the ware, with some description of their technical characteristics and processes of manufacture, threatens to make a rather ponderous tome, so that the complete story of American pottery may have to wait until someone has time and patience to write two more volumes.

If this single volume were meant to be a study of the manufacture of pottery, it would be necessary to preface it with an apology. If it were intended as a history of the pottery industry of the United States, further apologies would be in order. Since I have written from the standpoint of a collector of pottery, both subjects have been considered, but topics of considerable historical and technical significance have been compressed into very small space, because their interest to the collector is slight, while other material, which does interest collectors, has been expanded to what may seem, to others, unreasonable length. Thus "collectible" pottery—its types, manufacture and makers—is considered in detail, while other wares, as well as much early and recent ceramic history, are covered only sketchily.

A great deal of the material included is necessarily a résumé of what has already been published on the subject of American pottery. In this, I have been able to include and correlate much which has appeared only in periodicals, or has been buried in reports and publications not available to the casual reader. Some practical knowledge of the processes of manufacture, and the ownership of several hundred examples of American pottery, plus, of course, thorough examination of hundreds, not to say thousands, more, has helped me to put the technical data into fairly understandable shape. This technical information is really necessary for a thorough knowledge of the subject, but its scientific terminology requires careful translation for the non-technical reader. In this, as in the historical outline, I have been able to add to, and even correct, previously published material, but have tried to do this tactfully. Any reader who knows this previous work will recognize my emendations and corrections, with my authorities for them in important cases, but I have found no reason to write in controversial style.

The two check-lists are possibly the most important sections of the book, and its strongest claim to a place on the collector's shelf. Neither is complete, although that of pottery types must be nearly so. The list of potters and potteries has involved a great deal of work, and still shows unavoidable blanks. But a complete and accurate study of any one of our early potteries includes a tremendous amount of research—historical, genealogical, technical and even archeological. Local records have to be searched for names and dates, and excavation of the site is often the only way to determine the types of ware made there. All this has been done by many investigators, but, after forty years of such work, less than three hundred potteries, many quite unimportant, have been so completely documented. Consequently, I have felt justified in including less definite information on five hundred more.

This check-list has been intended to include the location of each pottery, the name of the owner or potter and his successors, the dates of foundation, of any changes in ownership, and of the final closing. To these facts are added the types of ware made, with any makers' marks used, or any distinguishing characteristics, and such pertinent facts as can be stated briefly, with occasional references to the text. This standard has been impossible to maintain, so all potteries for which approximate dates and production data are available have been included. As it happens, the most difficult date to pin down is that of the final closing of a pottery. So many of them were operated as side lines by farmers or small business men that, unless terminated by fire or flood, they "just petered out" over a period of years.

The list of pottery marks is entirely tentative. The statement "no mark" in the check-list itself means only that no mark used by that maker is known to the writer or the authorities on whom he depends, but there are only a few cases in which this statement can be definite. Absolute it can never be, since the individual potter might always be seized by a whim to inscribe his name on the soft clay of a piece he had just made. Marks in general are the most difficult to locate of all the information I have tried to compile. Most histories, particularly the technical and geological ones, omit any mention of them, so that I have had to depend largely on examination of the ware itself. This again is difficult, since very few potteries marked their entire output, and many, of course, never used any formal mark. On the other hand, the existence of a piece marked with its maker's name is conclusive evidence of his existence, and a number of potters are included in the check-list on that evidence alone.

The information included in the list, and consequently in the text, has come from many sources. Previously published books and articles, which are listed in the bibliography, are naturally the sources for much of it. John Spargo's *Early American Pottery and China* is the most complete from the collector's standpoint, but Ries and Leighton's, Barber's and Jervis' books have also been most helpful. These have been supplemented by many local histories, which usually mention their "first potter", but are distressingly vague about his products and his successors. Again, early directories and the files of old newspapers, usually tedious but in this case fascinating reading, have added many details. Finally, various reports of federal and state Geological Surveys have occasional paragraphs on early potteries, and odd bits of information have been picked up here and there, from marked examples of pottery, local traditions, even old grave-stones. These have been fitted together like picture puzzles, so that the complete history of a particular pottery, given in the text or outlined in the check-list, may have been gathered from half a dozen sources. Exact references to these sources, either in the text or as foot-notes, have been almost entirely omitted, largely because of the amount of space they would require.

This work is, unfortunately, decidedly "spotty", practically complete for some sections of the country, and sadly incomplete in others. This, of course, is due entirely to the amount of research which has been carried on. I have been able to work only in territory which has already been adequately covered, rather than in those states where really important material remains to be developed. Yet the government census of 1840 states that the county in which I have spent four years had eleven potteries in that year. I have been able to locate only six, with two additional possibilities, which seems a fair indication of the extent to which the industry as a whole has been documented. So far as the industry itself is concerned, it has been difficult or impossible to secure information from those connected with it today, either in the field of production or research. Dr. Ries, writing in 1908 after a similar search for material, comments on the "startling lack of knowledge in nearly all quarters", and the same condition seems even more startling thirty years later.

For those sections which are really adequately covered, I have to thank many people. In addition to the books already mentioned, Dr. Stout's monograph on the clay industries of Ohio, Dr. Weygandt's *The Red Hills* and Mr. Belknap's study of the artists and craftsmen of Essex County, Massachusetts have been particularly valuable. For more personal, and more valued assistance, I am greatly indebted to Mrs. Knittle for her contributions on the Ohio potteries; to Mr. Reinert, who has given me more unpublished material than anyone else; and to Dr. Weygandt

INTRODUCTION

again, for material on the eastern Pennsylvania potteries; to Mrs. Buxby for additional data on the long story of the industry in Essex County, and to Dr. Norton for other information on New England; to Mr. Mallory and Mr. Van Huyning for their help in the problem of Southern pottery; and, for additional information, Miss Anna Nixon, Mrs. Charles H. Watkins, Miss Mabel Weber, Mr. George L. Whitlach, Mr. Walter J. Sparks, Mr. J. J. Dronenburg, Mr. George S. McKearin, Mr. Richard C. Smith, Mr. Eugene Houghton, Mr. W. T. B. Gordy. In fact, I have been asking questions about pottery for so many years that I cannot remember all the kindly people I have pestered. I do remember, gratefully, that, while some of those who might reasonably have been expected to show some interest failed me, many others went out of their way to help. Much technical information, as well as historical data, has come from Mr. Reinert, and finally, I very gratefully remember the late Mr. Homer Eaton Keyes, editor of *Antiques,* without whose encouragement and advice this book would never have been written.

TABLE OF CONTENTS

TABLE OF CONTENTS

PART IV

LIST OF ILLUSTRATIONS

(*Top*) "Blue Rockingham" and White Granite, Wm. Brunt, Jr., East Liverpool, Ohio (*1866-1878*); (*center*), Brownware, opaque cream slip, brown glaze markings (*Mogadore, Ohio, c. 1870*).

(*Bottom left*) Redware, modeled by hand, probably Bell Pottery, Waynesboro, 1833-1880; Redware, Solomon Bell, Winchester, Va., c. 1830; Brownware, Ohio, c. 1870.

(*Bottom right*) Brownware hounds, modeled by hand, unglazed, painted, Tuscarawas County, Ohio, c. 1860; Brownware, buff glaze, Eastern Ohio, c. 1870-80 (*Author's Collection*).

(*Frontispiece*)

PART I

CHAPTER I

Definition

THERE are almost as many classifications of clay ware as there are studies of the subject, each criticizing, directly or by implication, its predecessors. Consequently, the introduction of yet another one is undertaken with regret, and only because it appears absolutely necessary. Collectors and students of that type of ceramic ware we know as early American pottery can afford to disregard many differences of definition and terminology in the existing classifications, but find them all extremely vague concerning their especial favorite. Previous writers have detailed the qualities and characteristics of hard and soft paste porcelains, Leeds, Liverpool and Wedgwood earthenwares, rouge flambee and Rose du Barry glazes and other details completely foreign to our simple American ware, and then added insult to injury by slighting that completely. Jervis, in his really excellent *Cyclopaedia of Ceramics*, published for American readers in 1902, devotes one short paragraph out of six hundred and seventy post quarto pages to the slipware pottery of Pennsylvania, and dismisses Dr. Mercer's experiments in that technique with the words, "the whole effort seems one of wasted energy." So it becomes evident that a study of American pottery which is to give a clear picture of the subject must begin with the tiresome detail of setting up specific types.

The previous classifications have neglected this ware so completely that they have given us neither a clear definition nor a specific name for it. Since it is generally spoken of as "pottery" or "American pottery," and those terms are clearly understood in the field of Americana, it seems best to retain them, or, more concisely, "pottery" alone. Yet some authorities, particularly in France, have applied this name to "any receptacle or vessel made of clay," while others draw a distinction between pottery and porcelain.

3

To be specific, the writers first mentioned divide pottery into "china"—a name derived, of course, from the country where the first porcelain originated—earthenware and stoneware. Other writers make only two main divisions according to paste or body, including as porcelain—or china—all wares having white, vitreous and translucent bodies, and as pottery all wares with opaque bodies. Still another school divides all ceramic ware into hard and soft bodies, classing true or hard-paste porcelain, stoneware, and some types of earthenware, such as basalt, jasper and Semi-Porcelain or Hotel Ware together. Their soft-bodied wares then include soft-paste porcelain and "Bone China," most white earthenware, and all our "American pottery" except stoneware, which, it will be noticed, appears in different company in each of the three classifications. In fact, the term is applied today to a type of hard-burned art ware made in Europe which would not be recognized by a collector of American stoneware. To add to this confusion, the general public has always insisted on calling all white tableware, irrespective of its technical composition, "china," whether earthenware or porcelain. Finally, this general public includes many of the historians whose scant references are often the only clues to the existence of early potteries, so that they frequently mention earthenware, and even more explicitly, queensware, when it is evident that they are describing only the crudest type of pottery.

Thus it is necessary to set up our own definitions, which, while open to criticism, may serve at least until better ones are worked out. The simplest and most understandable criterion appears to be the color of the body, that is, of the clay itself, not of any glaze or covering. So pottery, both our American ware and similar ware from other lands, is defined as table, household and storage vessels and utensils, or ornaments, made from colored bodies. These bodies may vary in color from brown through red and salmon to yellow or buff, even deep cream shades. They may be hard and vitreous, as in much stoneware, although never translucent, or may be extremely soft and porous, as in most redware. Incidentally, they are always coarse in texture compared to the average white

4

tableware, and this, with the difference in manufacturing technique, means that pottery is always heavier and thicker than whiteware.

This definition may not have been stated before, but the name "pottery" has been applied so frequently to the ware it describes by English and American authors, that it should be generally understood. It is admittedly less logical than the division of bodies into "hard" and "soft." But this distinction is sometimes difficult for the amateur, and the suggested one has the advantage of holding in one class all the many types generally included in "pottery."

There is another method of classifying ceramic wares, obvious but less reliable, that of "handmade" and "machine-made". These terms are entirely too sweeping, but there is undoubtedly a distinction between those wares which exhibit the maker's own skill and individuality, and those which have been reproduced, completely or in part, by mechanical processes or aids. At first glance, our pottery may seem safely described as the product of manual skill, while white tableware is obviously a factory product. But even the early redware potter, the complete individualist, carrying out every process of manufacture himself, duplicated his plates, bowls and platters on moulds or forms, while whitewares, necessarily reproduced exactly to insure uniformity, and passed through the hands of specialists in several departments, still shows occasional individual touches, particularly in decoration. In general, however, earthenware and porcelain may be considered factory produced wares, while the cruder types of pottery were made by hand. But the types to be defined as "brownware", having a buff or cream body covered by brown glaze, the typical ware of Bennington, East Liverpool and other sections, was made in factories, and reproduced by the use of moulds. Further, many small potteries of the earlier one-man-and-horse type used these same buff bodies, and similar glazes, for cruder handmade ware.

Returning to the preferred division of clay wares according to body colors, those made from white clays or bodies are termed "whitewares" by the trade today. These are then classed as porcelain and earthenware, porcelain, of course, describing vitreous bodies. Earthenware is very generally understood as white or cream bodies which are opaque, even in thin sections, with some absorption of moisture and granular fracture. Strictly speaking, earthenware cannot be vitreous, but, for the sake of convenience, several hard-paste or vitrified, but opaque, bodies may be included, such as "Ironstone" or "Hotel China", and the basalt and jasper wares originated by Wedgewood. These last are apparent contradictions, as is the so-called "Majolica" made late in the nineteenth century, since none of them are white. But the basalt and jasper are actually white bodies colored by the addition of ceramic oxides, while Majolica, under its coating of colored glazes, has a cream body.

In the development of the American ceramic industries, pottery plays a much greater part than whiteware, and it is also of greater interest to the collector. So it is naturally considered in greater detail, but must first be divided into four main classes. The first is redware, which has a comparatively soft, porous and fragile body, softer in many cases than that of any other clay ware. The color ranges from pinkish buff through the common red-brown to an occasional true brown, and it is usually covered by a colorless, soft lead glaze. Similar bodies have been used for fine ware, notably the ancient Greek vases and English lustre, but they have never, because of their fragility, been utilized for tableware.

The second division of pottery, stoneware, shows bodies made from finer, denser bodies, frequently but not invariably burned to vitrification, that is, to the point where no water can be absorbed, and usually showing buff colorings. These bodies are covered by the characteristic salt glaze, secured by throwing common salt into the kiln when the ware is burned. The result is a thin film of glaze, usually with a pebbled or irregular surface and stony lustre. The usual color of salt glaze is light gray, but this may vary to deep cream and shades of buff or grayish tan to dark gray and dark brown.

A third type of pottery was made from very similar clays, burning to the same shades, but covered with brown glazes, so that the term "brownware" seems to describe it best. These brown glazes vary through a wide range, from bright glossy mottled "Rockingham" colorings to dull flat browns, and brownware also appears in many forms, from the simplest cylindrical crock to finely modeled ornaments. The fourth and last type of American pottery is very similar to brownware in body, and appears in simple kitchen and table-ware often made from the same moulds as brownware. But it is covered by clear or colorless glazes, which intensify the buff body to yellow or cane color, so may be christened "yellow-ware."

A more detailed classification or check-list of pottery types is included in a final chapter. This list includes all possible sub-divisions according to form, glaze and decoration, with those few transitional types whose description here would only be confusing. Locations and dates have been attributed to each section, to show the range of time and territory in which they were made, but they cannot be considered absolutely accurate, for reasons which will be detailed farther on. Whitewares are included in the check-list, in order to complete the picture, although they have been covered only sketchily.

CHAPTER II

Technical Notes

THE previous chapter classified American pottery into four clearly distinguished types, differing in body and glaze and, to a certain extent, in age. While we are not certain which of these types was made by the first pottery in the country, that built by Daniel Coxe at Burlington, New Jersey in 1684, or in the earliest Massachusetts, Virginia and New York potteries, we know definitely that the potters of Pennsylvania were making redware, the oldest of the four types, in 1735. Since redware clays are found in all the original colonies, in almost every state of the Union, in fact, this type soon appeared elsewhere. Stoneware, the second type, being stronger and more durable than redware, came into popular favor about 1800, largely supplanting the earlier ware. This again was partially supplanted by brownware and yellowware, since these types were adapted both to factory production and to inexpensive duplication by means of moulds in the ornate designs of the Victorian era. While intermediate types exist, and all four were made simultaneously in some periods and localities, the division is so clear that no alternative classification may be suggested. Redware, however, is much the most interesting of the types, and presents the widest variation in technique. Hence a description of the methods of pottery manufacture must be largely devoted to this type.

The clays used in redware pottery are invariably shales, deposits of which are found at or near the surface of the ground throughout the country. This clay is also used for common red brick. It burns at a low temperature, around 1700° Fahrenheit, to a rather soft and porous body, red-brown in shade, darkening to a sepia brown if the temperature is increased, or showing orange or pink-

8

ish buff tones if the temperature is too low to develop full strength and color. The earliest center of the industry was in the German settlements of Bucks, Montgomery and Chester counties, Pennsylvania, From these counties, the people and their wares spread west and south to Berks, York, Lancaster, Cumberland and Adams counties, through Maryland into the Shenandoah Valley of Virginia. Likewise, occasional enterprising potters migrated to New Jersey, Ohio and even Vermont, invariably leaving traces of their technique wherever they went. An independent but very similar ware was made in early potteries throughout New England, in New York, especially on Long Island, in the Western Reserve and by Moravian settlers in the South.

While over a hundred and fifteen potteries making this colorful ware are recorded between 1750 and 1900 in eastern Pennsylvania alone, some operated by three or four generations of the same family, all the establishments were small. The Bell pottery at Waynesboro, which boasted six potters' wheels, was considered a large plant. Also, many of the potteries of this and other sections were part-time industries. The owner might be a farmer or small trader, making and burning his ware at intervals dictated by demand, other interests, or even the weather, many, called "blue-bird potters," operating only in Summer. In certain cases he might lease his plant to a more experienced potter. Thus the equipment was of the crudest. It included one small kiln, some simple horse-driven machinery, and the all-important throwing or potters' wheel.

The clay, dug from banks or swamps, usually required several months of exposure to the weather to develop full plasticity. It was then ground and mixed with water to the correct consistency for the potter. Occasional wet-pans or ring-pits, shallow circular pits lined with boards or masonry, around which heavy wheels, as much as six feet in diameter, sometimes iron, sometimes stone similar to mill-stones and sometimes nothing more than logs, were driven by horse power, were used for grinding. In some sections, this was replaced by the pug-mill, either a horizontal semi-circular

9

tank in which a shaft set with heavy knives revolved, or a similar shaft in a vertical cylinder like a huge ice cream freezer, with an opening at the base, also horse or pony driven.

From the wet or plastic clay, reduced to an even and smooth consistency by several hours of grinding in wet-pan or pug-mill, and further tempered by repeated pounding with a batter or wooden block rounded on one side, the potter made the great majority of his production, especially all hollow-ware, on the potters' wheel. This wheel, old as history and still in use, consists of a flat disc mounted horizontally on a vertical shaft or spindle, at the base of which a larger wheel was revolved by the operator's foot. More efficient wheels, known as "kick-wheels," had a pedal or treadle for the foot, and even more elaborate ones were driven by a series of belts, which "stepped up" the speed of a vertical wheel four or six feet in diameter, which an assistant or apprentice turned by a crank. The potter placed a lump of his prepared clay on the horizontal disc or wheel, revolved the latter rapidly, and by centrifugal force plus the shaping action of his wetted fingers and thumbs, turned out simple or incredibly complicated forms. The process is nothing less than impossible for the amateur, but is so easy for the trained hand that a good workman could "throw" hundreds of pieces in a day.

The common jar or crock thus fashioned is found in a wide range of shapes, all suited to their particular purpose, but otherwise limited only by the wide bounds of method and period. The ridges left in the soft clay of the shaped piece were removed while it was still on the wheel by a smoother or rib, a small piece of wood or leather with rounded edges and a hole in the center for the potter's thumb, while a small brush of hog bristles finished parts the rib could not reach. Then the jar or other vessel was cut loose from the wheel with a wire about a foot long, with a wooden frame or handles. Separately shaped handles were applied where necessary, spouts or lips pressed into shape, and the piece was removed to a covered shed usually next to the kiln, where the gentle heat it radiated and some circula-

tion of air dried it. For common pie-plates and platters, the clay was flattened on the workman's bench with a wooden rolling-pin, somewhat improved over that of the old-fashioned housewife by the addition of a handle or axle. Then a disc cutter or wooden arm revolving on a pivot or wooden block, with a metal or wooden point on the free end adjustable in a series of holes for the required diameter, cut round shapes, which were then decorated, and later given their convex shape on half-moulds or forms. In the case of the rare modeled or relief decorated ware, moulds of burned but unglazed clay, wood, or, at a rather late date, plaster of Paris, were used, the soft clay being pressed into them.

When a sufficient number of pieces to fill a kiln had been made, and all were perfectly dry, they were glazed. Some authorities quote the use of powdered lead oxide dusted on the surface of the ware, producing a glaze when fused by the heat of the kiln, but a simple lead glaze was commonly used. Professor C. L. Norton of the Massachusetts Institute of Technology gives a typical redware glaze, maturing to a smooth glassy coat at 1700° Fahrenheit, and frequently showing the characteristic crazing, a network of fine surface cracks, due to uneven expansion and contraction of body and glaze. This glaze is,

114 parts	red lead
39 parts	silica sand
10 parts	white clay.

These ingredients, or others having approximately the same chemical composition, in approximately the porportions given, were thoroughly mixed together. For this, the dry materials were placed in a small mixer similar in construction to the pugmill described above, but more like a large old-fashioned coffee-grinder, later supplanted by a pottery jar full of very hard flint pebbles revolving in a frame, the water being added later. Or a small cylindrical wooden pugmill, in which water and the dry materials were placed, was used, the mixing, in either case, being continued for several hours.

Enough water was used with the dry materials to form a smooth liquid mixture with the consistency of thin cream. The bone-dry ware was dipped quickly into a tub of this, so that it received a thin even coating. The glaze was occasionally brushed on, and pie-plates and the interiors of bowls were coated by pouring the glaze into and then out of them. The bottoms and bases of all pieces were invariably left unglazed because any glaze there would, when fused during the burning, "glue" them together and to the kiln floor, so that they would be broken in separating them. Barber, in his *Lead-Glazed Pottery*, states that some pieces were burned unglazed, and then glazed and re-fired, but this refinement was confined to the most elaborate types. Occasionally, too, fine pieces were burned in "saggers" or pottery boxes, to protect them from direct contact with the flame and any impurities it might carry with it, another refinement borrowed from the makers of fine whitewares. Very occasionally, unglazed ware was burned in saggers whose interior walls had received a heavy coating of glaze, sometimes mixed with salt. This glaze was vaporized during burning and deposited on the ware in a thin even film, known as a "smear glaze."

After glazing, the ware was placed in the kiln, set as close together as possible without touching to conserve space. The kiln was built of brick, sometimes reënforced with stone, and was usually quite small. At its simplest, it was rectangular with an arched top, having a single grate, furnace or fire box at one end separated from the body of the kiln by a low wall, and a chimney or stack at the other, so that the flames were drawn through the ware. More efficient kilns, as used in Eastern Pennsylvania, were of the circular "updraft" type, about twelve feet in diameter and eight feet high, with a domed top resembling a flattened beehive. These had two or three small fire-boxes around the outside wall, the flames passing through the kiln to the top. Wood was used for fuel, making a high temperature difficult to secure.

The kiln door was sealed up when it was filled, and it was fired or burned for about thirty hours until the glaze fused to a smooth glassy coat, ending with a period of intense heat when dry pine wood was used as fuel. It was then cooled very slowly to prevent the crazing of the glaze caused by uneven or rapid contraction of the ware. The body itself remained rather soft and porous, and only in the South and Middle West do we find redware burned to a dense and strong texture.

It is easy to understand the wide variation of temperature and burning conditions entailed by this process, so different from the carefully planned uniformity of modern procedure. The color of the body and the texture of the glaze thus produced were then correspondingly varied. In addition, the early potters were naturally limited to rather impure materials from any sources at hand. The glaze might be made from fine white glass sand or from brown river sand. One old potter even records that his first work as a boy was the Saturday morning collection from the town merchants of the sheet lead in which Chinese tea was once wrapped, to be reduced to lead oxide for the glaze. Consequently, redware glazes show a yellowish or straw-colored tint, which intensifies the red color of the base clay. Many potters, however, particularly those of Pennsylvania, used plain glazes only for very crude or common ware, and liked to add some coloring material, either as a solid shade or, more frequently, in splotches and streaks, producing endless variegated effects, made more individual by the uneven burning.

Even the utilitarian and simplicity-loving New Englanders used these colored glazes, and they are found on all types of redware. Spargo and Weygandt state that the splotched effects were secured by daubing the surface of the ware with dry or damp colors before glazing, but Professor Norton has duplicated them by applying spots of liquid colored glazes over a coat of the clear glaze. The most commonly used coloring material was manganese dioxide, which gives shades ranging from sepia or nigger brown to dead black, and appears in solid colors, often with a distinct metallic lustre, or in streaks, splotches, mottles or fine specks. The red-brown tones of iron were also used, although they are difficult to distinguish over the hues of the clays used. The warm green shades occasionally found, more often as mottlings than as solid shades, were secured by the use of copper salts, made by burning jars of scrap copper in the kiln. Oxide of cobalt was the source of the blue decoration on stoneware, which the later redware potters often made in addition to their earlier favorite.

Blue, however, is rarely or never found on redware. This may be explained by the fact that a blue glaze over a red body results in black. Certainly this is the formula of the rich black "jet ware" teapots and other pieces made by English potters from the eighteenth to the twentieth century. But unless the "red and black" earthenware advertised by several Philadelphia potters between 1800 and 1850, answers this description, "jet ware," as such, was not made in this country. Certainly the common black glazes show the presence of manganese salts quite plainly. Further, much of the later Pennsylvania and Virginia redware, which shows a wide variety of colored glazes, was first covered by a coat of light-colored clay or slip, and was made by potters who also produced blue-decorated stoneware, and had the color at their finger-tips. Rare examples of very early slip-decorated and of late slip-covered redware do show touches of blue, so that the reason for its general avoidance by the redware potters must remain something of a mystery.

The few colors used by the potters show innumerable combinations and variations. Even the solid blacks range from a bright mirror glaze through satin and matte effects to pebbled or "orange-peel" surfaces. Occasional pieces show the sheen of mica particles in the glaze, sometimes resembling the stone known as goldstone. Browns in all depths of shade are found, and the iron salts in the clay, or possibly added to the glaze may, under certain burning conditions, usually accidental, result in dull maroon or even soft rose shades. Even salt glaze and the natural Albany slip are found at times on redware. The vari-colors range through the carelessly applied splashes, dappled or speckled effects to mottled tortoiseshell glazes in imitation of Rockingham, and to the vivid orange, green, red-brown and ivory marbled or streaked glazes of western Virginia, faintly reminiscent of Whieldon.

In addition to glaze colors, the redware potters decorated some of their ware in other ways. A quite common ornamentation is that produced by incising designs in the soft clay as soon as the piece was made. At its simplest, as found in all localities, this consists of rings or wavy lines scratched with an awl or sharp-pointed tool while the piece was still on the potters' wheel. Toothed or coggle wheels produced "milled" bands or rows of dots, according to their width, and heavier ones made the indented or crimped edges of plates and platters, as well as the heavier fluting on Pennsylvania and Virginia flower-pots and vases. Even occasional star or cross designs like those of the Boscawen, New Hampshire, ware, are found. The Pennsylvania German potters elaborated this decorative technique into what is known formally as "sgraffito," and to the makers themselves as "scratched ware." This type, brought by the first settlers from Germany, shows designs incised through a coat of light-colored slip, so that they appear in the darker hue of the base clay. It was used for the potters' finest show-pieces, mainly plates and platters intended purely for ornament. The designs, usually traditional, sometimes even duplicated by stencils, are frequently elaborate, forming a record of Pennsylvania Dutch motifs, conventionalized tulips, lilies, roses and pomegranates, hearts and vases, doves and eagles, with mottoes and inscriptions and sometimes vigorous, if crude, figures.

Another method of decorating redware is that of tracing designs in white or light clay on the red body. This process was known in most European countries, and was used as early as 1733 in Berks and Chester counties, Pennsylvania, where a white kaolin or slip clay exactly suited to it occurs. The clay was mixed with water to the consistency of cream, and applied to the partially dry ware through a quill, or with a slip-cup having one or several quills or clay spouts applied to its base. The slip-cup of the European potters had a closed top with a small air-hole, by which the flow of slip was regulated on the principle of the oil-can, but the Americans used an open cup, raising the spout or quill to interrupt its flow.

In its simplest form, slip decoration consists of lines, often waved and often in parallel series, and dots as accents or rows. These may be elaborated by touches of green slip, or by forming words. Pie-plates, platters and bowls of this type are found in Pennsylvania, but were also made in New Jersey, Maryland, New York, Connecticut and Ohio. More elaborate designs, birds, flowers, even scenes and figures in slips colored green, dark brown, olive, black and blue as well as cream, are found in Eastern Pennsylvania and in the Moravian settlements of North Carolina, but apparently were not made elsewhere. The designs, simple or complicated, were necessarily applied free-hand, rather quickly and with no retouching possible, so that the effect is almost always crude. For the ornamental ware, the pattern was left in the slight relief built up by the thick clay slip, but for pie-plates and other household articles, it was pressed or beaten down flush with the body. Barber describes Pennsylvania slipware covered with a dark brown manganese glaze, decorated over this with colored slips, and then reglazed, but it is probable that the first coat is a clay slip and not a glaze, making two firings unnecessary, and these pieces are so similar to South German and Swiss examples that they may not be American productions. The later potters of Waynesboro, and their cousins in Strasburg, Virginia did cover their red body with a cream slip, on which brilliant colors, either in or under the glaze, were applied, but, strangely enough, they seem never to have used the slip-cup or the sgraffito technique, while the early red-ware potters of the Middle West used a similar slip, but plain glazes with no coloring oxides.

These two types, with the colored glazes, include the great majority of decorated pottery. Variations are the combination of slip painting and sgraffiito, the use of a glaze splotched with green on sgraffito, incised sgraffito designs on the base clay without slip, and an ornamental type developed about 1850 in southwestern Pennsylvania, having tulip designs painted in transparent glaze on the unglazed ware, showing dark brown on the lighter brown or tan clay. The possibilities of the plastic clay naturally appealed to the workmen, and we find a wide variety of tableware and household utensils, modeled ornamented figures and vases, flower holders and children's toys, dolls, whistles and banks, as well as occasional simply modeled bands or mouldings on jars. The dry clay might be carved in relief or openwork and basket pattern bowls and plates. Occasionally, too, moulds of plaster of Paris or unglazed redware were used to duplicate decorative pieces. The dog door-stops, picture-frames and other moulded pieces which characterize the final flowering of the type in the Shenandoah Valley of Virginia, while they owe their inspiration to Staffordshire via Bennington, are definitely Pennsylvanian in workmanship.

Interesting, even fascinating as redware is to the collector, its fragility, and the tendency of its soft lead glaze to scale off in everyday use were serious defects, and, with increasing knowledge of their natural resources, the potters were able to provide, from their European background, a sturdier substitute. This is stoneware, made from finer and denser clays, and burned to a higher temperature, around 2100° Fahrenheit, producing a vitrified body actually closer to porcelain than to pottery in ceramic classification. Stoneware as we know it was made in England and Germany during the sixteenth and seventeenth centuries. The Staffordshire potters of the next century developed it into a fine white tableware, but the Americans followed only the earlier tradition.

The finest stoneware clays were found in northern New Jersey, from where they were shipped by water to potteries as far distant as New Hampshire. The Crolius and Remney plants in New York City made stoneware as early as 1775, but it is entirely probable that they, like many others, began by making redware, changing to stoneware later. Certainly they were producing stoneware soon after the Revolution. There were other potteries in New Jersey and Connecticut by 1800, and stoneware came into general use, especially in the North, within the next thirty years. It is interesting to notice a genre picture of a poverty-stricken American home—Rip Van Winkle's—painted in 1815 by Charles B. Key, and reproduced in *Antiques* for February, 1932. Several utensils of pottery are plainly recognizable, and include one stoneware jug and several redware jars.

As a matter of record, the Government reports for the year 1900 show a production of about one million, eight hundred thousand dollars worth of stoneware for that year, while the production of redware is valued at four hundred thousand dollars, the states of Ohio and Pennsylvania leading in the amount made. This total includes much cheap glazed "art ware", in the form of the beloved jardineres and umbrella stands of the period, but shows that the earlier ware never quite disappeared from the market. The conservative Pennsylvania Germans made stoneware, but continued to turn out their earlier favorite, in the old designs, up to the present day. Redware was never a favorite in the South, largely because hard-burning white or buff clays are distributed through so much of this section. The potters of western Pennsylvania and the Middle West, with quantities of fine stoneware clays at their disposal, concentrated largely on this type, and Greensburg, Pennsylvania, Muskingum County, Ohio, Akron, Ohio, and Clay County, Indiana, became centers of stoneware production. The important characteristic of stoneware is its glaze. Being burned to a much higher temperature than redware, the soft lead glazes known to the earlier potters were impractical, being vaporized or absorbed into the body in burning. These were replaced by the glaze secured by throwing common salt into the kiln full of ware at its highest temperature, the salt or sodium chloride vaporizing and being deposited on the surface to form with the silica present in the clay a glassy silicate or glaze. As a siliceous clay natually reacts best with the salt, sand was often added to the natural clay. The salt glaze is rarely smooth or bright, and usually shows a decided "orange-peel" or pebbled surface, with a stony lustre and considerable irregularity. Hollow-ware, being set mouth to mouth in the kiln to conserve space, the salt vapor could not reach the interior of the pieces, which very often received a wash of lead glaze or the natural Albany clay before burning.

The manufacturing processes of stoneware are, except for the glazing, much the same as those of redware, with larger potteries and kilns, and a narrower range of output. A sketch of the "first stoneware furnace, built near the Collect Pond in 1730" is shown in Valentine's *Manual of the City of New York* for 1854. This was rhomboidal in plan, with the single fire-box, six and a half by five and a half feet, set at the wider end, and a door opposite, the exterior measurements being about thirteen by fifteen, with a height of six and a half or seven feet. The ware made by the stoneware potters, mainly storage pieces, such as jars, pitchers and jugs, shows little decoration, compared to redware, even in its finest examples, since the glaze affords no opportunities for it. The inequalities of burning, and the different clays used, as when the potters of New England adulterated their expensive imported New Jersey clay with native material, result in a fairly wide color range, the usual clear gray varying, even in the product of the same pottery, to light cream, buff, mustard yellow or deep reddish brown, and from pale pearl gray to dark blue-gray.

For actual decoration, the makers of stoneware relied chiefly on the blue of cobalt salts, since this shade is not affected by the high burning temperature of stoneware, which alters or fades the oxides of iron, copper and manganese used to color redware glazes. This cobalt was usually applied in the diluted form of "smalt" or "zaffre," a powdered blue glass, obtained by burning cobalt ore and sand together. This was first imported from Europe, but, by 1787, was being produced at East Haddam, Connecticut. The clear bright blue it produces rarely varies, although the stoneware of Virginia shows an odd purple blue, probably due to the use of a local cobalt ore. This blue coloring was never used as a solid coating, but was applied in designs, usually quite simple. Flowers, "feather" scrolls, and conventionalized birds, simplified versions of those which were such favorites of the Spencerian school of handwriting, drawn with a deer-tail brush, were favorites. More ambitious effects were, of course produced at times, and the later ware often bears elaborate stencilled patterns. There are occasional examples of incised designs, sometimes very simple, but also, in rare instances, quite elaborate, with the incised lines filled in with blue. Applied modeled decorations are found in widely separated localities, as well as rare examples which received a relief design from moulds in which they were pressed. It is noticable, however, that the potters of Eastern Pennsylvania, who made so many types of decorated redware, produced only very simple stoneware. The miniatures, toys and other products of the potter's leisure time continued to be made in stoneware, but are rarer than in redware.

Since stoneware, more by tradition than by necessity, was confined to heavy plain vessels, another type of pottery was developed, in which more ornamental pieces were produced. This was made from fine cream-burning clays, which, in the plastic state, are smooth enough to be pressed into moulds easily and quickly. This body is very similar to that of crude earthenware, or cream-colored ware, but the American potters covered it with brown glazes, so that it is best described as brownware although the makers themselves particularly in Ohio, called it "Queensware," or "Rockingham." The first brownware was made in the modern type of factory by quantity production methods, so that it represents a radical departure from the earlier types. D. & J. Henderson of Jersey City were making brownware as early as 1830, and it is best known as the typical ware of the pottery at Bennington, while very large amounts were also produced at Baltimore, in the Ohio Valley from Pittsburgh to Cincinnati, and in many other localities.

Rockingham brownware of this type was not made by hand, the

potters' wheel being abandoned. The pieces were formed in moulds of plaster of Paris, the soft and plastic clay being pressed into the separate sections, forming a thin wall or layer. These sections were then joined, and the clay layers worked together, so that, when the clay became dry enough, through absorption by the plaster of the excess water, the mould could be removed. The perfect piece then appeared, with, of course, any decorative motifs which had appeared in intaglio or reverse on the inner surface of the mould, repeated in relief on its outer surface. Handles and spouts were then applied, and the ware was dried and burned.

Through the use of this process, brownware is often quite thin and light in weight, and appears as tableware, cups, plates and bowls, as well as finely modeled ornaments in full or high relief. These pieces, however, are rarely unique, since hundreds of pieces could be produced from the same mould. The delicately modeled animals of Bennington and the Gothic pattern sugar or cracker jars of East Liverpool are distinctive, but such popular designs as the Bennington hound-handled pitcher and the Baltimore Rebecca Teapot were copied, with more or less fidelity, by as many as twelve manufacturers, and even the "Flint Enamel" glaze patented by Fenton of Bennington was duplicated. Consequently the maker, and even the provenance, of an unmarked piece of brownware is difficult to identify.

Unlike the earlier types of pottery, this brownware was burned twice, coal being substituted for wood in more efficient kilns after about 1850. The first burning developed a dense, even body, which was then glazed and burned again, at a lower temperature. The glazes were developed from those used in England and known as Rockingham glazes, which contained manganese or iron salts in addition to the lead oxide. They have a high lustre, and show a dark brown mottling resembling tortoiseshell, varied occasionally to black or deep brown-black, and, in the later ware of the Middle West, to a light brown and cream stippling. Another very common glaze is a natural clay, found only along the Hudson River near Albany, New York, and called "Albany Slip" which, according to a report of the New York Geological Survey for 1843, was then "known and shipped all over the country." Although it fuses to a perfect glaze in burning, it is sometimes called a slip glaze, a technically impossible description. This glaze, alone or in combination with a lead glaze, is a bright transparent dark brown, whose uneven thickness on modeled ornament may give it a mottled or streaked effect.

The potters of the entire country knew this Albany Slip well, and used it for all types of ware. The Bennington factory added another glaze, patented as "Flint Enamel," which shows finely mottled green, brown, blue, yellow and orange flecks in a brilliant glaze. These colors were, according to the patented process, dusted over the surface of the glazed ware with a pepper shaker. They are thus in the glaze, rendering it opaque, not on the body under it. This glaze was copied elsewhere, but other Bennington originations, the combed, scroddle and marbled wares are less commonly found in the products of other potteries.

Another and coarser type of brownware was made, not in factories, but in the same individual potteries as redware and stoneware, and by the same methods. It was, however, produced largely after 1850, when the Rockingham type had been accepted for tableware and ornaments, so is strictly utilitarian. Thus it appears in a limited range of storage pieces, usually fairly heavy and clumsy, with little attempt at ornament. The usual range was jars holding from one quart to ten gallons, quart to five-gallon jugs, fruit jars with lids, quart to two-gallon pitchers, two to six-gallon churns with covers, milk pans and flower-pots, and the usual "off-hand" pieces and toys were made at times.

This type of brownware was made largely in the South and Middle West, and is very similar in body and glaze to the hard-burned redware of the same sections. The glazes generally used are the Albany slip described above, or combinations of this with a lead glaze, sometimes with the addition of manganese oxide as coloring. Since the ware was not always burned to the maturing temperature of the Albany slip, the coating is often a hard and stony opaque brown, dull matte or semi-matte in texture, which is an enamel or vitreous slip rather than a glaze. The potters of the South combined two types by salt-glazing their ware on top of this immature coating of slip, thus securing a nearly mature glaze. The classification of brownware may also be extended to cover similar crude pottery, whose body is the same as that discussed above, or between it and a red body, covered with hard alkaline glazes, usually immature and rough in texture. This ware is found especially in Georgia and the Carolinas, where the combinations of clays used result in natural shadings which are almost anything but brown.

There is one other type of pottery, made by the same methods as the Rockingham ware, and in the same factories. It is made from the same clay, burned to the same temperature, and is distinguished from brownware by the clear lead or alkaline glaze which intensifies the buff color of the body to the shade so characteristic that we have called it yellowware. Naturally, there are intermediate types, particularly in Ohio, where some of the so-called Rockingham shows the yellow coloring plainly between light brown stippling, and other examples have a putty-colored body under a transparent glaze, but are too coarse in texture to be classed as earthenware; Other late examples are bi-colored, partly solid brown and partly buff or cream, and others are yellow with white bands. In general, this ware shades into brownware on one hand, and into the coarse earthenware known as cream-colored ware on the other, with no clearly defined demarkations. It was limited to strictly utilitarian pieces, modeled or relief decorated examples being rare. A few mugs, bowls and plates do show lines or bands of white or blue, like, but much cruder than, the English Mocha ware. Those factories which made Rockingham made yellow-ware as well, except Bennington and others in New England. It was a favorite in the Ohio valley, and is still produced in quantity.

The manufacturing processes of whiteware follow the general procedure which has been described, but are necessarily more involved. Like Rockingham and yellow-ware, whitewares were never made by the individual potter, but passed through the hands of several workmen. Thus one mixed the clay, another pressed the pieces in moulds, or reproduced them in forms on a variation of the potter's wheel, often with an assistant to apply handles or ornaments, while still another mixed and applied the glaze, almost invariably alkaline, after they were burned, when they received a second or "glost" firing. This system was developed in Europe long before the inception of the industry here, so may be considered general. Decoration, too, was applied by specialists, artists who painted designs in gold and colors, or, on most tableware, artizans who only applied printed transfers, sometimes coloring them later. Any detailed description of these processes would demand another chapter, which, being of little interest to the collector of American pottery, is not included here.

CHAPTER III

Pottery Forms

THE previous chapters contain some account of the manufacturing methods of the early potters, and some knowledge of these is necessary for any true appreciation of their ware. The most casual collector can understand the importance of pieces bearing dates, makers' marks, or certain favorite types of decoration, but examples of unusual shapes or glazes are actually equally rare, and even more interesting, technically and artistically. Chapter II and the check-list of pottery types, attempt to give an idea of the usual, and some of the unusual glazes found on American pottery, but these glazes are very difficult to classify. Only two—at most three—basic formulae, and three or four coloring ingredients were used, but these, with intentional or accidental variations in the basic clays and in the processes of manufacture, produced an almost endless range of shades and textures. The most general and characteristic of these have been listed, but more probably exist, and may even be common in some localities.

After glazes, the forms in which pottery occurs may also be considered as affording information on its provenance, while they are in themselves a fascinating study. Any attempt at classification here must first separate pottery in general into the same main divisions which have already been discussed, hand-made and factory-made, or, more correctly, mould-made. The latter class, of course, includes the Rockingham type of brownware and the similar yellow-ware, which occupy little space in any list of pottery types because they show so little variation in form, glaze or body. Their most outstanding characteristic is that each piece was duplicated, possibly only once, probably hundreds of times, in the same mould, and that each design, except the occasional show-piece, was simplified to meet the requirements of the moulding process. Since especially popular models required more than one mould, and might also be copied by several makers, and since a fairly wide range of kitchen and table-ware was made in Rockingham and yellow-ware by some eighty plants, from Vermont to Illinois, there are a multitude of types and variations. Thus some thirty different hound-handled pitchers are known, and even more of the familiar dog door-stops. This ware was made in the United States in enormous quantities, largely by recent emigrants from the Staffordshire potteries and their sons, its European origin being clearly shown in the shapes, glazes and bodies It would be possible to classify and describe all known patterns of Rockingham and yellow-ware, as has been done with other early American wares produced wholly or in part, by mechanical means, such as lithographs, cup-plates and flasks. But a complete and adequately illustrated list of this sort would form a book of itself, while a partial one would be of so little value that no attempt has been included here.

To return to hand-made pottery, which, in general, was thrown on the potter's wheel, the problem of classification is much more difficult, since, with no mechanical reproduction, infinite variation of form is possible. Pottery is made on the wheel very rapidly, and with no guides beyond an idea, a memory, or, at most, a model to be copied by eye. In fact, a potter must be fairly expert to reproduce even his own pieces. Yet, among any number of transitional outlines, some clearly defined ones can be recognized. These show clearly the influence of environment, economic conditions and purpose on the traditions of what must be our oldest and most conservative handicraft, but the results of these influences are not always apparent. The potters' craft is very old, yet has long known true artists. Mechanical and technical progress also began at an early period, but, long before the Christian era, the potters of China and Greece were making superlatively lovely forms in soft red-burning clays. Later craftsmen of all ages and countries copied or adapted these, and recent investigation has shown that the classic curves follow certain definite mathematical laws, the equations of conic sections or the rules of dynamic symmetry. Certainly these old shapes are so universal that the very recent *Twentieth Century Ceramics,* written by Gordon Forsyth, shows more traditional than original designs. Incidentally, redware, stoneware, sgraffito and slip-decorated pieces appear among its illustrations.

Our early American potters knew little or nothing of the history of their craft. They lacked all knowledge of the great potteries of the past, or of laws and theories, and, uneducated and usually bucolic, lacked even the artist's training in line and curve. Further, they were limited in their choice of forms by the fact that their products were made for use, and hard use. Their severely practical customers demanded jars, jugs, pitchers and the like which could be filled and emptied easily and would not tip over in use, so that all the beautiful and slender amphorae, stamnos, chalices, trumpet vases and flagons of Greek, European or Oriental art, with their narrow mouths or bases, were not to be thought of. Yet, working within these limits, and with none of the guides, mechanical or otherwise, of the more sophisticated potters, our native craftsmen produced many lovely shapes. Further, they not only obeyed those unknown laws of dynamic symmetry, but reproduced, with surprising fidelity and frequency, those Greek urns and early Chinese bottles of which they had never heard.

Thus the form of pottery, as much as its decoration and body, reflects the economic and sociological conditions under which it was made. The democratic but progressive society of New England appreciated fine, durable ware, especially stoneware, whose makers, valued citizens of the community, had sufficient pride in their handiwork to put their names on much of it; and the conservative sectarians of Pennsylvania whose tenets forbade all useless show, loved their redware pie-plates, milk-bowls and jars, so like those of their German ancestors, their graceful lines and frequent decoration easily excused on such obviously utilitarian articles. In the South, on the other hand, the luxury-loving planters were completely uninterested in crude pottery, and, even before the disastrous days of the war, its makers in that section completely forgot the very high degree of science and craftsmanship their ancestors brought from England. The pottery of the Middle West, made by potters from all sections of the East, shows a variety of traditions, but, in general, is rather plain and heavy, showing the influence of quantity production, even on the individual craftsman. Full consideration of these influences could easily fill a long chapter, but the few shapes, chosen from thousands as typical, sketch them fairly well.

Thus the jar—or, more familiarly, crock, sketched as Number 1, which may have been made before 1750, or, not impossibly, after 1890, shows careful and skillful throwing, as well as a good eye for line and proportion. This example has the "loop" handle set horizontally, a characteristic of New England ware. Number 2 is also handsome, also one of the earliest shapes, and shows the handles placed vertically, attached to the rim, as was customary outside New England. Both these jars, like most early pieces, are embellished by the small foot, or base moulding, which, however, was added, not for its decorative effect, but to assure the safe separation of the soft finished piece from the wheel when the cutting wire passed under it. Similarly, the well-proportioned mouldings around the rims of these jars were added, not for any decorative effect, but simply as re-enforcements, and, on late ware, are often simplified into an unimportant bulge.

These jars are the common products of all times and localities. They were made in sizes holding from one pint to thirty gallons, and used for storing commodities of all kinds, from oysters to sauerkraut, although they are mostly referred to today as "apple-butter crocks." That shown as Number 3 appears with unglazed exterior oftener than the other forms, probably for some use now forgotten, and was a favorite with the Pennsylvania redware potters. Number 4 is also a characteristic eastern Pennsylvania shape, more likely to be covered by the soft mottled glazes of that region. Number 5 is a particularly graceful and less localized design, with wide mouth for storing apples, eggs, butter and the like, while the sharp shoulder of Number 6, difficult to produce on the wheel, shows a conscious attempt at decorative form.

In outline, the jar shows a somewhat chequered course, from beautiful urns, finer than those sketched, to the useful but un-lovely cylinder of today, but, in general, its lines show a gradual straightening through the years. It is naturally impossible to limit shapes to one period, or even, since the same potter often made both redware and stoneware, to one type of pottery. But Number 7, like as it is to Number 1, is slightly less rounded. It may thus be considered as rather later in date, and actually does appear in stoneware as well as redware. It also has the later "ear" or solid handles, easier to make and less liable to be broken than the ear-lier loops. Numbers 8, 9, and 10 are definite stoneware types, and also show the first appearance, chronologically, of the cylinder in the straight neck or collar, wide ones being particularly noticeable in New York and New England stoneware. The loop handle of Number 10 is found occasionally with these shapes, but is unus-ual. Number 11 is an example of the shape designed for a par-ticular purpose. It is a churn, a piece common in all sections, in redware, stoneware and brownware, and, since a too rounded shape would not be suited to its use, there is a noticeable flatten-ing of outline. Number 12, directly inspired by the cylinder or cone, appears in many small jars from the stoneware and brown-ware potteries of western Pennsylvania and the Middle West.

Numbers 13, 14 and 15, variations of the common pickle jar of our grandmothers, all exhibit nearly cylindrical or conical forms narrowed to small mouths, usually covered by flat pottery lids. Number 16 is actually very similar, but has a wide mouth, again for storing butter and the like. Number 17, a very simple shape, is included with the late examples, but its very simplicity made it a favorite always and everywhere. Number 18 is another cylin-der, evidently modeled after a barrel, and also appears in mould-made high-glazed brownware. Numbers 19 and 21 are unusual shapes for special purposes, a butter-crock and a flower-pot, and are frankly utilitarian and straight-lined, while Number 20 is the plain cylinder produced by machine in present-day factories. The adaptation of form to purpose is shown in illustrated price-lists sent out by several New England stoneware potteries during the 1850's. "Pots," similar in shape to Number 9, are advertised in sizes holding from one to five gallons, churns, like Number 11, hold from two to five gallons, butter pots, like Number 20, with covers, from one to four gallons, while cream pots are as shown in Number 19. "Sweet-meat jars" resemble Number 17, with covers, and made in one-quarter to three-gallon sizes, and "cake pots" look like Number 14.

American pottery shows, within its rather utilitarian limits, the gradual progress common to all art, moving from crudity and heaviness to full technical skill, then declining into facile and uninteresting productions. Like other American handicrafts with European backgrounds, pottery manages to pass quickly and easily through the first stage. Yet, as the makers followed the frontier West, always with new materials to work with, and unfamiliar equipment to control, the cycle began again. The final decadence, too, is delayed by two factors. One is the innate conservatism of the potters, many of whom, living in small communities and isolated from "advancement," continued to use the traditional forms and methods actually into the present day. The other is the influence of the machine and the ideal of quantity production. Even though the true product of that influence has been excluded from this chapter, the tendency toward simplicity, not necessarily of form, but of forming, that is, of manufacture, can be seen clearly in the jugs which are, after jars, the most common pottery vessels.

Jugs were used, of course, for storing liquids, from the fiery "moonshine" of the Southern mountains to innocuous vinegar, maple syrup or plain water. The jug has a much more limited range of form than the jar, but shows the same progression from pronounced curves to the straight line. Number 1 may be considered an approximation of the most common shape, and was made in all localities and periods, in redware and stoneware. In

Number 2, the outline varies to that of an inverted pear, and in Number 6 to an upright pear, while Number 3 approaches the sphere. Numbers 2 and 3 are characteristic redware forms, but were also made in stoneware, especially in Pennsylvania and the South. The redware potters of New England liked wide-mouthed jugs, as in Numbers 4 and 5, although these are really more like pitchers without spouts than jugs. Returning to the typical shapes, Number 7 shows two handles, which were usually applied for convenience in moving large stoneware jugs and water-coolers. Number 8 is another stoneware or brownware form, repeating the bell shape of jar Number 15. Number 9, with its two oppositely placed spouts and handle over the top, appears in the pottery of several foreign countries as a water-jug, but American potters hit on the same idea, possibly independently, for heavy, slow-moving liquids like molasses. Number 10 may be considered the first form of stoneware jug; with the addition of a bearded mask, modeled or separately pressed and applied, on the front just under the neck, these were first made by the sixteenth century stoneware potters of Flanders as caricatures of a Cardinal Bellarmine whom they particularly disliked, and were copied for centuries, there, in England and possibly in the first New York and New Jersey stoneware plants. Jug Number 11, again, is a late brownware modification of the syrup jug Number 9, often pressed instead of thrown, fitted with metal cover and bail handle, and used for very heavy liquids, particularly pancake batter. Numbers 12 and 13 show the final flattening of curves in stoneware and brownware jugs, toward Number 14, the combination of cylinder and cone which is made today. Thus jugs show the same variation of form through the years as jars, but the shapes are more clearly limited, and the few examples whose provenance can be given are more clearly localized.

It must always be remembered that the personal element in thrown or modeled pottery not only increases the difficulty of classifying shapes, but also makes it impossible to formulate any infallible rules for determining the age of any particular piece. A

31

thick, heavy jar or jug, with the ridges left by the thrower's fingers evident, and badly worn glaze, may be an extremely early one, but it may also be the carelessly finished and used production of a careless apprentice of 1860, or even of an old and tired potter of 1900. Toward the end of his eighty years, Jacob Medinger of Montgomery County, Pennsylvania insisted that he could still throw ware as thin and finely finished as in his younger days, but found it not worth the effort for an unappreciative generation. Again, a thin, beautifully formed, finely finished and decorated piece may have been thrown by a master potter of the great age before 1860, but it may just as well be a show-piece made by his son in 1890. Even those redware jars with unglazed exterior, which sometimes appear to be very old, were turned out occasionally, possibly for the sake of economy, by potters of all periods.

The personal element is particularly evident in the case of pitchers, which are also common examples of American pottery. There is some possible confusion here, since some authorities, particularly in England, describe these vessels as jugs. But, in our American parlance, the jug has a small mouth which can be closed by a stopper, while the pitcher has a comparatively wide mouth, pinched or shaped to form a spout for pouring. Pitchers were designed to appear in public, if only on the kitchen table, not for storage in cellar or shed. Consequently they show, as might be expected, considerable attempt at ornamental form. Although pitchers in general, silver, pewter, glass, porcelain and earthenware, have been made in a wide range of graceful designs, our American potters could, as usual, choose only the most substantial ones, with solid bases and wide mouths.

The pitcher sketched as Number 1, which certainly meets these specifications, is an early New England piece, very similar to the jugs Numbers 4 and 5 of the same genus, but otherwise a clearly defined local type. Pitcher Number 2, on the other hand, may be a modification of Number 1, and is also found in New England. But it also shows great similarity to a favorite model of the late eighteenth century English potters of Liverpool and Leeds, and is a later form than Number 1, occurring in both redware and stoneware. Number 3 is a Pennsylvania piece, while Numbers 4, 7 and 9, alike in general outline, are much more common, found in early and late pottery from all sections of the country. Actually, the design is a very old one, the cylindrical collar on globular base being found in examples of medieval English and Germanic ware. Number 5, another modification of this, directly inspired by the European flagon, is found in Pennsylvania, but infrequently, since it is less substantial and practical than the others. Of the remaining pitchers sketched, Numbers 6, 7 and 8, stoneware and brownware types, show the progression toward the straight line which was traced for jugs and jars, although this is less pronounced in the case of pitchers. Numbers 9 and 10 are slightly decadent but rather unusual and interesting forms developed in the Middle West about 1840, representing an attempt at originality by the makers. After the turn of the century, thrown pitchers continued to be made, but, being less decorative—to the contemporary taste, at least—and no cheaper than the moulded ones in Rockingham and yellow-ware, they were less popular.

When the other forms in which American pottery is found are considered, so many come to mind that it is hardly practical to attempt any such outline as can be traced for those already discussed. Also, they are found to be either entirely individual in design, or confined to a narrow area, or a limited period of time. A few of the more common types are worth mention, and the six mugs shown will serve to show how such a simple and quite common form can vary. The severely solid New England redware mug, Number 1, changes to a rounded shape, or takes on decorative mouldings in Numbers 2, 3 and 4, which are Pennsylvania redware made at different times from 1780 to 1880. Number 5, late redware from Virginia, copies a whiteware teacup closely, but Number 6 is again a plain heavy mug for beer, cider or milk. It occurs in late redware, stoneware and brownware in New England

33

and in the Middle West. With the addition of a small saucer balanced on the rim, for soap, it even appears as a shaving mug.

Another very common piece, the familiar bean-pot, shows a similar diversity of form. That of New England, Number 7, with its straight handle, was made in redware, stoneware and brownware, through a wide range of time and territory, and even copied in moulded brownware, ornamented with rose relief. The Pennsylvania potters, on the other hand, preferred a different shape, Number 8, slightly smaller, and with a loop handle. The one sketched was covered with a cream slip and lead glaze, and was bought "right off the stove," from a septugenarian whose health was obviously not impaired by the much discussed glaze. Any number of other pieces might be mentioned, but most of these are so definitely localized that it would be rather a waste of space to catalogue them here. Out of hundreds, the redware roach trap of central Pennsylvania is only one example. Designed by some ingenious potter with ridged and sloping unglazed sides leading the insects by an easy ascent to the well whose glazed and vertical sides made escape impossible, it is fairly common in a few counties, and unknown elsewhere. Another piece made for a particular purpose is the "harvester's jug," a hollow ring with a small neck, traditionally designed to be carried over the arm, so that field workers, with both hands occupied, might still have drinking water available. These are not limited to any particular locality or period, and are found in all types of ware. Actually, the potters probably made them as exhibitions of skill rather than with any particular use in view.

This list, of course, could go on indefinitely, but a few of those shapes whose age can be guessed at, at least, by reference to their purpose are worth mentioning. Flower-pots, for example, were hardly needed by the early settlers, and first appear in New England shortly before 1800. By 1830, they were popular enough to appear in a price-list of stoneware issued by D. & J. Henderson of Jersey City. The redware potters of Pennsylvania and Virginia made many flower-pots, handsomely glazed and sometimes decorated, while the final type, straight-sided, pressed by machine and unglazed, was the sole product of most of those redware potteries which survived into the last years of the nineteenth century. On the other hand, a pottery "fat-lamp" might well have been made by any of the first American potters, but would not have been salable after this style of light went out of use. This, however, did not occur until well after 1850, in the Middle West and South, at least, so that such pottery lighting appliances are not excessively rare. There are many other pieces, barber's bowls, wash-bowls and pitchers, colanders, foot-warmers and tableware in general, which were made, more or less frequently, by the early redware potters only as long as no substitutes in lighter and more durable materials were available. These substitutes were stoneware and brownware to some extent, but also white earthenware, glass and metal. So late pottery, especially the later bodies, is found in a narrower range of shapes, and many of these were finally replaced by other materials, leaving only storage vessels and flower-pots as exclusive pottery types.

This must not be taken as a dogmatic rule, because the occasional decorative or exceptional piece, made by the potter for his own use, or as a gift, will always turn up to confound it. Only three of these are sketched. Number 9 is an apparent contradiction of the statement that jars always had wide bases, but this one owes its graceful outline to its purpose. It is an Ohio beer-crock, made with a narrow base so that the sediment of the brew could collect and be drawn off there. Numbers 10 and 11 are real exceptions to the demands of utility, being purely decorative vases. Number 10, with its rope moulding, was made at Strasburg, Virginia, but the shape, very similar to that of a bottle found in Chinese ware of the Han dynasty of 200 B.C., occurs also in Virginia, Ohio and North Carolina. Number 11, from an unknown Pennsylvania pottery, is unglazed redware, but actually a very late piece, since it was painted black and decorated with pasted paper decalcomanias in the style of the seventies. Many more types and pieces could be discussed, but this very general outline should be sufficient. Intensive study of the forms used in definite localities of potteries could add a great deal to it, but will also show that it has some application in every case.

PART II

CHAPTER IV

Potters and Pottery of Eastern Pennsylvania, New Jersey, Delaware and Maryland

THE earliest pottery recorded within this territory is that of Daniel Coxe, later governor of New Jersey, established at Burlington, New Jersey, in 1684. Potters are known to have lived in New York, Massachusetts and Virginia before that date, but we have little evidence that they ever produced their ware on a commercial scale. And, while we know that this pottery existed, as shown in contemporary advertisements and inventories, we do not know what ware was made there. Some authorities have concluded that it was cream or white salt-glazed tableware, like that developed in England about the same time, but no examples of this made at Burlington or at any other American pottery exist.

The discovery of this process of salt glazing is attributed by some to John Dwight of Fulham, who patented a process of making "porcelane" in 1671. According to other accounts, it was discovered by Staffordshire potters between 1680 and 1691, but it is agreed that the process was a trade secret for many years. In general, we find the Americans of colonial and later times from ten to thirty years behind their English cousins in adopting any new fashion, process or invention, so that it is decidedly stretching a point to assume that Coxe's pottery was making the new salt-glazed ware within thirteen years of the earliest date when it could have been made in England. John Spargo has unearthed the records of a law suit brought in 1685 in the Court of Sessions of New Jersey against James Randall, one of Coxe's potters. James Budd, apparently the manager, sued for £200, which Randall had agreed to pay if he failed to carry out an agreement, apparently to make whiteware. The witness in Randall's defense praises his skill as a potter, but fails to mention any knowledge of the process of glazing, which, at a time when

39

this was a closely guarded secret, would certainly have been conclusive evidence of his ability. So, in default of any known examples or definite information, we may dismiss as an exaggeration intended to impress the English authorities Coxe's statement that "£1200 worth of white and chiney ware" had already been produced by 1688. This is not unusual in the records of early American industries, and may be considered the first of many similarly over-blown claims.

Of course, very fine cream-burning pottery clays are found in New Jersey, but we find little record of their use, except as "pipe-clay" for whitening uniform belts and facings, until after the Revolution. Prior to that time, the colonists undoubtedly imported most of their pottery, with other manufactured goods, from Europe. Pottery, being heavy and cheap, was likely to be slighted by importers in favor of lighter and more profitable commodities, so that, in all probability, little of it was used. Certainly, early inventories, such as that of Michael Burst of Lebanon, Pennsylvania, are not uncommon. This, drawn up in 1741, in a section where pottery was made in quantities only a few years later, gives the value of Burst's "earthenware" as four shillings, while his "wooden vessels" are worth fourteen shillings.

The first center of pottery production in eastern Pennsylvania was in Chester, Montgomery and Bucks Counties. The German colonists there began to utilize the red, soft burning clays soon after their first settlement, and shortly discovered the white or cream-burning slip clays of Chester County which have been mined on a commercial scale since 1839. From these clays, they made ware very similar to that of their South German fathers. The earliest known dated pieces are a platter inscribed "1733," and a sugar-bowl with the figures "1742," both accepted as American in spite of their close resemblance to pottery brought from Germany during the same period. The first recorded pottery in this district is that of the Vickers at Caln, Chester County, built about 1740, later moved to Lionville, and carried on by the same family until 1878. Other pre-Revolutionary potteries are that of the Ephrata Community in the Kloster at Ephrata, founded, with other communist or community industries shortly after 1740, of Conrad Mumbauer at Haycock, Montgomery County, founded in 1760, and carried on by his successors, the Singers to 1912, and the pottery at Wrightstown, started in 1763, and operated by various owners until 1900.

The redware of Pennsylvania has been described in a previous chapter, which devotes much space to it. The elaborate sgraffito and slip-decorated pieces were made largely in those counties mentioned, and show unmistakable German influence in their decorative motifs. These very often include the conventionalized tulip, whose history would of itself form an interesting study, following it from its origin among Eastern civilizations in the dawn of history to its appearance on an illuminated citation from the Emperor of Abyssinia of 1910, or on a "Pennsylvania Dutch" pie-plate of 1850. The potters also used other flowers, some conventionalized almost beyond recognition, but the rose, lily, fuschia, lily-of-the-valley, forget-me-not and pink are familiar. From the animal world, we find the eagle, always with wings spread, and often the double-headed one of Teutonic heraldry, the dove—usually a pair to symbolize love, the peacock—rarely with spread tail, and occasional ducks and drakes, cocks and hens from the potter's "back yard," swans, orioles, parrots, pelicans, deer, horses, lions, rabbits and dogs. Other favorite motifs include the star which averted evil "hex" spells, the true-lovers' heart, fish, swords, houses, trees, and occasional human figures. Patriotic and political designs are known, with at least one advertisement proclaiming "Singer's Superior Earthenware for Sale Here", and the emblematic scissors of the barber's bowl in Figure 14.

The glazes and colors of the Pennsylvania redware are not uniform. The invariable lead glaze always has a yellow tinge, intensifying or darkening the red-brown color of the clay used, which actually varies in unglazed surfaces from salmon to dark brown. The white or cream slip used as a coating for sgraffito ware, and for much of the slip decoration shows as yellow, cream or buff under the glaze, while the copper green often used as a contrast, and the rarer chocolate brown, olives and black are unchanged. Where slips are used, the glaze is usually left untinted and clear, but on otherwise undecorated ware it is very frequently colored brown, olive, black or green, occasionally as a solid shade, much more often in specks, splotches, mottlings or combinations of these. Other characteristics of the Pennsylvania ware are the use of decoration applied to the soft clay before drying, ranging from carved all-over flower and fruit relief or simple ropes and swags, to fluted bands or rims, or even incised lines made with the coggle wheel or awl. It is a fair assertion that the average piece of Pennsylvania ware is decorated in some way, if only with a colored glaze or incised bands. Consequently, many of the simplest crocks or jars show great beauty and interest, while finer examples, which have received more elaboration, are not too difficult to find.

A most important characteristic of this ware is the wide variety of domestic utensils and modeled or unusual decorative pieces in which it occurs. Another is the fidelity with which the potters repeat, not only themselves, but their fathers and grandfathers, until there may be little difference between a piece made in 1760 and one of 1860. The simpler pottery, of course, is much less specifically localized than the fine sgraffito and slipware. Pie-plates, bowls and platters decorated with simple lines of slip, possibly traced in parallel, waved, or elaborated with dots and scrolls in green, occasionally bearing the owner's or donor's name, or such suggestions as "Mince Pie" "Lemon Pie," "Shoo Fly," were made in quantities in Eastern Pennsylvania, but also occur in Connecticut, New York, New Jersey and even Ohio. In contrast to their redware, the Pennsylvania potters made quite plain stoneware, with, at most, simple blue flowers or scrolls on a medium gray ground. The clays were mainly secured from New Jersey, and the ware is, in general, very similar to that of the latter state. It was made by many of the later redware potters, but there were very few potteries devoted solely to it, and it obviously remained a step-child to its producers. In western Pennsylvania, on the other hand, stoneware was an important type, which may be considered in the chapter devoted to Mid-Western potteries. The later Rockingham brownware and yellow-ware were, of course, not suited to production in small potteries of the Pennsylvania type, but were made in a number of factories in Philadelphia, none of them large or particularly successful.

These Pennsylvania potteries were all small, with one kiln and one or two wheels. The owners were frequently farmers or small tradesmen, some of them not potters at all, but leasing their plants to others, although in many other cases, members of the same family carried on the business through several generations. As was generally the case in redware potteries, makers' marks were only rarely used, and the names found on some of the fine sgraffito and slip ware pieces are often those of the decorators or recipients. But the innate conservatism of the German race appears in the adherence of each pottery to certain types of glaze or decoration, so that unmarked pieces can often be identified by reference to marked or authenticated examples. Among the best known of these eastern Pennsylvania potteries are those of the Renningers, father, son and grandson, at Gerysville, of Johann Neesz and his son John Nase at Tylersport, and that of the Vickers at Caln and Lionville, whose traditions and methods were carried on by one of their workmen, Thomas Cope, at Lincoln University until 1920.

In all, about a hundred and twenty potteries made this type of redware, and most of them produced a fairly full range, from common storage pieces to the finest sgraffito. Two-thirds of these were concentrated in the four counties of Bucks, Berks, Montgomery and Chester, although the last had comparatively few. Several small villages boasted a number of potteries, particularly Nockamixon, Bucks County, which had five. One family, the Herstines, operated a pottery there for four generations, from 1785 to 1910. In Rock Hill, in the same county, two brothers, Andrew and John Headman, built potteries about 1800 which their descendants carried on until 1870 and 1890, and a third plant, that of the Diehls, was in business from 1832 to 1915. In Franconia, Montgomery County, John Leidy, a boy of 16, started a pottery in 1796 which he and his successor Joseph Groff carried on until 1832, and in Carversville, again in Bucks County, there were three potteries between 1800 and 1860. Quite naturally, these potteries situated close together used the same clay, and very often the same workmen drifted from one to another, so that it is difficult to distinguish the ware of each. But Vickers or Leidy pottery, or that from the plant at Haycock, Montgomery County built by Conrad Mumbauer in 1760 and carried on by the Singers to 1913, is easier to place. And among the later potteries, that of the Stahls at Powder Valley in Lehigh County, made between 1847 and 1898, and of the Bells of Chambersburg and Waynesboro, Franklin County, can be distinguished. The latter, alone of those mentioned, seem to have made little or no sgraffito or slip-decorated ware, but developed the use of a coating of slip under a colored glaze. They also made much stoneware, having a large pottery, and, again differing from the others mentioned, marked a large porportion of their ware with their name and address impressed. The last of the old Pennsylvania potters was Jacob Medinger of Neiffer, Montgomery County, who burned sgraffito in the old designs up to his death in 1930 at the age of eighty. For comparison, one of these is shown in the Frontispiece. The Stahl pottery at Powder Valley has recently been reopened by the sons of the founder, making pie-plates and other redware intended for everyday use.

In Philadelphia, the potters had to meet the demands of urban and sophisticated customers instead of the quiet and conservative inhabitants of the back country. So, while many of them made the plain and decorated redware described above, they also branched out in other directions. Several early potters made "red and black earthenware," which is also mentioned in advertisements of others from Boston to Baltimore, and was presumably black-glazed redware copying the "jet-ware" tea-pots and table-

1. Potter at foot-operated or "Kick-Wheel."

2. Potter's ball of prepared clay centered on wheel, top flattened.

3. Potter's thumbs start depression for hollow interior, fingers holding outside diameter. (Courtesy of Antiques Magazine.)

4. Thumbs have formed interior down to thickness of bottom, opening widened by outward pressure.

5. Fingers of one hand and knuckles of other make walls of cylinder thicker and higher.

6. Cylinder widened at rim by reversing pressure.

7. Cylinder widened at shoulder by greater pressure of hand inside vessel.

8. Interior of vessel smoothed by same method. (Courtesy of Antiques Magazine.)

9. Partially dried vessel cut from wheel and reversed, base formed and surface smoothed with ribstick whose support allows greater accuracy.

10. Pennsylvania redware lamp, redware slip-cup, used for applying lines of slip decoration, metal coggle-wheel for "crimping" rims and incised lines. (Clement Collection, Brooklyn Museum.)

11. Pennsylvania Sgraffito barber's bowl, dated 1793. (Courtesy Philadelphia Museum of Art.)

12. *(Top)* Pennsylvania sgraffito mug (same). 13. *(Bottom)* Pennsylvania
pie-plate decorated with sgraffito and colored slip, dated 1838 (same).

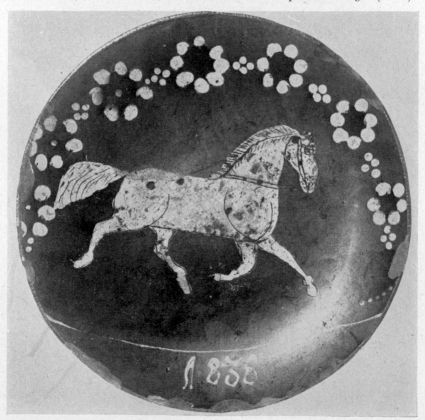

14. (*Top*) Pennsylvania slipware bulk-jar (c. 1830), (same).

15. (*Bottom*) Pennsylvania sgraffito flower-pot, incised rim with rope moulding (1826). (Courtesy of the Philadelphia Museum of Art.)

16. (*Top*) Pennsylvania redware jar, slip and incised decoration (c.1792). (Courtesy of the Metropolitan Museum of Art.) 17. (*Bottom*) Pennsylvania redware "Puzzle-Jug," mottled glaze with incised decoration (c.1809). (Courtesy of the Philadelphia Museum of Art.)

18. Redware tile, from a pottery near Bethlehem, Penns., c.1790. (Clement Collection, Brooklyn Museum.)

19. Stoneware money-bank, blue decoration (Richard C. Remney, Philadelphia), 1859-1900. (Courtesy of the Philadelphia Museum of Art.)

20. Pennsylvania redware; slipware plates and platter, coffee-pot and flower-pot, mottled glazes, money-bank, modeled bear and dog, dark manganese glazes. (Author's Collection.)

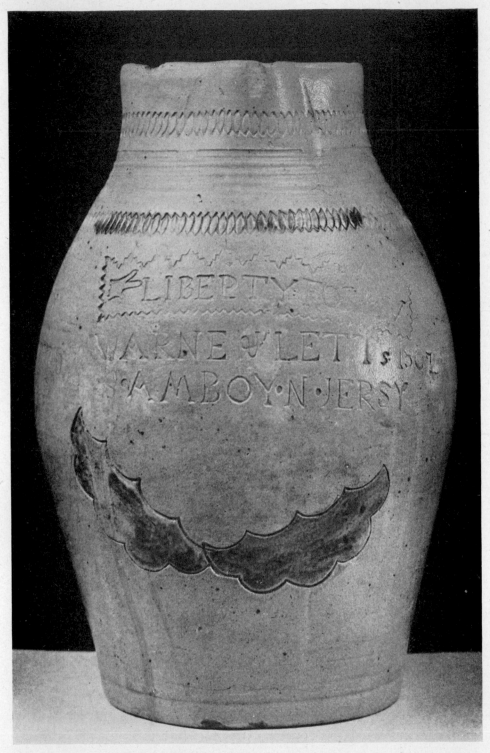

21. Stoneware pitcher, incised and blue decoration, Warne & Letts, South Amboy, N. J., c.1807.

22. (*Top*) Rockingham "Apostle" pitcher, modeled by Daniel Great-
bach at the Jersey City Pottery, c.1839-1845. 23. (*Bottom*) Rockingham
Pitcher, Salamander Works, Woodbridge, N. J., 1845. (All Clement
Collection, Brooklyn Museum of Art.)

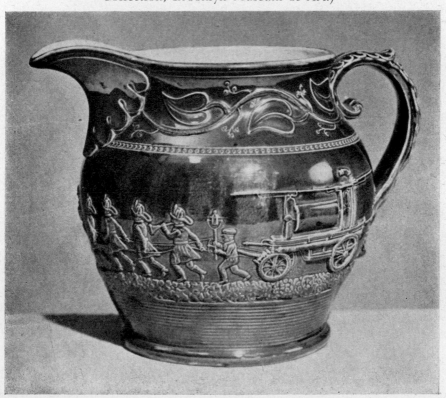

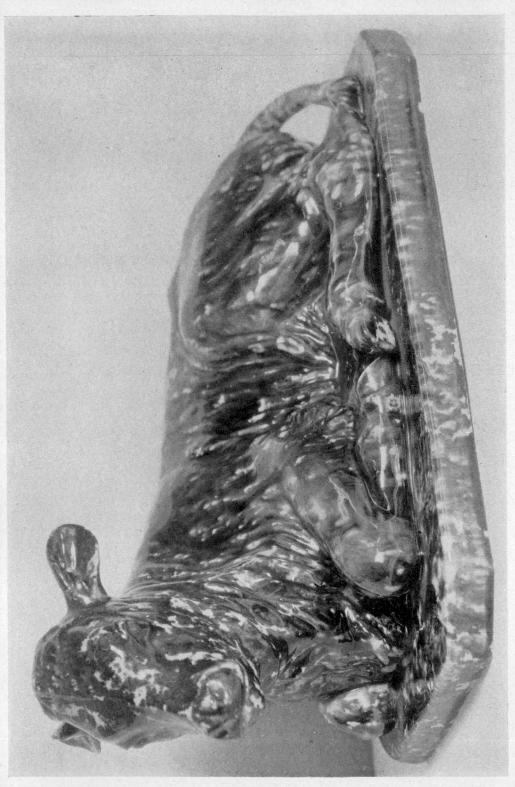

24. Rockingham bull-calf, Abraham Cadmus, Congress Pottery, South Amboy, N. J., c.1850. (Clement Collection, Brooklyn Museum of Art)

25. Rockingham hound-handled pitchers; New Jersey, probably Trenton, c.1860. Bennington, Vt., c.1852; Jersey City, N. J., modeled by Daniel Greatbach, c.1839-1845; Ohio, probably East Liverpool, c.1870. (Author's Collection.)

26. Rockingham "Rebecca-at-the-Well" and "Rose" teapots, Edwin Bennett, Baltimore, Md., 1856-1900. (Courtesy of the Philadelphia Museum of Art.)

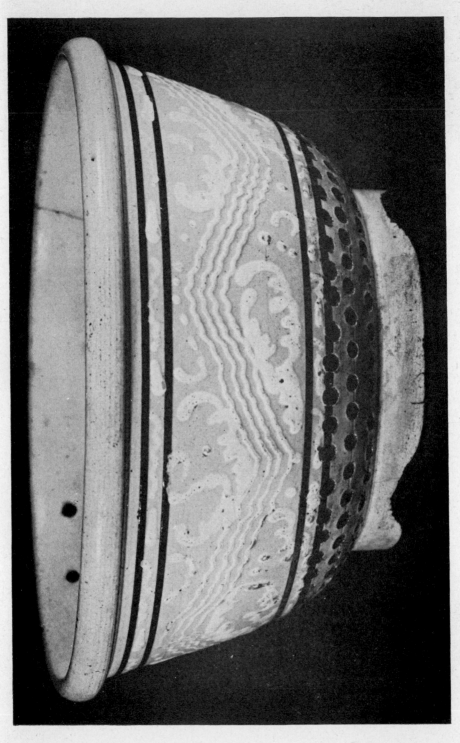

27. Yellowware bowl, white slip decoration, New Jersey, 19th century. (Clement Collection, Brooklyn Museum.)

28. (*Top*) New England slip-decorated redware, early 19th century. 29. (*Center*) Stoneware Jar, Blue Caricature of Stephen A. Douglas, Lewis & Cody, Burlington, Vt., 1860. (Both Courtesy of George McKearin.) 30. (*Bottom*) New England redware, early 19th century. (Both Courtesy of Antiques Magazine.)

31-32. Stoneware jug, blue and incised decoration, John Crolius, New York, dated 1775. (Courtesy of the Metropolitan Museum of Art.)

33. Stoneware water-cooler, blue and incised decoration, Paul Cushman, Albany, N. Y., c.1806-1832. (Courtesy of George S. McKearin.)

ware of England. One Jeremiah Warder even advertised in 1784 "Gen. Washington's bust, ditto in medallions, similar images etc." The later potters made Rockingham ware and even White Granite, while more or less successful attempts to produce whiteware, especially porcelain, went on from 1769 to 1857.

The first of these was the possible porcelain and known white earthenware of Gouse Bonnin and George A. Morris about 1769 or 1771, continued with the also possible Queensware or creamware of John Curtis, Alexander Trotter and David G. Seixas between 1790 and 1822, and culminated in the hard-paste porcelain of William Ellis Tucker and Tucker & Hemphill between 1826 and 1837. Little is known of most of this ware, the makers, like most American manufacturers of the period, marking very little or none of it. Consequently, several of the types mentioned may never have been produced successfully. Three earthenware pieces marked with a small "p" in blue under the glaze are ascribed to Bonin and Morris. Tucker, having received a medal from the Franklin Institute in 1827 for his first efforts, and his partner and successor, Judge Hemphill, having brought French workmen to this country to help him attain the standards of Sèvres, felt justified in marking a few of their pieces with the current firm name and address in red. From these, we know that they made rather clumsy pieces painted with flowers and scenes in brown, with or without other colors and gold, and followed these with finer copies of the ornate and much-gilded Sèvres ware of the 1830's.

Those of the Philadelphia potters who confined themselves to simpler ware were more successful. Andrew Miller founded a redware pottery there in 1785, and his son Abraham, who carried it on until 1858, experimented with Queensware, silver lustre using the platinum glaze made by a Dane—Dr. Eric Bollman in 1814, and white glazed and unglazed earthenware between 1824 and 1842. He made Rockingham ware as a staple but also produced the first floor and wall tile made in the United States about 1845. Rockingham was also made by the Haig Pottery between 1830 and 1890. A pitcher showing Washington as a Mason is

45

ascribed to this pottery, and rather doubtfully dated before 1830, but they later made cow creamers, head pitchers and log cabin banks in Rockingham, and possibly, a variation of the hound-handled pitcher having the figure of Columbia on the sides, which appears in Figure 20. The Spiegels made Rockingham between 1837 and 1880, as did Ralph Bagnall Beech, between 1844 and 1853, the origination of the "O'Connell" head pitcher being credited to him. It is noteworthy that these potteries were not like those which manufactured Rockingham in other sections, because they all made redware as well, including the finest types. They apparently could not compete with the more or less standardized factories, and the Haigs turned to stoneware after 1858, while the Spiegels made bisque or unglazed moulded redware vases and other art pieces from 1880 to 1890.

The only Rockingham factory, as such, in Philadelphia was the Port Richmond pottery of J. E. Jeffords & Co., built in 1868. Stephen Theiss of Bennington was the designer, and they made toby pitchers and cow creamers very similar to those of Bennington. Later, they went into the whiteware field, and continued to manufacture White Granite and Semi-Porcelain, plain and decorated, until 1890. Another important name in the history of Philadelphia pottery is that of Remney. Henry Remney, grandson of John Remney I of New York, came to Philadelphia about 1810, and issued his first price-list of stoneware in 1833. He and his descendants continued to make the same type of stoneware, including some fine pieces (Figures 18 and 22) as late as 1895, and the firm is still in business.

In New Jersey, redware was never an important product. Several potters made it during the nineteenth century, and the Prudens at Elizabeth turned out quantities of simply decorated slipware and some sgraffito from 1818 to 1879. At Trenton, John McCulley was making redware jars and plates from 1779 to 1852 while Charles Hattersley later built the City Pottery as a redware plant, but gave it up very shortly. The New Jersey redware is not common, especially as it is very difficult to distinguish from

that of the neighboring states, but few of the elaborately decorated pieces found across the Delaware were made by the Jersey-
men.

The clays of northern New Jersey, from Staten Island to Gloucester County, are, however, admirably suited to the manufacture
of stoneware. Hence it was natural that the potters of this section should turn to this type of ware as its advantages became
known. This New Jersey stoneware has a fine dense body, light
gray or cream in color, with a smooth glaze. In contrast to the
ware of Pennsylvania, some of it is finely decorated. The invariable cobalt blue was used for colored designs, but the conventionalized tulips and nondescript birds in Spencerian curves which
have been christened, without much reason, "robins," were supplemented by cockatoos and exotic specimens, by roses, feathers and
graceful scrolls, as well as by human, animal and even fish forms.
These designs may be emphasized by incised outlines, and applied
modeled relief motifs, alone or in combination with blue, are occasionally used. The "Bellarmine" jugs, whose origin is not too
definite, were probably made in New Jersey, and the shape was
certainly copied there. The later potters made stoneware pressed
in plaster moulds, and the "off-hand" pieces all collectors prize
are found here as elsewhere.

The earliest of these stoneware potteries of which we have any
record is that of General James Morgan at Madison, which was
producing stoneware by 1775, from clay obtained at near-by South
Amboy. Xerxes Price started a pottery at Sayreville, then known
as Roundabout, in 1802, some of his ware being marked with his
initials and the latter address. J. Letts or Warne & Letts began
business at South Amboy in 1807, marking their pieces with
their names or initials, which read "T. W. J. L." not "W. & L.",
as might be expected. Joseph Henry Remney, another member
of the New York family, may have moved to South Amboy in 1826,
after the closing of the old Remney pottery, and brought some of
its equipment with him. Many other potters worked in this section, some of those whose marks are found including T. W.

Whiteman of Perth Amboy, B. J. Krumeich of Newark, and the Fulper pottery at Flemington, which, founded in 1805, first made redware, then stoneware, and is now noted for its art pottery.

New Jersey, with fine pottery clays at hand, became the original American home of those types of pottery which have been described as brownware or Rockingham and yellow-ware, and which are generally ascribed to the plants in Vermont and eastern Ohio. The Jersey City Pottery was built by local capitalists in 1825, and employed several French potters, who made the first commercially produced hard-paste porcelain in the United States. They were less successful financially, and the plant was taken over for the production of simpler and cheaper ware by D. & J. Henderson in 1829. They made "Flint Ware," examples of which show a grayish buff stony glaze, only occasionally clear and bright, and a price-list of 1830 shows two-quart tobies (Figure 42), coffee and tea-pots, flower-pots, covered butter pots, nursery lamps, water coolers, tea tubs, spittoons, jars, toys and other pieces. In 1833, the business was incorporated as the American Pottery Manufacturing Company, the younger Henderson withdrawing from the firm. About this time, too, a true but light-colored Rockingham glaze was introduced, although the few marked examples known bear either the D. & J. Henderson mark, or the title "American Pottery Company" adopted in 1840.

Daniel Greatbach, later to become famous as a designer at Bennington, came from England to Jersey City in 1839. There he made the first of his hound-handled pitchers, copied from models made at Brampton and Denby in England, which he was to copy for James Carr at South Amboy and Fenton at Bennington. This first attempt differs from the later and better-known Bennington type in having a sharper, less rounded shoulder, a slightly different relief decoration, and a less well-modeled hound, whose head sometimes, but not always, touches the rim of the pitcher. Other Jersey City Rockingham pieces, presumably modeled by Greatbach, include a "mask" pitcher, and a small toby having the familiar head grafted on a paneled body.

48

White earthenware was introduced after 1833, and has been found with spatter decoration, and in an uncolored cream-colored tea-set having a fine all-over relief design, also modeled by Great-bach. Tableware in this white body, printed in a "Canova" pattern pirated from one introduced by the great English firm of Ridgeway in 1839, was issued in 1840, and is accepted as the first transfer printed earthenware made in the United States. Other printed ware, pitchers and mugs showing portraits of William Henry Harrison, and similar pieces followed this until the factory was taken over by Rhodes, Strong & McGeron in 1845 for the production of whiteware exclusively. The Jersey City plant was thus a pioneer in several lines, but it was also a "nursery" for the industry in general, being the first employer, or the first American employer, of a number of potters who later became important elsewhere. These include James Carr of South Amboy and New York; William Taylor, James Bennett and William Bloor of East Liverpool and Trenton, Daniel Greatbach of Bennington, H. W. Farrar of Bennington and Kaolin, South Carolina, and others.

Other manufacturers of Rockingham and yellow-ware in New Jersey were James Carr, or Carr & Locker, who operated the Congress Pottery at South Amboy, with Daniel Greatbach as a partner, from 1852 to 1854, L. S. Beerbauer and Company, who took over the Pruden Pottery at Elizabeth, with William Leake of Bennington as a partner, in 1879, copying the Bennington "Flint Enamel," and several Trenton firms. Taylor and Speeler, William Young and Millington, Astbury & Poulson all established potteries there for the production of this ware in 1852 and 1853, but Young's introduction of cream-colored earthenware in 1854 changed the trend of the industry in that city. In a few years these and a number of other potteries were making crude whiteware, undecorated, which was known as "White Granite," and Trenton soon became the pottery producing center it has remained.

The Rockingham of the New Jersey plants is, like all ware of this type, very rarely marked. Of course, it was not the policy of

49

the early American manufacturers to mark their products, but the dark thick glaze of Rockingham, applied, in contrast to cruder types of pottery, to the bottom of the piece, was likely to render a mark illegible, so that there was good reason for neglecting to use one. This ware is, in general, lighter in tone than the finest of the dark tortoise-shell glazes of Bennington, but never shows the pale mottling of some of the Ohio ware, and, like the others, shows so much variation that identification is not easy. It is noticeable that the New Jersey potteries were factories, planned and operated on the English system, with many of their "key men" brought from Staffordshire. The Philadelphia plants followed the traditions of the old potteries, and made Rockingham, redware or anything they thought would sell, sometimes simultaneously, but those of New Jersey had only one product. The crude ware with the same body and a similar but less perfect glaze, thrown by hand, which we call brown-ware also, was almost unknown, even in the earliest of the Rockingham potteries.

The pottery of Delaware and Maryland is very similar to that of Pennsylvania, although the more elaborate redware types were not made. Delaware, of course, was largely supplied from her neighbor, but had several small potteries. In Maryland, the manufacture of pottery began at an early date, and by 1750, one Thomas Baker of St. Mary's was advertising in the Maryland Gazette, "milk pans, butter-pots, jugs, pitchers, quart mugs, porringers, churning pots, painted dishes, plates, etc., of the same kind as imported from Liverpool or made in Philadelphia." Redware continued to be made at Catonsville and Bacon Hill, near Baltimore, until very recent times. In western Maryland, the potters were largely of Pennsylvania German blood, and made redware and stoneware indistinguishable from that of Central Pennsylvania. One of the Bells of Waynesboro was in Hagerstown, Maryland, from 1800 until 1834, making redware and some stoneware. The Baechers at Thurmont, who later moved to Winchester, Virginia, as did Peter Bell, and a number of others, made this ware, and, as far west as Cumberland, in the mountains, Christian Neff was potting at the time of the first census in 1790.

The Baltimore potters of the first half of the nineteenth century made, according to their advertisements, both redware and stoneware, and seem to have specialized in tea and coffee pots, those puzzling black-glazed redware pieces mentioned previously. Baltimore also had two women potters, Catherine Brown and Margaret Parr, who carried on inherited businesses during the thirties. Henry H. Remney, son of Henry Remney of Philadelphia was in business in Baltimore from 1818 to about 1835, when he returned to Philadelphia; Maulden Perrine was making stoneware in 1824, and one of these, probably Perrine, is credited with the technically important achievement of turning out the first stoneware drain pipes in the country. The Perrines are still in business, and later made Rockingham and the similar ware covered with a black high glaze, especially the seated dog doorstops copied from those of Staffordshire earthenware, and so popular in Ohio.

In 1846, Edwin Bennett, who came from England via Jersey City, Troy, Indiana, East Liverpool and Pittsburgh, finally settled in Baltimore and started a business which grew and lasted. He made some stoneware and much Rockingham, including copies of the Flint Enamel and scroddle types originated at Bennington. He later made a great deal of the Victorian Majolica, and still later changed to whiteware, issuing the printed platter showing "Pickett's Charge at Gettysburg" (Figure 86) in 1870, to copy it in 1901. Although the Bennett brownware is rarely marked, many designs are identified with the factory. Among these are the first Rebecca-at-the-Well teapot (Figure 12), introduced in 1851, which has a flower finial on the cover to distinguish it from many later copies. Charles Coxon, the Bennett's able designer, also modeled a series of Rockingham pitchers, the wild boar, Daniel Boone or hunting, dolphin-handled, snake-handled and mask-spouted, and still another version of the hound-handled pitcher, in several sizes, differing in shape from those of Greatbach, and with a relief design of hanging game on the sides. These Rockingham pieces often show a fine rich glaze, dark and deep. Coxon's designs also include an early majolica bust of Washington, and a green pitcher with fish relief, produced twenty years before the ware commonly known as majolica became popular.

CHAPTER V

Potters and Pottery of New England and New York

FROM the beginning the earliest European settlements in North America had to be, and were, self-sufficient and self-supporting, and their governors and promoters, realizing this, sought to attract skilled artisans who could supply the necessities of life. Pottery could hardly be listed among these, but, as soon as life in the New World began to be stabilized, potters appeared. The colonists, set down in a wilderness, with three thousand slow miles between them and the only available markets, found, as their families grew and the table and kitchenware they had brought with them went the way of all such things, that they needed a source of supply nearer than "home." And certainly the moving spirits of the settlements would see that they were supplied by inducing potters to emigrate.

So, while no examples of ware made before the middle of the eighteenth century exist, there is much evidence that potters were living and working, both in Massachusetts and New York City, a hundred years earlier. On this evidence, ancient Essex County, Massachusetts, can well claim to be the first permanent center of the pottery industry in the country, with New York a close, but less evident, second. There, Dirick Claesen, "Pot-Baker," is named in the list of burghers of April 18th, 1657. Dirick Benson and William Croylas, potters, appear in 1698, but it is only possible to guess at the character of the ware they made.

Actually, it is fairly safe to assume that the first potters of the English settlements made redware. This was a common type in England, appearing commonly from Roman times until about 1750, and more rarely, up to the present day. Further, since this clay can be burned at a low temperature, very simple kilns and equip-

53

ment can be used, and, what is most important, red-burning clays are found throughout New England, while satisfactory stoneware clays are not available within the territory of the earliest settlements. The process of salt glazing did not become generally known in England until well into the Eighteenth Century, so it seems certain that the pottery of New England was redware at least until after the Revolution.

In New York, on the other hand, it is far from safe to offer any such conclusion. Stoneware was made in Flanders and South Germany before 1600, and it is entirely probable that most of the Dutch potters who crossed the ocean were familiar with it. Again we are confronted by the lack of evidence, since the sketch of "the first stoneware furnace in New York, 1730" in Valentines *Mannel* for 1854 cannot be accepted as conclusive. A stoneware jug in the Metropolitan Museum, inscribed "1775, I.C." and attributed to John Crolius I, is the earliest dated piece of American stoneware known. Certainly both the Remney and Crolius families were making stoneware in the city at a very early period, while no authenticated examples of redware from either exist. Also, stoneware clays of good quality were within easy reach of the potter, possibly on the island of Manhattan itself, certainly across the bay on Staten Island and along the Raritan. On the other hand, redware clays were even easier to secure. A Philadelphian, Jonathan Durrell, who worked in New York from 1753 to 1774 or later, advertised kitchen and storage ware, "striped and colored dishes of divers colors," but no tableware. These, in so limited a range, could hardly have been white earthenware, and could never have been stoneware, so we may believe that he was making slip-decorated redware, although we know that other potters were making stoneware in the city at this period. We also know that the Hudson River Pottery made redware as late as 1840. So a safe conclusion is that both types were made in New York City, with stoneware introduced there at a much earlier date than anywhere else in the country.

Of the two important New York potteries, that of Crolius is

apparently the earlier. William Croylas appears in the records of 1698, and we find William and Peter Crolius, potters, listed in 1732. A not too reliable map of the city "As It Appeared in 1742-1744" shows the "Remmey & Crolius Pottery" as well as those of Wilson and Corselius on Potter's Hill near the old City Hall, not far from the present corner of Centre and Read Streets, but this conjunction has been proven an error, no other evidence of the partnership existing. The first William Croylas is also rather hazy, but the William and Peter of 1732 are known to have operated a pottery at that date, and William's son, John, having taken the side of the colonists during the Revolution, was forced to leave the city, and even had his property confiscated during the British occupation of New York, from 1776 to 1783. He later returned, and became a prosperous and influential citizen, as was his son, Clarkson, sachem of Tammany Hall in 1821, whose "Elegant Mansion" adorns the pages of Valentine's Manual for 1858. Clarkson Crolius, when Potters' hill was leveled and Collect Pond filled in 1812, to make room for new streets of the growing city, moved the pottery to 65 Bayard Street. Stoneware, usually brown, not gray, in shade, was the sole production. Clarkson died in 1830, but his son, another Clarkson, carried on the pottery until 1870, while John, William and George Crolius, apparently cousins, are also recorded as potters in the same period.

The competitor of the Crolius pottery during most of these years was that of the Remmeys first heard of in 1732, when John Remney, or Johannes Remy, is listed as a potter along with the Crolius brothers. Three generations of Remmeys operated their pottery, even working through the troubled days of the Revolution, and the last John Remmey became a prosperous and prominent citizen. The pottery was closed in 1820, but Henry Remmey grandson of the first John, settled in Philadelphia. The firm he founded there is still making stoneware under the family name, and must be the oldest business firm in the country. Again it is uncertain if the Remmeys ever made redware, and this must remain a question. Examples of both Remmey and Crolius stoneware, bearing either initials or full names, impressed or inscribed, with the address "Manhattan Wells" or "New York," are graceful and well made, quite similar in design, as might be expected, varying in color from tan or brown to gray, with the Remmeys' ware slightly darker in color and heavier in body than that made by the Crolius family. Some pieces show elaborate decoration, with graceful conventional scrolls and flowers in cobalt blue outlined by incised lines. It is not easy to identify an unmarked piece, and even difficult to determine the age of a marked one, the same Christian name occuring over long periods in both families. The address, "Manhattan Wells" alone, is usually attributed to Clarkson Crolius I, while "C. Crolius, Manufacturer, New York" is probably his son.

To return to the eighteenth century, there were a number of potteries in existence throughout New England before the Revolution. Litchfield, Connecticut, had three potters in 1753. Adam States was working at Huntington, Long Island as early as 1751, and Abraham Hews was at Weston, Massachusetts in 1769, establishing a long-lived enterprise. The Revolution forced most of these men to cease operations, at least temporarily, but most of them started again as soon as the British troops left the country. An energetic Asa Smith is first heard of in Norwalk, Connecticut, in 1780, while the war was still raging, and his business was continued until 1898.

New England was the first manufacturing center of the country, and our present industrial system may be said to have originated there. The first signs of "mass production" may be in the tendency of artisans of one trade to settle in the same localities, as the hatters did at Danbury and the clock-makers at Waterbury. Potters have always done so, largely, but not altogether, attracted by a supply of good clay. So the first American pottery center grew up in Essex County, Massachusetts. In 1639, the town of Salem granted ten acres of land to Lawrence Southwick, William Osborne, Ananias Conklin and Obediah Holmes, for the purpose of producing pottery and glass. Two of these men, with the glass, disappear from sight, and Southwick is said to have been banished, for his Quaker faith, to a desert island off the coast, where he died. However, William Southwick and Joseph Osborne were making pottery in the same location a hundred years later, and their descendants carried on the trade through several generations. Salem also had two potters, John Pride and William Vinson, in 1641, and the latter name appears among the potters of the next century. Most of the Essex County potteries were in Peabody, although the best clay deposits were in Danvers. By 1775, there were seventy-five potteries in the two towns, and twenty-two Peabody potters were under arms at the Battle of Lexington. The best-known of the potter families are the Osbornes, seventeen of whom were master potters. William Osborne's pottery was in existence in 1742, remained in Osborne hands until 1860, and is still operating.

These potteries all made redware, with only occasional experiments in stoneware. Potters from Essex County built plants in other sections of New England, where they continued to turn out the ware they knew best. Other redware potteries were that at Huntington, Long Island, started by Adam States about 1751, and carried on under various managements until 1900, and that built by Abraham Hews at Weston Massachusetts, which his descendants carried on, with a change of location to Cambridge, as late as 1900. They always made redware, but, during the last years of the century, it was flower-pots and unglazed moulded "art ware," in the taste of the period.

The New England redware reflects the rather hard simplicity of early New England life. There are well-defined regional types, but fewer individual ones than in Pennsylvania and the Middle West. Since so much of it was made in a comparatively few potteries or groups of potteries, this is entirely natural. A few distinctive pieces were developed, notably an ovoid wide-mouthed jar, which, with the addition of a single loop handle, becomes a jug, and, when a spout is added as well, appears as a pitcher.

Other pieces are the jars with loop handles set horizontally on the shoulder instead of vertically, and, as might be expected, the useful bean-pot.

Much New England redware is covered by a clear and colorless lead glaze, but the potters also added color to this at times. Black glazes were popular, and are found on the earliest examples—jars, bowls and platters. The first potters, of course, brought their formulae from England, where black-glazed redware has been made for centuries, especially in tea-pots for the benefit of those who are sure that tea cannot be properly brewed in any other ware. The New England black glaze, however, is not the blue-black shade secured by the use of cobalt oxide, but the brown-black of manganese, or of the clay known as Albany clay, which is a natural glaze. Green glazes are also found, usually mottled or streaked, but are less common than they are in Pennsylvania. A number of the New England potters, particularly in Connecticut and Massachusetts, also made the simple slip-decorated ware generally identified with Pennsylvania. This is not surprising, since slip-ware is an English as well as a German type, and emigrant English potters might be expected to carry on, and hand down to their successors, the same technique. English slip-decorated ware was made until about the middle of the eighteenth century, and has a red body decorated by lines and dots, the familiar tulips and inscriptions, in white or cream slip, colored yellow by the glaze. Sgraffito ware was also made in England, but rarely, and it is significant that the potters of New England hardly attempted it. The marbled or streaked agate-ware of Whieldon is even echoed in the Connecticut slip-ware pie-plates of (Figure 32), on which the colored slips have been mingled in a fashion unknown in Pennsylvania.

The years after the Revolution saw a great increase in the amount of pottery produced in the country. The American people, with imported wares expensive and difficult to secure, were forced to buy the cruder and less durable American ware, for common use at least. But, in New York and New England at least, the superior qualities of stoneware were becoming known, and many of the potters began producing it in preference to red-ware. There were exceptions, of course, the Essex County potters mentioned, and others. The German Charles Mehweldt made decorated and plain redware at Bergholtz, New York after 1852, while Jacob Merz, a Pennsylvania German who had drifted to Bennington, started the same line after the closing of the United States Pottery in 1859. But the potteries of Connecticut were changing shortly after 1800.

Another pottery center grew up in the Connecticut towns, especially Hartford and Norwalk. There were, of course, redware potters in the state before the Revolution, but the greatest development of the industry came about 1890. Nathaniel Seymour and Seth Goodwin both made slip-decorated and plain redware at Hartford before 1800, but their successors, "Major" Seymour, who was in business until 1842, and Goodwin & Webster and other partnerships who carried on the Goodwin pottery until 1900, made stoneware and brownware. Adam States, driven from Huntington during the Revolution, built a pottery at Stonington, where he and his sons and grandsons made stoneware until 1884. The Smith pottery at Norwalk was another of these family potteries which was in business for many years. The potters of New York state also became active about 1800 or a few years later, and concentrated on stoneware. At Albany, Paul Cushman was working between 1805 and 1825, and the Nash pottery at Utica, built in 1819 and later taken over by Noah White, continued until 1875. Nathan Clark at Athens began making stoneware in 1820, continuing until the Civil War, with branches at Lyons and Mount Morris. In western Massachusetts and Vermont, redware apparently continued to be made until a slightly later period. The Crafts' pottery at Whateley did not turn to stoneware until 1833, while the Farrars of Middlebury and Fairfax and the Fentons of Dorset, Burlington and St. Johnsbury, who worked in the first half of the century, apparently made both types until 1850.

This New England and New York stoneware is unlike that

made in the territory to the South in many respects. So little good stoneware clay is found in this section that the potters were compelled to import New Jersey clay, bringing it as far north as Nashua, New Hampshire by rail and water. .Consequently, the uniform clear gray and buff shades of New Jersey and Pennsylvania stoneware were attained only by those plants so close to the clay deposits that they could use the stoneware clay alone, as in Connecticut and along the Hudson River. Where distance and transportation costs made this expensive, native and imported clays were mixed. Thus some finely made and decorated ware made in New Hampshire is a reddish brown, and all shades between this and light gray appear, including yellow, mustard and buff. Jars and other hollow-ware were given a coat of Albany Clay, lead glaze or vitreous brick clay on the interior, where, as they were set in the kiln mouth to mouth to conserve space, the salt glaze vapor could not penetrate. The shapes and decorations are usually simple, but incised, modeled or finely painted pieces, while not common, are found more frequently than in Pennsylvania, some of them being obviously show-pieces of their makers. Some large pieces were reproduced in moulds, as is seen in two handsome water coolers with classic relief decoration and ring handles, which are identical except that the one marked "L. W. Fenton, St. Johnsbury, Vt." has added scrolls in cobalt blue, while that made by Hastings and Belding at South Ashfield, Massachusetts is plain. These potters were business men, and believed in advertising, so that much of their ware bears the makers' name and address, usually stamped or impressed.

Between 1825 and 1850, the stoneware industry continued to grow in this territory. But a new type of ware was being developed, which was to reduce stoneware to a strictly utilitarian material. Bennington, Vermont, had a pottery as early as 1793, when Captain John Norton began the manufacture of redware, to be succeeded by his son, who introduced stoneware, and by two more generations, who made it until 1894. But Julius Norton became interested in the possibilities of the Rockingham type of brownware and of yellow-ware, which had been made in New Jersey by several firms since 1830, and was just beginning to become popular in the Ohio Valley. He formed a partnership with his brother-in-law, Christopher Weber Fenton, son of another pioneer Vermont potter, in 1844. The firm continued to make stoneware, with an increasing production of the later type, and some experiments with white porcelain bodies, until 1848, when the two separated, Norton continuing with his stoneware business.

It should not be necessary to give a detailed story of the Fenton pottery and its wares here, as John Spargo has given a very complete account of them in his book on the potteries of Bennington, and has covered the subject adequately in a later work. But, in spite of a strong objection to poaching on others' preserves, and a rather faint admiration for the types of ware made at Bennington, the subject cannot be slighted. Fenton's influence on the pottery industry of the country is so considerable, and Bennington ware means so much to the collector, that the story must be given in full.

Fenton began business, first on his own account, then with several very temporary partners, then with A. P. Lyman as Lyman & Fenton from 1849 to 1852. Finally, with Oliver A. Gager, who was later with Carr & Morrison in New York and after 1881 was American representative for the Havilands of Limoges, he formed the United States Pottery Company in 1853. As early as 1847-48, he developed the porcelain body into the production of the ornamental pitchers and ornaments in white bisque or unglazed porcelain which we know as "Bennington Parian." These were supplemented with other pieces and designs, and with variations in the way of a fawn body, hammered effect grounds, or white figures on a blue ground. The factory, however, also continued the manufacture of the Rockingham type of brownware, with the mottled dark glaze which Fenton probably introduced in this country, and he built up a good business in this. They made large amounts of common ware, pie-plates, milk pans and soap dishes, as well as relief decorated tableware, pitchers, tobies, tea-pots, sugar-bowls and book flasks bearing such ambiguous titles as "Parting Spirits," "Ladies Companion," "Hermit's Companion," "Bennington Battle" and "Indian's Lament." The ornamental pieces include figure bottles, candle-sticks, lamps, picture-frames, curtain tie-backs and vases copied from a Sandwich glass celery vase, and culminate in the large and beautifully modeled dogs, deer and lions which are the masterpieces of Bennington or any other Rockingham ware.

The importance of the Bennington factory in the history of the American pottery industry or to collectors, lies in the wide variety of types originated there. Other factories copied, only too freely, the models and glazes of the United States Pottery, and did so with such success that only fifty per cent of the Bennington ware being marked, according to Mr. Spargo, the remaining fifty per cent is indistinguishable from the best ware turned out by competitors. This "best" is an important qualification. Much of the Rockingham of other factories is heavier in body, cruder in modeling, and shows a lighter, less brilliant and less clearly marked tortoise-shell glaze than that of Bennington.

In brownware, Fenton also originated the "Patent Flint Enamel," whose distinctive feature is the fine mottling of colors, green, blue, orange or yellow, in, not under, the glaze. These were applied by a patented process, by which finely ground coloring oxides were sprinkled on the glazed ware while still wet, an ordinary pepper-pot being used for the operation. In spite of the patent, the glaze was successfully copied by Bennett of Baltimore, Beerbauer & Company of Elizabeth, New Jersey and others. Another Bennington specialty was the "scroddle ware," in which layers of plastic clay, each containing a different coloring material, were mixed together just enough to give a marbled or veined effect, and then pressed in moulds. This was copied from an early English earthenware type, and was again imitated by competitors, including Bennett. Rarer types, which are confined to Bennington ware, are the "combed" pieces, in which a coating of slip, differing in color from the body, has been scratched through with a steel comb like that used in graining wood to show fine waved lines, and "marbled ware," in which coloring oxides, brown or tan, are veined or marbled with a rag or sponge over the surface of the piece before glazing.

These coatings or glazes, possibly with the porcelain body already described, which was developed from local clays, are Fenton's claim to fame as a potter. His designers and modelers were competent and very successful in meeting the demands of popular taste, and the process by which his ware was made allowed them to comply easily and cheaply with that rule of Victorian art that all surfaces must be covered by ornament, regardless of its quality or appropriateness. Daniel Greatbach, an Englishman of a family of potters, is the most famous of the Bennington designers, and his hound-handled pitcher is probably the best-known production of the factory. It was copied extensively by other plants, yet Fenton never thought enough of it to put the factory mark on it, nor to duplicate it in Flint Enamel, Parian or White Granite, as he did many of the other Rockingham models. Greatbach copied the design from one he had already made for D. & J. Henderson at Jersey City and James Carr at South Amboy, and it was again copied, more or less closely, by Bennett, by Nichols & Alford at Burlington, and by Harker, Taylor & Company at East Liverpool and others. In the closing years of the century, the Vance Faience Company at Tiltonville, Ohio, issued a hound-handled pitcher which they claimed was from the original mould, but usually were considerate enough to mark their product.

Greatbach also copied at Bennington his own Jersey City toby pitchers, adding, however, a vine handle, and a pitcher with a twisted rope handle, as well as a grapevine-handled pitcher he had modeled during his brief partnership with James Carr in 1852. Several of his other designs, including the cow creamer, are identified with English originals, and even his fine standing lion is a copy of an English one.

Our American potters' habit of copying foreign styles, only too often copying them badly, and their entirely logical reasons, will be discussed later. These especial instances are mentioned here because of the common tendency to acclaim Bennington ware as typically and originally American, which, so far as the designs are concerned, can hardly be true. Rockingham ware remains, however, in spite of its British origin, an American type, more fully developed and more used here than abroad, and the United States Pottery was easily first in this field. Its so-called Parian is also important, but deserves less consideration, since it is so largely an adaptation and simplification of the English ware.

The closing of Fenton's factory in 1858 was only the beginning, not the end of the production of Rockingham ware in this country, as enormous quantities continued to be made, especially in the Ohio Valley, up to 1900. Parian, the other specialty of the pottery, was also made in several places. Fenton and most of his workmen left Bennington, he going as far as Peoria, Illinois to start another factory, others appearing at potteries throughout the country, where their technical knowledge obviously improved the quality of the ware. But the pottery industry was gravitating to the new centers at Trenton and East Liverpool. Consequently, there was little production of yellow-ware and Rockingham in New England and New York, and less of White Granite during the last forty years of the century. Boston had two factories—the short-lived Boston Earthenware Factory of Frederick Mear and the New England Pottery, which, founded in 1854 for the production of yellow-ware and Rockingham, followed the general trend by making some White Granite about 1875, but finally turned to the manufacture of porcelain and art ware.

In New York, with its large and prosperous buying public, there were several manufacturers of finer pottery, none of them particularly successful. The Salamander Works made some Rockingham about 1848, and disappeared. James Carr came from South Amboy in 1853, and as Carr & Morrison, made Rockingham until 1858, then the Majolica ware just becoming fashionable, including the first cauliflower-shaped teapot, and finally the usual

White Granite until he retired in 1888. Charles Cartlidge made soft-paste porcelain at Greenpoint about 1848, later changing to the bisque hard-paste porcelain or Parian, with some handsome figures and imitations of the Wedgwood Jasper, but failed in 1856. The Union Porcelain Works in Brooklyn was founded in 1850 and became, after a false start, the first successful porcelain factory in the country.

New York was also the home of the first really successful "art pottery" in the country. This was the hard-burned pinkish terra-cotta made by John Rogers in large figures and groups, covered with drab-colored paint, from 1860 until about 1890. These "Rogers Groups", found on all correct parlor tables for a generation or more, were pressed in moulds, but they show considerable technical skill. The figures, redolent of Mid-Victorian sentimentality, were actually modeled by some talented sculptors, notably Daniel Chester French. The factory also produced large and fine figures in white "Parian". Although he has escaped previous notice in American ceramic history, John Rogers is actually a figure of some importance in the field.

CHAPTER VI

Potters and Pottery of Western Pennsylvania, West Virginia and the Middle West

THE Mason-Dixon Line and the Ohio River form entirely political boundaries, while the Allegheny Mountains are the actual dividing line in the settlement of the country and in the development of its industries. The territory beyond the mountains was a wilderness until after the Revolution, and was the frontier, with no industries, until 1800. These industries, when they did come, were the natural extension of those already in existence in the country. The early pottery of the Atlantic seaboard shows characteristics which reflect the racial origins of its makers, modified by American life and thought, so that Pennsylvania ware differs materially from that of New Jersey, which is again unlike that made in the northern states. West of the mountains, we find pottery which reflects the origin and training of its makers, but these are now American, not European, influences.

These influences are seen most clearly in the pottery of Ohio, which must be considered in some detail, since this state has been an important producer for generations. Ideal raw material, fuel, and its great artery of transportation made the Ohio River valley a pottery center of national importance. The inherited traditions of the first settlers of Ohio are reflected in the pottery they made, but are clearer, to the most casual observer, in the homes they built, the architectural types of seven hundred miles along the seaboard being compressed into a hundred and fifty along the Ohio. Thus the Western Reserve to the north has villages of New England white-painted wooden houses in the style of the Classic Revival and the salt-box, grouped around greens on which sit white tall-spired churches. Only a few miles to the South, these

66

are replaced by plain solid red brick farmhouses, and small towns whose brick homes are set directly on the street around the central square which we associate with Pennsylvania. Farther south again, there are dignified white columned mansions transplanted from the Southern states.

The first known pottery west of the Alleghanies was built at Morgantown, West Virginia, by a man named Foulke about 1784. He made redware covered by a yellow slip, similar to that of some Philadelphia potters, and plain redware. The pottery was taken over about 1800 by John W. Thompson who was succeeded by his son, Greenland Thompson, in 1840. From then until 1890, stoneware was made, including some vases and pitchers with applied relief of roses and leaves, and blue-decorated jars.

Beyond the Ohio, the first potter of whom we have any record is William McFarland, who came from Kentucky to the small settlement on the Ohio shore known as Losantiville, later to be Cincinnati. He built what was, according to local historians, "a manufactory of earthenware, probably the first factory of any kind in the place," and was either joined or succeeded by James and Robert Caldwell, also from Kentucky, who advertised that they were making "earthenware at the house of William McFarland" in 1801. Since the alluvial clays of this section are all red-burning, we are safe in assuming that this earthenware was redware, but no examples are known. Two more potters, William Sanders and William Iler, came to Cincinnati a few years later, and the city directory of 1819 lists three, employing fourteen men. A number of others, including James Vance, who had left a thriving plant at Greensboro, Pennsylvania to drift down the river, came within the next few years. By 1826, stoneware was being manufactured, improved transportation having made the deposits of stoneware clays farther up the Ohio available.

In Pittsburgh, Bracken & James were making redware before 1803, Thomas Bracken carrying on the pottery until 1825. William Price is listed as making "delft-ware", which is difficult to identify, in 1805, but the pottery industry never thrived in this city. Even as late as 1857, only five potteries are contrasted with thirty-four glass factories. In Greensboro, on the Monongahela south of Pittsburgh, Alexander and James Vance were making redware about 1800, to be succeeded by Alexander Boughner and his sons from about 1812 to 1890. They originated a distinctive type with a fairly hard-burned brown, not red, body, glazed inside only, and ornamented with tulips and scrolls painted or, later, stencilled in bright glaze, showing as a darker brown than the body. This type was carried to Ohio, probably by that James Vance who went "down the River" to Cincinnati about 1830, but the Boughners turned to stoneware, and made this small village an important center of its production. This ware, bearing the names of A. & W. Boughner, Williams & Reppert, the Eagle Pottery of James Hamilton and others, found its way from Philadelphia to Indianapolis during the last half of the century.

Early potteries are recorded all through the Middle West, one at Detroit as early as 1820, but most of them naturally sprang up in Ohio. J. C. Fisher was making redware, glazed and unglazed, at Steubenville in 1806; Samuel Sullivan, later head of Ohio's first glass factory, the White Glass Works built in 1825, was making redware plates, cups and saucers at Zanesville in 1808; Thomas Hughes was working at Salem in 1812; while Solomon Purdy was turning out "red and yellow ware," obviously slip-covered or decorated redware, at Putnam in 1820. But, by 1814, Joseph Rosier had built a small plant for the production of stoneware at Jonathan Creek in Muskingum County, near Zanesville. He was followed by so many others, attracted by the fine stoneware clays of the vicinity, that by 1840 there were twenty-two potteries in the county, representing a capital of eighteen thousand dollars, nearly half of that invested in the industry in the entire state at that date. Being close to the Ohio River, they were were able to take advantage of the transportation it offered, and supplied the entire Ohio and Mississippi valleys as far South as New Orleans with stoneware.

The pottery industry in the Middle West naturally centered in those sections where good stoneware clays occur. In eastern Ohio, north of Zanesville, there were several potteries in Tuscarawas County. In Canton, Stark County, John Shorb, Jr. was making stoneware in 1817 and later so many names appear that it is impossible to mention them all. Edward Houghton, a Vermonter who had worked at Bennington, built a plant at Dalton, Ohio in 1842, which is still in operation, and made brownware and stoneware, including a log cabin bank. Summit County had only five potteries in 1840, one of them started by Fiske and Smith in 1828, but by 1870 there were thirty-five or more in the district, and Akron, the county seat, was the Stoneware City before its present title of the Rubber City was thought of. The usual "line" of stoneware and coarse brownware was made, but stoneware beer bottles were the chief product, and miniature brown jugs, some less than an inch in height, the favorite toys.

Farther west, there was a thriving stoneware center in Indiana, where H. R. Atcheson built a stoneware plant at Annapolis in 1841. Others appeared at Logotee in 1842 and Clay City in 1846, and an important industry grew up in Dubois, Clay and Parke counties. Illinois, which in 1900 was second only to Ohio in the production of stoneware, saw its first pottery at Ripley in 1836. By 1880, there were twelve potteries there, one of them, that of John N. Stout, making brownware, with some carefully modeled ornamental pieces, as well as stoneware. C. W. Fenton of Bennington came to Peoria in 1859, and built a plant where some white earthenware and yellow-ware were made with little success. He gave up the attempt in 1865, and stoneware and brownware were made until 1889, when some White Granite was produced. Iowa had a pottery at Sargeant's Bluff in 1838, which operated, under several owners until 1900, and another at Vernon in 1841, while several others, all making stoneware, were built before 1860. In Missouri, there was a pottery at Caldwell, Calloway County in 1827, which also ran until about 1900, and several at Washington, Franklin County, where a Mr. Walford is said to have made some white earthenware in 1848. And, finally, the plant at Red Wing, Minnesota, built by Joseph Pohl in 1858, was the largest producer of stoneware in the United States in 1888.

Among the most interesting of the early Mid-Western settlements are the religious or communistic communities. These were actually numerous, the Mormons successively at Kirtland, Ohio, Nauvoo, Illinois and Independence, Missouri; The Harmonists or Rappites at Harmony, Pennsylvania, New Harmony, Indiana, then again at Beaver, Pennsylvania, succeeded at New Harmony by Robert Owen's Community; the Shakers at Dayton, near Cleveland and elsewhere in Ohio, and in Amana, Iowa; and the Zoarites or German Separatists at Zoar, Ohio. In accordance with their ideals of common ownership and self-sufficiency, several of these owned potteries, particularly those at Beaver, at Amana and at Zoar. This last was one of the most interesting of these communities. Founded in 1817, and incorporated in 1832, this small community of less than a thousand inhabitants was worth the then large sum of one and a half million dollars in 1875. It was not disbanded until 1898, and the village is largely untouched by time or modern improvements today. The beautiful church and impressive "King's House," built for the leader, are surprisingly fine examples of late Georgian architecture, while the old houses and barns, many with red tile roofs, and the communal flower-garden are decidedly lovely.

The Zoarites set up a tile plant soon after they settled in Ohio, but it was abandoned when new houses ceased to be built. The membership counted no potters, and the enterprising leader apparently engaged an outsider, Solomon Purdy, who had made red-ware at Putnam. The records are not clear, but the Society was selling "porringers," which may have been small shallow bowls, to the people of the neighborhood by 1834, and those early pieces known to have been made at Zoar are typically Ohioan, even to the yellow or buff slip used by Purdy at Putnam. Purdy was settled farther north at Atwater about 1840, and made much fine stoneware there, but the Zoar pottery was carried on by his assistants until about 1853. Sales of "stone crocks" are recorded in 1841 and later, but little of this ware seems to have been made. Coarse brownware, occasionally decorated with simple incised lines, often covered by a dark brown or black glaze—dull or bright—but very rarely marked, is characteristic, and some more sophisticated Rockingham was attempted.

The Economy Society at Harmony, Pennsylvania, a similar but more worldly organization, also owned a pottery as early as 1810. In their later home at Beaver Falls, they had one operated entirely by water-power from the Ohio River, which produced redware, stoneware, and crude brownware from 1834 to 1889. It was then sold to the Mayer Pottery Company, who made White Granite there until after 1900. As far west as Amana, Iowa, the Shaker colony there built a pottery in 1850, and made redware, with some attempts at cream-colored earthenware, until 1900. The ware made by these societies is, as might be expected, very plain and simple, and rarely bears makers' marks, which would be contrary to their communistic tenets.

This Mid-Western pottery naturally developed certain definite characteristics. The first redware of Ohio was made by potters who had learned their trade in their Eastern homes, so is very like that of Pennsylvania and New England. The true Pennsylvania sgraffito is unknown, but incised ornament was used, and considerable slip-decorated ware was made. Black and rare colored glazes were used, while much of this early ware was covered by cream slip, colored yellow or buff by the glaze over it. Since the red clays of the Middle West are superior to those of the East in burning qualities, the potters soon discovered that, by carrying them to higher temperatures, they could produce dense and strong ware. Further, while Eastern red clays will not take salt glaze, but absorb it with little change of color and only a slight surface lustre, some Ohio clays of this type take it so well that the characteristic gray color is fully developed. Thus when, as is usually

71

the case, the interior has been covered by a brown glaze, Ohio salt-glazed redware is difficult to distinguish from the usual stoneware.

This salt-glazed redware is exceptional, and much of the early Ohio redware, like the pieces shown in Figures 49 and 52, is difficult to distinguish, except by a slight heaviness and crudity of glaze, from that made farther east. The "slip clay" imported from Albany was used by many Ohio potters, both for hard-burned redware and over the light-burning clays common in the Middle West. These were, of course, the ideal material for stoneware, and for the later factory-produced yellow-ware and Rockingham, but a great number of the small potteries also utilized them for rather heavy thrown ware, jars, jugs, churns and pitchers, and many other pieces. Toys and whistles appear in this ware, and were a specialty of the potteries of Mogadore. Well-made fat lamps and occasional ornamental pieces, such as the flower-pot of Figure 57, with its incised design, were made occasionally. This type of brownware was burned in crude kilns, in which the temperature and conditions necessary to develop full fusion of the Albany clay could not be secured, so that the coating is very rarely a smooth high glaze. Coloring oxides, or lead glaze mixtures, were also added to the clay, so that there is much variation from a clear transparent glaze to the more usual hard stony enamel or slip, in colors from sepia or red-brown to black-brown.

This brownware forms a distinct and common Mid-Western type. But the Mid-Western potteries also made a great variety of stoneware, most of it rather plain and solid, which, during the latter half of the nineteenth century, they supplied to the entire country. This ware is usually a medium gray in shade, with some buffs and browns, but with less variation than is found in the stoneware of New England. Blue decorations are common, rarely with the incised outlines of the finest Eastern pieces, but with occasional elaborate floral designs and rare figures and scenes. In the later productions, stencilled patterns appear, ranging from the name of the maker or distributor in blue to the large and spirited eagle designs used by Hamilton of Greensboro and others. Since this was the everyday product of most of the potters, they amused themselves with occasional show pieces having relief or incised decorations, toys and the odd examples which can only be described as inspirations. One local fashion is seen in the jugs made by E. Hall of Tuscarawas County, Ohio, which have the applied relief motif of the clasped hands seen so commonly on whiskey-flasks from the Mid-Western glass factories of the sixties and seventies.

Hall also made the jug of Figures 54 and 55, which seems to be his masterpiece. Intended to commemorate the presidential campaign of 1856, it bears the date, the inscription "Buck and Breck" for Buchanan and Breckenridge, and full details, "Made by E. Hall Newton Township, Muskingum County, Ohio, at W. P. Harrises Factory, Holesale and Retail Dealers in Stoneware, For Joshua Cites." The reverse is covered by a quite elaborate relief design, much of which is applied, as are the bands of moulding at base and neck. By contrast, the jar of Figure 58 is plain and crude, but it is also a stoneware campaign banner, as the balloon issuing from the odd creature's mouth bears the words "Hurra for Van Buren." The provenance is not definite, but the piece was made in western Pennsylvania or eastern Ohio for the presidential campaign of 1836.

The rural potteries of the region were, like similar ones in other sections, usually small. That 1840 census report which shows ninety-nine potteries in Ohio gives the total number of men employed in them as only two hundred. As in the East, too, many of these potteries descended from one generation to another. But pottery plants of the modern factory type also grew up, even stoneware being produced in them during the last part of the century. The yellow-ware and Rockingham wares which came into general use after 1845, supplanting the heavier hand-made pottery for many purposes, were suited to quantity production rather than to the methods of the individual potters, and the men who made them were not stay-at-home countrymen but, employers and workmen alike, drifters, in the manner of our early glass- and metal-workers.

The first production of yellow-ware and Rockingham in the Middle West was in Pittsburgh, where two Englishmen, Vodrey and Frost, with several workmen from Staffordshire, built a pottery in 1827. According to a contemporary newspaper report, they planned to manufacture porcelain. This was reportorial exaggeration; they expected to make white earthenware of the Staffordshire type, but found the local clays unsuitable. They did make some yellow-ware, and probably stoneware as well, but became discouraged after three years, and traveled down the river to Louisville, Kentucky to manage a yellow-ware plant which had been built there. This was more successful, but its owners were inveigled into financing James Clews' whiteware factory at Troy, Indiana. When Clews gave this up as hopeless, Vodrey moved his organization there and made yellow-ware and brownware until 1847. Then he was attracted by the possibilities of East Liverpool, Ohio, and made his final move, founding a plant for the manufacture of Rockingham and yellow-ware which, first with partners and then under his sons, flourished until after 1900.

This city of East Liverpool produced the great bulk of the yellow-ware and Rockingham, particularly of the simpler types, made in the United States between 1840 and 1900. There was a red-ware pottery, operated by John Koontz, in the vicinity as early as 1807, but the real pioneer of the industry was James Bennett, an immigrant from Staffordshire who had worked at Jersey City, Troy and Cincinnati. With Anthony Kearns as his financial backer, he established himself at East Liverpool in 1839, burning his first kiln of ware, mostly yellow-ware mugs, in 1840, and peddling them through the surrounding country himself with some profit. His success was so immediate that George Breed was advertising "Bennett's Liverpool ware" in Pittsburgh the following year. In later life, he claimed that he made the first Rockingham ware in America, but this honor should probably go to the Jersey

74

City Pottery, since a few pieces of this bearing a mark which would hardly have been used after 1840 are known.

James Bennett's brothers, Daniel, Edwin and William, came from England to join him in 1841. But some difficulty in shipping their products, and the Ohio River floods, caused dissatisfaction with their location, and James, Daniel and Edwin moved to Pittsburgh in 1844, leaving William to sell their first pottery to Croxall Brothers, who became one of the most important firms in East Liverpool. Bennett's Pennsylvania Pottery, in Birmingham, the southern section of Pittsburgh, made Rockingham and yellow-ware, exhibiting a distinctive paneled pitcher with a mask spout at the Franklin Institute of Philadelphia in 1846. Edwin, still restless, moved to Baltimore in this same year, founding this time a permanent business. James retired, while Daniel and William carried on the Pittsburgh plant for several years, being listed as a manufacture of "domestic Queensware" in the directory of 1847. In 1849, William rejoined Edwin in Baltimore, while Daniel carried on the Pittsburgh enterprise, being listed in the local directory of 1856 as a "manufacturer of fancy colored Iron stoneware" and appearing again in 1860.

In East Liverpool again, Benjamin Harker, who had been interested in Bennett's enterprise, built a pottery in an old log house in 1840, and Isaac W. Knowles, who had sold part of Bennett's first kiln of ware went into business in 1853, both founding firms which became large and important producers of the East Liverpool specialties. Another English potter, John Goodwin, built a factory in 1844, but sold it to Baggott Brothers in 1853, and financed two of his workmen, William Taylor, who had been a thrower at Jersey City, and Henry Speeler, in starting the manufacture of Rockingham and yellow-ware at Trenton, New Jersey. Their success there soon brought others, establishing Trenton as a pottery center, but Goodwin returned to East Liverpool and bought another pottery, which he and his sons carried on until after 1900. The pottery industry in the town grew so rapidly that by 1880 twenty-three potteries with sixty-seven kilns were operating there. These were factories representing capital beyond the means of the average potter. In all, nearly a hundred individuals, partnerships and corporations succeeded each other in various combinations. An attempt to chronicle them would be entirely too confusing, but it is interesting to note that the same names occur again and again.

The ware made in these potteries was naturally very similar and, since Rockingham and yellow-ware are rarely marked, particularly those of East Liverpool, is difficult to attribute to any particular source. Some of the Rockingham made here is finely potted and shows a beautiful bright dark mottled tortoise-shell but much is streaked, not mottled, and more shows a duller glaze, in which the manganese appears as a film on the surface. In others, also rather heavy and thick in body, the tortoise-shell marking is very light in tone, actually a brown and yellow stippling, and this is characteristic of the late Rockingham which East Liverpool turned out in quantity until after 1900. The finest early ware, however, is indistinguishable from unmarked Rockingham made at Bennington, Baltimore or elsewhere. In 1856, Woodward, Blakley & Company, predecessors of Vodrey Brothers, advertised, "The Highest Premium awarded by the American Institute, a gold medal, was recently awarded to the ware manufactured by us, 'uniting the beauty and finish of the Bennington ware with the durability of other wares manufactured in the United States.'" The East Liverpool potters copied the Bennington "Flint Enamel" glaze as early as 1852, but rather poorly, sometimes with a mere sprinkle of green, or streaks of green and dark brown over the relief design. Others, especially the innovator William Bloor, used mottled glazes which were blue or black instead of brown.

Bennington's designs were also copied fairly closely in Ohio, where several variations of the familiar hound-handled pitcher appear, as well as a tall octagonal paneled one, book flasks entitled "Coming Through the Rye" and "History of Bourbon," even the picture frames of Figure 57, and, of course, the common mugs, soap dishes, pie-plates and milk pans. In addition, many original designs were developed, including plates with relief modeling around the rim, cake, pudding and butter moulds, like the cup-cake pan of Figure 64, covered tureens and vegetable dishes, flower-pots and paneled cylindrical sugar or cookie jars. The Ben-nington paneled candlesticks and dog door-stops also appear in local variations, as in the dog of Figure 66. Yellow-ware was, of course, the cheapest and plainest form of common earthenware, but even in this a few graceful fluted bowls and mugs with col-ored bands showing some similarity to the English Mocha-Ware are found. Another specialty of several potteries, here and else-where, was the common door and furniture knob, graceful de-scribed by contemporary reporters as "Door Furniture" or "Min-eral Door-Knobs."

All this ware, made at East Liverpool, Zanesville, Cincinnati, Akron, Putnam, Ohio, Pittsburgh, New Brighton and Beaver Falls, Pennsylvania, and other towns along the rivers, was natur-ally distributed throughout the Ohio and Mississippi valleys by boat, as far south as New Orleans. More of it was sold by ped-dlers going from door to door throughout the country, a method of distribution which the Ohio potteries did not abandon until well after 1900.

East Liverpool was the center of the production of Rockingham and yellow-ware, but, as might be expected, was rivalled by other towns. Uzziah Kendall and Sons built a stoneware pottery in Cin-cinnati in 1834, and made some of the later ware before they moved farther west in 1850. George Scott made the same wares after 1846, William Bromley between 1842 and 1860, and there were several other producers in the city. In Zanesville, more Eng-lish potters, Bernard Howson and his partners, were making yel-low-ware and Rockingham by 1850, building a pottery which is still the site of a ceramic industry, and George Pyatt started an-other in 1849, to move on to Cincinnati and farther west and then return. Some of this ware was also made in Akron, and Clews' Indiana Pottery at Troy, after Jabez Vodrey abandoned it,

77

was carried on by other potters, who made some Rockingham. Christopher Weber Fenton, after the closing of the Bennington factory in 1858, moved to Peoria, Illinois, where he built a plant to manufacture the Bennington specialties. He operated this from 1859 until 1865, without much success, and was succeeded by other managers, who made the simpler stoneware and brownware, with some White Granite between 1889 and its final closing in 1894. In Kaolin, Missouri, Elihu H. Shepard, a St. Louis capitalist, built a plant to utilize the white clays of the vicinity in 1851. He engaged George Pyatt to manage it, and some yellow-ware was made when it proved impossible to achieve whiteware.

The Mid-Western factory potters were too enterprising to confine themselves to Rockingham and yellow-ware when those of Trenton and elsewhere were making a success of whitewares. William Bloor bought part of the Woodward Blakley & Company plant in East Liverpool in 1860 and turned out biscuit porcelain or Parian in the style of Bennington, frequently copying their blue backgrounds, but painting the color in the ware after it was made instead of introducing it into the body. He made busts of "noted statesmen," butter dishes, mugs and other pieces, like that shown in Figure 23, some glazed and decorated, but sold his factory in 1862 and returned to Trenton. In 1867, Tempest, Brockman and Company of Cincinnati, who had been making yellow-ware since 1862, produced the first White Granite in the Middle West, and were followed by other firms, George Scott, Michael and Nimrod Tempest, who made some biscuit porcelain between 1860 and 1865, and were then succeeded by Frederick Dallas and others. Many of the East Liverpool potters remained faithful to their first standby, but others, headed by Knowles, Taylor and Knowles in 1872, changed to White Granite, until by 1884, sixty-three kilns out of a total of eighty-seven were devoted to whiteware, mainly White Granite and cream-colored ware.

The development of art pottery in the United States does not come within the chronological scope of this study. Of course, the airs and graces of the "Parian" and "Majolica" wares certainly destined them for this classification, but today's standards are much higher than those of Victorian days. Art pottery, as we know it, had its American origin in the Rookwood Pottery of Cincinnati, founded by Mrs. Bellamy Storer. As Maria Longworth, of a wealthy Cincinnati family, she dabbled in the then fashionable and lady-like art of china painting for five years, then, with growing interest, spent a year at the Dallas Pottery, making, glazing and firing her ware. Finally, in 1880, she built her own "Rookwood Pottery." After nine years of experiment and failures, during which Joseph Baily, a practical potter, came from the Dallas pottery as manager, W. W. Taylor became a partner, and the famous matte glaze was developed. Success was recognized by the award of a gold medal at the Paris Exposition of 1889. Those critics who complain that American wares never equal the standards set by the European factories, such as those of Sèvres, Dresden, Copenhagen and Berlin, forget that all these were able to establish their standards, and to disregard many failures in attaining them, because any deficits in their finances were met by interested rulers or governments. This burden was carried by Mrs. Storer at Rookwood, and, when she retired in 1890, Mr. Taylor organized a company to take over the business, erecting a new plant in 1892. Rookwood has had less pressure from dividendless stockholders to withstand than its competitors, but has spent much more in developing its wares, particularly in the field of fine glazes, so that it is rather a tribute to the American public's appreciation of fine ware that the factory is still in business. Much of the Rookwood ware undoubtedly "dates;" its designs are still, as they have always been, somewhat conservative; but its forms, glazes and decoration are quietly fine.

Another pioneer in the field of art ware was also a Cincinnatian, and also a woman, Miss Mary Louise McLaughlin. Graduating from the art school there in 1876, she became interested in china decorating, and, in 1871, was the first American to experiment with underglaze painting, working on unglazed ware from the Coultry Pottery. After twelve years of work in other mediums, she conceived the ambitious idea of making porcelain, building her own kiln. Later, in 1900, she achieved the technically difficult feat of making single-fired porcelain.

CHAPTER VII

Potters and Pottery of the South

IN the light of our present knowledge, it is possible to write the history of the pottery industry of the South only in very general terms. Even the local characteristics of the Southern ware, which are apparent here as in other sections of the country, are confusing. In fact, they make the ware difficult to fit into any general technical classification. These characteristics are largely due to the clays used by the Southern potters, which are very different from those known in the North and Middle West. Then, also, the Southern potters have been isolated for generations from the current of improvements in modern manufacture and technique. One result of this is that the production of hand-made utilitarian pottery is still a living industry in the South, with scores of small plants operating, where at most three or four Northern potters of the old school survive. This ware is still made by the most primitive methods, although it has, within recent years, been more or less standardized into "art ware," with some unfortunate experiments with commercial colored glazes. But it still remains an interesting subject to the student of pottery.

It is extremely difficult to secure adequate information on the potters of the South. Historical details are difficult to obtain and are then not too reliable. There are several adequate reasons for this obscurity. Since the industries of the South played a negligible part in its development, Southern historians have confined their attention to past glories, political, military and social, and few of those studies of local industries so valuable to a compilation such as this have been made. Further, in the aristocratic, almost feudal, civilization of the South, the potters were individuals of slight importance, so that local historians give them scant

81

attention, and the problem of reconstructing their lives and work is a difficult one. In other sections of the country, where the potter's trade furnished, if no great men, at least selectmen to the towns, majors to the militia and deacons to the churches, it is always possible to locate some records, but these are largely missing in the South.

The present-day Southern potters are almost unanimous in the opinion that they are descended from immigrant Staffordshire potters, and that the trade has been carried on, in many cases, through generations of the same families. This opinion is probably based on fact, but has been largely disregarded in the following check-list because so few definite names and dates are available. The potters's names show a common English ancestry, but it is noticable that few or none of them are familiar to the student of English pottery. Many names appear among both Staffordshire and American potters—Goodwin, Beech, Wood, Hancock, Greatbatch, Bennett, Vodrey, and others, but the Americans are not in the South, which casts some doubt on the legend. But, whatever their origin, these Southern potters form an unusual class in many respects. Much has been written in the past few years on the "mountain folk" and "poor whites" of the South. We know that, originally of good British blood, they have spent many generations outside the current of American life, with results that are never entirely good, and are often disastrous. But, even among these highly individual people, the potters were a class apart.

There were potteries in the cities and in the coastal plain, some of them important ones, employing slave labor. But the best pottery clays are found in the hills, so most of the potters were there also. The other people of these back-waters of civilization were small farmers, laborers or, at most, insignificant tradesmen, but the potters were artisans, not to say artists. Anywhere in the North. they would have found the company of their own kind. For these men, this was impossible, the few skilled workmen being largely the property or dependents of the great planters. These they despised, but they also rather looked down in their own people as unskilled field hands, so that they necessarily kept very much to themselves. Unquestionably, many of these small potteries have been in the hands of the same families for as much as six or seven generations. But the attempt to trace them back to their foundation is extremely difficult. The usual sources of information, contemporary newspapers, court records and legal transactions, show few traces of the potters, and even family records are negligible. One man, who spent considerable time in the attempt to trace the histories of some of these potter families, came to the conclusion that there had been so much carelessness about the legality of the line of descent in the past that family trees were, in many cases, too close to family skeletons to be popular.

In the *Travels* of Captain John Smith, he states, referring to the colony at Jamestown, "the furnaces for glass and pottery are in decay." This is, of course, the first record of the industry in the United States, but the pottery, while undoubtedly in existence as early as 1611, cannot have operated over any period of time. Excavations on the site of Jamestown have yielded white enameled tiles, obviously Dutch, several examples of sgraffito ware of English type, and some plainer lead glazed pieces. It is said to have made large covered jars for storing grain which may be of local origin, but, from the collector's point of view, these must remain more or less legendary. Georgia, last settled of the Southern colonies, contributes their first known potter, one Andrew Duché who came from Philadelphia about 1732, and established a thriving business, which continued for some thirty years. Duché's father had been a potter in England and Pennsylvania, so that his son probably made the plain and possibly slip-decorated redware which was common in England before 1700, although no examples of this exist. Duché, however, must have been an unusual man, as he discovered the possibilities of the white-burning clays of Georgia, and is definitely recorded as producing "China Ware" in 1738.

The next potters of whom we have any record in the South were the Moravians, who settled in North Carolina about 1740.

By 1756 their town of Betharaba boasted a pottery, and they continued to make slip-decorated and plain lead-glazed redware of the South German type for eighty years. They were of the same race and religion as the first German settlers of Pennsylvania, and theirs was also a religious community. Consequently, their potter is known only as Brother Aust, and Joe Kindig, Jr. has found several references to his work in the records of the community. From these, it appears that the pottery was eminently successful. In fact, the authorities of the colony were disturbed because people came from a radius of fifty or sixty miles to buy the ware. This pottery at Betharaba continued until 1777, but Brother Aust was enticed to another Moravian settlement at Salem, now Winston-Salem, by the promise of "his own house-keeping and a certain sum annually." Here again, he was so successful that the leaders of the community ordered him to discontinue sales to outsiders "on account of the crowd it draws."

This pottery continued until about 1830. The ware made was, as might be expected, very similar to that of South Germany and, of course, to that of Eastern Pennsylvania. In addition to the usual plain, undecorated ware, quite elaborate slip-decorated pieces occur, of which plates and the rather large covered jars known as sugar jars are the most common. The designs are traced in cream, green and brown slips, in designs showing conventionalized flowers, with quite elaborate borders as shown in Figure 43. Unlike the similar ware of Pennsylvania, no figures, animal or human, and no names appear, and dated pieces are very rare. Sgraffito, which flourished in the same potteries as slipware in Pennsylvania, was unknown in Carolina. These Moravian potters left a legacy of methods and formulae to their successors, but pottery of the type they made has never been common in the South. Actually, some of their pieces show the use of a very light, almost white, body, rather than the red-burning clay which the potters knew and, being conservative after the manner of their tribe, undoubtedly preferred.

Another early venture in the South continues to be fairly mysterious. Duché's experiments with white-burning clays do not seem to have received much publicity in England. But these clays, which have, within recent years, become an important product in some Southern states, were one of the first raw materials of the region to attract attention. Champion and Cookworthy experimented with them at Plymouth for the hard-paste porcelain which they were the first Englishmen to make, and Josiah Wedgwood, "Father of the Potteries," tried them for the fine earthenware he was gradually developing. So that it is no wonder that a "Mr. Bartlem," a master potter of Staffordshire, should have conceived the idea of utilizing these clays at their source, nor that Wedgwood should have been disturbed over the prospect of losing a profitable export trade to the new venture. John Bartlem, then spelled "Bartlam" was advertising the manufacture of Queensware—white or cream-colored earthenware—in Charleston in 1770, but the records are only fragmentary, and no examples of his "Queensware" exist. The clays which attracted him are suitable for white-ware, but only after the impurities have been removed, and, of course, differ sufficiently from those he knew in England to make his formulae and processes useless. So it is safe to assume that the enterprise was a technical and, probably, a financial failure. Of Bartlem's potters, one named Ellis is recorded as appearing at Winston-Salem in 1773, claiming to know the secrets of making stoneware and queensware, while Peter Craven, the first of the family at Jugtown, near Steeds, North Carolina, is said to have come from Staffordshire "about 1750." Also, the founder of the Long pottery at Byron, Georgia came from South Carolina around 1820, so both may have been members of the same clan.

It is quite possible that these and others of Bartlem's workmen scattered through Georgia and the Carolinas, and established themselves as potters. Also, there were probably, among the English redemptioners and bondsmen who formed a large part of the early population of the South, some ne'er-do-well potters who also engaged in their trade. With slight financial resources and not too much knowledge, their equipment and ware might be expected to be very crude. Unfortunately, the individual potters do not begin to emerge from obscurity until about 1830, and again followers of the German tradition are best known. The Bells of Waynesboro, Pennsylvania have been mentioned, and one of them, Peter, was in Hagerstown, Maryland, as early as 1800. From there, he followed the Pennsylvania German migration south to Winchester, Virginia in 1824, and his son, Samuel, went farther down the Shenandoah Valley to Strasburg in 1834. There he built a plant which was operated by the Bell family until 1900, and established a pottery center, no fewer than five potteries congregating in this little town.

The history of the Bells, and their ware has been thoroughly covered in Rice and Stout's book on the pottery of the Shenandoah. They were not of pure German blood, and their pottery is not a pure Pennsylvania type. They evolved many distinctive types, which have had to be listed separately in the technical classification given later and consequently need only be mentioned here. In general, they made slipware, but not what is generally understood by that term. Like their cousins of Waynesboro, they covered their red clay with a coating of cream slip, and, instead of inscising designs through it, or painting them on with colored slips, were satisfied to use colored glazes, which, over the light slip, became bright and almost gaudy. The colors used were the familiar ones, copper green, manganese brown and iron red-brown, usually mottled or streaked, occasionally in solid shades.

These potters, as is shown in Figures 79, 80, were obviously interested in decorative effects, and made full use of the methods and materials at their command. Some of their variations are an unglazed rough cream slip, decorated with "curliques" of bright green slip seen in the flower-pot of Figure 38, a light reddish tan glaze, dull from the use of too much coloring material, with sepia brown markings (Figure 79), and any number of modeled and moulded pieces. These include wall pockets for flowers, ornamented with birds in full relief, lamb door-stops in the rough slip, whippets, statuettes and "comforter" spaniels, copied from those of Bennington, picture frames, soap dishes, and pitchers, even the hound-handled type, copied from Bennington originals, and the jars, flower-pots, vases, grotesque toys and other pieces, often decorated by heavy fluted moulding, whose inspiration can be found in Pennsylvania redware. Even the Strasburg stoneware differs materially from that of other sections, being a dark smoke gray with the familiar flower decorations in a deep purple-blue, probably due to the use of a native cobalt ore in place of the "smalt" used by all other potters. Also, as if these strongly-marked characteristics were not sufficient for identification, the Strasburg potters marked most of their ware.

Thus two best authenticated types of early Southern pottery are soft-burned, lead-glazed redware, with more or less decoration. Yet these appear to have had little or no effect on the typical Southern ware, which is either stoneware or hard-burned brown-ware, with a hard alkaline glaze. During the 1840's, or earlier, the Meaders were making one or both at Cleveland or Walkerville, the Longs at Byron, the Halcombes and Hewells at Gillsville, Georgia, and the Cravens and Foxes at Jugtown, North Carolina. William Wolfe made some decorated redware at Blountsville, Tennessee about 1850, before he moved across the border into Wise County, Virginia, where he changed to stoneware, which was also produced by Moro Phillips at Wilson's Landing, Virginia, before 1853. In the deep South, the Cribbs family had a stoneware pottery at Tuscaloosa, Alabama, as early as 1830, and stoneware was also made at Brandon, and Natchez, Mississippi in the fifties. There were other ante-bellum potteries as far west as Arkansas, and several in Kentucky and Tennessee. The first pottery in Lexington, Kentucky was built by John Carty and Ward Menelle, a Frenchman from the French settlement at Gallipolis, Ohio, about 1796, and probably made redware, but the later establishments, including the long-lived Lafever pottery at Baxter, Tennessee, made stoneware. The importance of the pottery industry during the early years of the South may be judged by the fact

87

that there are "Jugtowns" in three states, and a "Pottertown" in Kentucky.

In this Ante-Bellum period, there was some production of more sophisticated pottery. In Kentucky, where several potters had been established before 1800, William Lewis established a yellow-ware plant in 1829, bringing Vodrey and Frost from Pittsburgh to manage it. Lewis and his associates were induced by James Clews to invest in a concern to make whiteware, and built a pottery at Troy, Indiana. When Clews was unsuccessful, Jabez Vodrey was sent there to replace him, and the Louisville pottery was closed soon afterward. In Kaolin, South Carolina, between Aiken and Augusta, the white clays of the region attracted H. W. Farrar, who had been at Bennington and at Jersey City. In 1856 he built a factory there, making Rockingham type brownware, White Granite, some decorated in gold, and bisque porcelain. In this, he copied the Parian of Bennington in white and blue and white, as well as some glazed porcelain, without color but in a few cases decorated in gold. Among his productions are wicker or basket-work pitchers, figures, a wheat syrup jug and a copy of the Cartlidge corn pitcher. The outbreak of the Civil War interrupted the progress of the pottery, as did a disastrous fire in 1865, and coarse ware only, including insulators for telegraph lines, was made until it closed in 1878.

The War may be considered to have established the typical Southern pottery, but it is certain that the same ware was made considerably before that time. The manufacture of some ornamental ware in the South has been noted, but it is easy to understand that there would be no great demand for it. In the North, the wealthiest farmer of a Pennsylvania county, or the leading citizen of a New England town would be quite proud to display the products of the local pottery on his table or in his cupboard, and the potters, appreciating this, did their best to produce ware worth such positions. But, to the owners of the great Southern plantations, such crude ware was common, to be banished to the kitchen and slave quarters, and, quite naturally, all Southerners

88

of any pretensions to gentility followed suit, The result was that the potters, with no inducement to make any but the plainest and cheapest ware, omitted the decorative touches which not only add to the charm of pottery, but identify many unmarked pieces. Nor did they mark their ware. The did, of course, develop the usual quirks of workmanship, body and glaze, by which the ware of one pottery or group of potteries can sometimes be identified, but these are rather insufficient evidence on which to build assumptions.

The War intensified this tendency to crude simplicity, as the tremendous scarcity of manufactured goods developed the domestic pottery industry. The potters were exempt from military service, so great was the demand for their ware, and they made coffee mugs, mess bowls and medicine jars for the Confederate hospitals, as well as tableware for domestic use. The Southern Porcelain Company at Kaolin made brownware insulators for telegraph lines, the Davies pottery at Bath, South Carolina, Henry Stevens at Milledgeville, Georgia and the Paducah Pottery at Paducah, Kentucky made brownware and stoneware for domestic use.

This pottery occurs in a rather limited range of pieces. Plates, known to the users as "dirt dishes," mugs, water bottles or carafes, candlesticks, fat lamps, soap dishes, sugar jars with covers to keep out the flies, bowls, from small ones up to stoneware wash basins, are among these. The usual jars and crocks in all sizes, vases, churns, flower-pots and pitchers are found, while jugs for the illicit spirituous liquors formerly such an important product of the mountain country, formed an important specialty. The decorative motifs are also very limited. Blue borders or designs on stoneware, and occasional simple incised patterns are found, but the show-pieces of other sections seem unknown, and any decoration is rare.

The equipment of these potteries was, and still is, extremely simple. The kilns are much smaller and cruder than those of the North, of the rectangular type, like a furnace, with a single fire-box at one end, and a chimney or stack at the other. Some examples of the primitive "ground-hog" kiln are reported in North Carolina. These, similar to the type used in China before the Christian era, are merely holes in the hillsides, lined with brick. In spite of this poor equipment, the variety of types it produced is larger than might be expected. Stoneware and brownware are both common in the South, but are supplemented by a hybrid type unknown elsewhere. In this, the ware is covered with the usual brown Albany slip and then, probably because the potters found it impossible to secure a sufficiently high heat to mature or fuse this, it is salt-glazed. The result, of course, is rarely a smooth high glaze, but is more or less rough and stony. Other potters achieved similar or finer results by mixing a lead glaze with the Albany slip. Some soft-burned red-ware with the lead glaze used in other sections was made, especially along the coastal plain, but most of the potters located in the hills.

There they found and used those white-burning kaolins and ball-clays which occur especially in north-western Georgia and western Carolina. These are often found in combination with red clays and shales, deposited along river banks and old stream beds. The potters saw that this mixture of clays had the proper plasticity or "workability," and burned to a hard body at a low temperature, so mixed the two types of clay if they did not find them together. Since this mixture, natural or not, is rarely thorough, the color of the burned ware varies widely. Its characteristic color is, of course, a pale salmon pink, orange under the glaze. But some of the clays, when burned rather hard, turn gray or even, under the glaze, gray-green, so that shadings or mottlings of orange and olive resembling those produced with colored glazes by Northern potters may result. The Southerners used colors in their glaze only very occasionally, then a brown or red-brown native iron ore, iron carbonate or limonite. The glaze, too, is not the soft lead mixture of the North, but a harder sand-lime or alkaline glaze. In effect, this is the glaze used for the finest porcelains and earthenware, but is made from crude and poorly prepared raw materials, common sand and lime, sometimes crushed glass, wood-ashes and native clay. This, burned under technically very unsatisfactory conditions, rarely becomes smooth or bright, but ranges from a stony lustre to the deeply pitted and irregular surface of the "Walkerville" jars.

The development of the pottery industry throughout the rest of the country follows a fairly regular pattern. Redware was always the first to appear, and, while largely superseded by the stronger stoneware, continued to be made in quantities up to 1900. The factory-produced brown-ware introduced Albany clay to the smaller potteries, but it was not used to any extent except in the Middle West. This general pattern, unfortunately, cannot be made to fit the pottery of the South. Lead-glazed redware, in the German tradition, was made, and the first English potters, settling along the coast, where red-burning clays are usual, must have made some redware. They surely knew it since it was made in England, much of the fine lustre ware, even that made after 1800, having a red body. But no trace of such potters, nor of their productions, can be found.

The stoneware which appears as the typical pottery of the South, would naturally be expected to appear, as good stoneware clays are found throughout the region. The English emigrants understood its manufacture, and it was also developed from American sources. Thus, the first of the Cribbs family, who operated two stoneware potteries, came to Tuscaloosa, Alabama, from Canton or New Philadelphia, Ohio, both stoneware centers, before 1827. The use of Albany clay, of course, was learned from the North, probably from the Bennington potters who worked in Kaolin, South Carolina after 1856.

This stoneware was produced mainly west of the Alleghenies, appearing even in Arkansas by 1840 and the pottery made along their eastern slopes is entirely different, presenting an interesting problem. The light-burning clays used in it are purely local, but the typical alkaline glaze is difficult to account for. Its earliest recorded user among the potters of Georgia and Carolina appears to be James B. Long of Byron, Georgia, working between 1840 and 1850. Thus it is just possible, chronologically, that he and his fellows learned this mixture, usually identified with fine white-ware, from the whiteware plant at Kaolin, South Carolina. But Long's father came to Georgia from South Carolina in 1820, presumably a son of one of Bartlam's Staffordshire potters, and, again, it is within the bounds of possibility that Bartlam knew the secret of the alkaline glaze, just beginning to replace lead glazes in the English potteries of 1765. Again, there is Richard Champion, certainly familiar with it, and living in South Carolina from 1784 to 1791.

Also, the "mountain potters" use a mixture of quite different clays to form a satisfactory body, invariable procedure in the manu-facture of whiteware, but quite unusual for pottery. So there is considerable solid fact on which to base the rather romantic story that these potters are not only lineal descendants of craftsmen who came to the South before the Revolution, but that they have carried the craft on from one generation to another, for nearly two hundred years.

PART III

CHAPTER VIII

Earthenware and Porcelain

THE story of the development of fine whiteware in the United States cannot be a happy one, including as it must a long catalogue of unsuccessful ventures. At the present time, American porcelain and earthenware are as fine as any made, but it has taken over a hundred and fifty years to reach this point, and those years covered many failures, technical, artistic and financial, and only too few successes. There are many reasons for this. On the financial side, American buyers were victims, during this entire period, of a fixed idea, amounting to a psychological complex, that foreign art and applied art were superior to our own. The result was that they refused to buy American attempts at fine ware, and, as late as 1879, Nichols could begin his work on pottery with the statement, "nearly all the fine pottery used in the United States is imported." The artistic failures were due to this same cause, since the earlier American potters copied European models too slavishly, and those of the last half of the nineteenth century were interested only slightly in design, neglecting it in favor of quantity production at low prices.

The technical failures of our whiteware makers were caused partly by the innate conservatism of the potter, which has been emphasised before, and partly by the determination of our early industries to show the mother country that American workmen and American materials could equal or surpass anything she could produce. They therefore attempted to use the new and unfamiliar clays and glaze materials of this country with the old rule-of-thumb formulas and methods they had learned in England, France or Germany, and, very naturally, found it impossible to make good ware. Few of our early potters could afford the long and

95

expensive experiments necessary to reconcile these two elements, and it was only after the experience of many separate failures was available and it was understood that certain materials should be imported from Europe, that fine earthenware and porcelain were produced commercially in this country.

The general characteristics of American whiteware before 1900 may be said to be non-existent. Most of the early factories were manned by European potters, who followed the technique in which they had been trained, and the later Americans copied whatever type of foreign ware would sell most readily and cheaply. Further, realizing that their public preferred imported ware, they very generally and intentionally omitted to mark most of their production. There are, in fact, actual records of orders given the United States Pottery Company at Bennington after 1850, specifying that the ware was not to be marked. And, of the marks used, several are plainly intended to deceive the purchaser, showing the knot device which was almost a trademark of the Staffordshire potteries of England, or even the British royal arms. Since the American factories whose existence is recorded prior to 1865 were all small, and most led short and chequered lives, the total amount of American whiteware produced before that date, marked and unmarked, is so slight that it is difficult to give a clear picture of the types and pieces made. And in the ware made after 1860, there is so much duplication, and so much copying of English designs, that only the marks which began to be used more freely allow us to identify our own.

If we dismiss as unconfirmed the claim that Daniel Coxe of Burlington, New Jersey, made white salt-glazed whiteware before 1690, the earliest of the many attempts to produce fine ware in this country was due to the discovery of white clays by settlers in the Southern colonies. The first record of these clays comes from Georgia. Andrew Duché, a Philadelphia potter, established himself in Savannah sometime between 1732 and 1738, and made "common ware", which was certainly the redware of his home and period. But in 1738, General Oglethorpe, founder of the colony, reported to the trustees in London, "an earth is found which Duché the potter has baked into China Ware." Duché, like many other pioneer American manufacturers, proceeded to secure a subsidy for his project of making porcelain, and was drawn into political squabbles, with the result that the enterprise failed, although his ware, experimental white earthenware as it probably was, must be recorded as the first whiteware made in the country.

This first discovery of white-burning clays seems to have escaped notice in England, although all Europe was interested at that period in locating deposits of Kaolin or China clay, the raw material which they believed necessary to duplicate the enormously popular and expensive Chinese hard porcelain. Similar clays were found in the mountains of "Virginia"—probably Carolina—and samples were sent to England in 1745. There William Cookworthy, the Bristol chemist whose researches brought about the production of the first English porcelain under a Royal patent granted in 1768, investigated them, and only twenty years later discovered a satisfactory clay for his purpose in England. Richard Champion, who also made hard porcelain at Plymouth, and later ended his days in Carolina, was experimenting with American clays in 1765. Josiah Wedgewood, greatest of the English potters, also tried them on an extensive scale for earthenware. They impressed him so favorably that he wrote to a friend in 1765, predicting the loss of his profitable American export business to a "new Pottworks in South Carolina," adding that "They have every material there, equal if not superior to our own, for carrying on that manufacture."

Wedgwood further stated that "they have got one of our insolvent master potters to conduct them," and "an agent amongst us hiring a number of our hands." This master potter was John Bartlem, according to Wedgwood, or Bartlam, according to the American records. He disappeared from view for five years, but the *South Carolina Gazette* for October fourth, 1770 stated that "A China Manufactory and Pottery is soon to be opened in this town, on the lot late Mr. Hougett's, by Messers. Bartlam &

97

Company, the proper hands, &c, for carrying it on having lately arrived from England; and there is no doubt that it will meet with great encouragement." Six weeks later Bartlam advertised for "five or six apprentices, immediately," and again on January thirty-first, 1771, "John Bartlam, Having opened his Pottery and China-Manufactory in Old Church-Street, Will be much obliged to gentlemen in the Country, or others, who will be so kind to send him samples of any Kinds of fine Clay upon their Plantations, &c, in order to make them Trials of. He already makes what is called Queen's Ware, equal to any imported; and, if he meets with suitable encouragement, makes no Doubt of being able to supply the demands of the whole province."

No further records of Bartlem's enterprise, and no examples of his "Queensware" exist. But the story must parallel those of so many early American industries, several of which are mentioned in this and other chapters. Wedgwood may have been right in hinting that he was not a good business man. In any case, his British formulas and methods cannot have been suited to the raw materials at hand, which, as a matter of fact, were not developed commercially for well over a century after his time. He probably struggled for several months or years, but "the rest is silence." Richard Champion of Plymouth, who bought Cookworthy's patent in 1774, and made porcelain for seven years, retired to a home at Camden, South Carolina in 1784, dying there in 1791. There is a tradition that he made some porcelain at Camden, but if Llellwyn Jewett's opinion of him as a promoter and merchant rather than scientist or potter, is correct, the tradition may be doubted.

In Philadelphia, another attempt at the production of porcelain was made a few years later. Gouse Bonnin, of uncertain nationality, but a former workman in the English porcelain factory at Bow, induced a native Philadelphian, George Anthony Morris, to join him in the enterprise, and by December 29th, 1769, they advertised that they were now making "as good porcelain as any heretofore manufactured at the famous factory in Bow, near London"—but mentioning their own factory as only "now erecting in Southwark." This was quite in the tradition of other infant American industries of the period, as was their application for a loan from the Provincial Assembly two years later, which, also according to precedent, was refused. Their advertisements during the two years, appearing in the *Pennsylvania Packet,* do give a picture of some technical success. On January 10th, 1771, a notice appears, "To prevent retail purchasers from being imposed upon, they are desired to take notice that all future emanations from the factory will be marked 'S'." Six months later, on July 25th, the advertisement reads, "The proprietors of the factory, having at length procured some zaffre, are ready to supply shop-keepers and country dealers with any quantity of blue and white ware." By January 10th, 1772, they amended this to "blue or enameled ware," and on August 3rd, the advertisement mentioned experiments with clays from South Carolina.

The demand for this American ware cannot have been great, as the factory closed toward the end of 1772, **Bonnin** returning to England. The plant and equipment were advertised for sale on December 21st, 1772, the itemized list giving interesting details of the equipment of the factory. "A pair of Large Mill Stones, each stone surrounded with a circle of cast iron, weighing about 2½ Tons, and run on a circular cast iron plate of the same weight. Also a wrought iron axis, and a large shaft on which they run. A Shaft and framework of a large mill which is surrounded by a cedar frame of set-work, hooped with iron, the inside is paved with very smooth flat stone; also a rolling press for copper-plate printing. A little study evolves two "pans" for grinding clay, with ball-mill for fine grinding, while the press obviously turned out the decorative designs.

The Bonin and Morris factory is the first of whose production any know examples exist. A well-authenticated openwork fruit-basket in the Pennsylvania Museum (Figure 77), and a similar basket all show simple under-glaze blue decoration, made with the zaffre referred to in the advertisement of July 25, 1772, and are marked with a small old-style "s," resembling our modern "p," under the glaze. But, in contradiction of the advertisements, they are not porcelain. As can easily be determined by the fracture of one broken piece, they are cream-colored earthenware, and not in the least vitreous.

Another early attempt to make porcelain was that at Braintree, near Quincy, Massachusetts, then known as Germantown from the German workmen brought to this country in 1753 by the promoters Joseph C. Palmer and Richard Cranch. They proposed to make glass and porcelain but made neither and are not heard of after 1760. Some fragments of ordinary stoneware found on the side of the factory may prove that they made this, but no authenticated examples of their ware exist. Again, advertisements appeared in the *Boston Evening Post* during 1769 of a new factory which expected to make "Tortoise-shell, cream and green color plates, Dishes, Coffee and Tea pots, cups and Saucers and all other Articles in the Potter's Business, equal to any imported from England" and asked hopefully for samples of white clay. Nothing more is known of the factory, so that it may have been the over-ambitious enterprise of a local redware potter. The advertisements of one Jonathan Durrell in Holt's *New York Journal* of 1774, offering "Butter, water, pickle and oyster pots, porringers, milk pans, jugs" and other pieces," equal to the best of any imported from Philadelphia," and "striped and colored dishes of divers colors," sound, especially when we learn that Durrell was a Philadelphian, very much like slip-decorated redware rather than white earthenware.

The Revolution naturally put a temporary end to attempts to produce fine ware, as it did to most American business. But by 1787, we find the Boston Porcelain and Glass Manufacturing Company incorporated in Boston, with a Mr. Thompson as manager, and building a plant in East Cambridge. They had a six-pot furnace for glass and kilns for porcelain, and experimented for about a year, with no success, and then closed, although the factory was later taken over by the very successful Cambridge

Glass Company. In 1789, one Samuel Dennis applied to the Legislature of Connecticut for financial aid in building a factory for stoneware and porcelain, but the hard-headed legislators refused, and no porcelain appeared.

By this time the excitement over porcelain and kaolin had subsided, and the earthenware developed by the Staffordshire potters had been so much improved that it was used in many fine homes. This was due, of course, partly to its lower cost, but also to the selection of Wedgwood's fine earthenware or Queensware services by such arbitresses of fashion as the Queen of England and the Empress of Russia. Consequently, the American potters turned their attention to this, and Philadelphia, then the cultural capital of the country, saw several attempts at its production. Alexander Trotter exhibited his products at Peale's Museum in 1810, and was in business until 1811, Daniel Freytag made similar ware, "colored and gilt" in 1811, and David G. Seixas is said to have made whiteware like that identified with Liverpool, although probably without its characteristic printed decoration, between 1816 and 1822. Abraham Miller, whose redware pottery had a long existence, exhibited experimental pieces of white earthenware, porcelain and silver lustre at the Franklin Institute in 1824, and made some earthenware commercially in 1842. A Dr. Mead of New York was also making porcelain ware in 1816, and one vase of his manufacture was exhibited at the Franklin Institute in that year.

The interest in French fashions, which was strong during the first years of the century, still encouraged the production of porcelain, an attempt to manufacture it from local feldspar and kaolin being made at Monkton, Vermont in 1810. Again, in December, 1825, a group of New Jersey and New York men formed the Jersey Porcelain and Earthenware Company. According to tradition, they brought experienced potters from France, and they obviously found them somewhere. In 1826, they received the medal of the Franklin Institute for "the best china from American materials." Competition was negligible, of course, but they did succeed in making whiteware within a very short time, and one authenticated example of porcelain decorated in gold re-mains to show its good quality. However, the company estab-lished its claim to the profitless honor of making the first com-mercially produced porcelain in the United States, made some white earthenware and yellow-ware as well, and then went out of business in 1827 or 1828.

At the same time as this Jersey City enterprise, William Ellis Tucker, son of a Quaker china dealer in Philadelphia, having had some experience in decorating china, and made some experiments in the manufacture of porcelain, established a factory in the old city water-works. With a young associate or partner, John N. Bird, he bought a feldspar quarry to supply part of his raw ma-terials, his china clay coming from the farm of Israel Hoppe near New Garden in Chester County, who discovered the deposit while digging post-holes about 1820. Tucker began the manufacture of porcelain in 1826, but, less fortunate than the potters at Jersey City, he experienced the usual difficulty in translating his experi-mental results into actual production, and exhibited his first satis-factory pieces at the Franklin Institute in 1827, with another showing of a hundred pieces in 1828. In this year, he also ac-quired a partner, Thomas Hulme, and, either by his aid, or by the natural improvement of experience, materially bettered the quality of the ware, and particularly of the decoration. The part-nership, however, did not last, and by 1830, Tucker, alone again, was following the usual procedure of applying to the government for a loan, sending samples of his ware to President Jackson. Also as usual, the money was not advanced, but in 1831 Judge Joseph Hemphill, a prominent citizen of Philadelphia, paid Tucker seven thousand dollars for a partnership for his young son, Alexander Wills Hemphill. Tucker died on August 22nd of the next year, and Judge Hemphill bought the Tucker interest in the firm for another ten thousand dollars in 1833. His son also died in 1834, but the Judge carried on the business alone. He completed a new factory at Chestnut and Schuylkill (now Seventeenth) Streets, and brought in experienced French workmen, with Thomas Tucker, William's brother, as manager. More elaborate designs, in the contemporary style of the very fashionable Sèvres porcelain appeared, and the factory continued with some success until Hemphill retired in 1837. Thomas Tucker, to whom he leased it, could carry it on only another year.

The Tucker, Tucker and Hulme, Tucker and Hemphill or Hemphill porcelain is rarely marked, then with the current firm name, "Philadelphia" or "Philad," and rarely the date pencilled in red or brown over the glaze, sometimes with a workman's initial inscribed in the soft clay. Enough of these, with some thoroughly authenticated examples and the factory's pattern book, are known, to give a fairly clear idea of the ware. The rare early pieces, the true Tucker porcelain, usually parts of tea-sets, show a good, rather creamy body, and good glaze, the decoration gradually improving from scenes or flowers and butterflies poorly painted over the glaze in brown or sepia, often with no gold, to flower motifs, well executed in natural colors, centered on the sides of pitchers and cups, and rather heavy gold lines. The pitcher of Figure 82, dated 1828, is an unusually fine example of this early ware. The factory advertised "A Superior Assortment of China, comprising Dinner sets, Tea Sets, Vases, Mantel Ornaments, pitchers, Fruit Baskets, etc., either plain or ornamented." Other productions included shell-, shield- and heart-shaped perfume bottles, cup-plates, "compotiers," funnels and cake stands, while there were a hundred patterns in services and vases. Of all these pieces, the few which can be identified by form include the perfume bottles, a vase-shaped pitcher with a fluted relief band at the base, a high and sharply marked spout and unusually high arched handle, and a similar but shorter design, without the fluted band, and a scrolled or waved lip. A cylindrical vase, shown from the pattern book in Figure 84, is also known, and some large and handsome footed vases were also made.

The decoration of this ware was very much in the French

103

taste, with heavy gold bands, flowers or compact floral motifs, roses, forget-me-nots or tulips, in natural colors, occasional flower bands or scattered sprigs, birds or fruit, and rarely portraits, as in the pitcher of Figure 85, with its handsome bust of Washington, or special-order services with crests or monograms; very occasionally, too, the decorators departed from their source of inspiration, as in a service decorated with sepia landscapes, and a large pitcher with a band of hunting figures in colored relief, reminiscent of one made in earthenware by Turner of Staffordshire. In general, it is very difficult to identify the porcelain of this factory. It is so similar to French ware of the same period that Barber complained in 1895 that much of it was sold as Sèvres, while today much Sèvres is undoubtedly classed as "Tucker." Even other American porcelain manufacturers of the period copied Tucker ware very closely, one of them being Smith, Fife and Company of Philadelphia about 1830.

Potters, like all other manufacturers, must meet the popular taste to remain in business. At that period, imported porcelain was still preferred, leaving to the American potters only the field of the cheapest and most durable ware. This, during the early factory period of the 'thirties and 'forties, was the Rockingham type of brownware, with yellow-ware as second choice. Some few attempts to popularize American porcelain continued, especially in Philadelphia, where Ralph Bagnall Beech, of a family of English potters, and Charles J. Boulter made some in addition to Rockingham about 1845, and Kurbaum and Schwartz tried it in 1853, Beech also developing an unglazed earthenware decorated with enamels, which he patented in 1851. But D. and J. Henderson, who had taken over the Jersey City Pottery in 1829, and incorporated it in 1833 as the American Pottery Manufacturing Company, played safe. While they marked none of it before 1840, we know that they made much Rockingham and yellow-ware, and they only gradually expanded their production of white earthenware. By 1840, they were ready to pioneer to a limited extent, and issued what is accepted as the first transfer printed tableware made in this country. It is, however, a romantic floral design marked "Canova," and pirated, name and all, from one issued by the great English firm of Ridgeways the year before. They also made for the presidential campaign of 1840 a large octagonal pitcher with a printed portrait of William Henry Harrison, "The Ohio Farmer," with his log cabin and the American eagle, and the more common large mugs bearing Harrison's portrait may also be their production. In addition, some octagonal tea-sets decorated with blue spatter, and handsome ones in cream-colored ware, with all-over floral relief decoration and no color, shown in Figures 81 and 83, bear the mark of the "American Pottery Company."

Farther west, Trotter and Company of Pittsburgh were advertising "Queensware, pitchers, coffee and tea-pots, etc., similar to those of Philadelphia" in 1815. This is probably the Alexander Trotter who made similar ware at the Columbian Pottery in Philadelphia in 1810 and 1812, but his Pittsburgh venture seems short-lived, and it is easy to guess at the reasons for his failure, with no raw materials available. Later, Vodrey and Frost brought a number of Staffordshire potters to Pittsburgh in 1827, establishing a pottery for the production of whiteware. The available clays being unsatisfactory, they fell back on yellow-ware, but gave up the attempt in 1830.

A more ambitious, but equally unsuccessful enterprise was that of James Clews. He had operated the Cobridge Works, not the Cobridge Pottery of Ralph Stevenson, in Staffordshire from 1819 to 1835, making fine tableware printed in dark blue, especially large quantities of the fine printed "Historical Blue" printed earthenware, including the "States" and "Landing of Lafayette" patterns. His father, Ralph, died about 1835, and James sold the "Works" to Wood and Brownfield and emigrated to the United States. He found his way to Louisville, Kentucky in 1836, and interested the group of citizens who had owned the quite successful Lewis Pottery Company, making yellow-ware, since 1829, in his scheme for a factory to produce white earthenware of the type he had made in England. They formed a new company, known as the

Indiana Pottery Company, and built a factory at Troy, Indiana, on the Ohio River below Louisville. Forty experienced potters were brought from England, and the first kiln of ware was burned in June, 1837.

The local clay on which they based their hopes proved unsatisfactory for whiteware, as occurred at Pittsburgh, and the white-burning clay they expected to find in the "chalk levels" along the Mississippi proved an illusion. Fragments of ware dug up on the site show only a dark cream instead of pure white. Then an epidemic of fever caused the factory to suspend operations, and Clews returned to England in disgust. Since he had been so successful there, many explanations have been given for the failure of his American enterprise. But Jabez Vodrey, who took over the plant in 1839, could not, with his experience in Pittsburgh and Louisville to guide him, make even good brownware or yellow-ware there, and gave it up in 1846, to become a very successful potter in East Liverpool later. The plant was carried on until 1846, but never turned out first-class ware, and it is also significant that a discovery of white clay in nearby Huron County, hailed with enthusiasm by Nichols and the State Geologist in 1879, was later found worthless for whiteware.

CHAPTER IX

Earthenware and Porcelain
(Continued)

THE year 1850 saw the rise of many new potteries in the United States, and the birth of the industry as it exists today, but general conditions and popular demands on it both changed at this time. The Staffordshire tableware, whose quality, beauty and cheapness had ruled the markets of the world for years, so that our American potters could only copy it at a distance, had degenerated greatly. Bodies were heavier and coarser, and the current printed decorations no longer showed the rich deep blue, in large areas from deep-cut engravings, of the early printed ware, but thin and spindly designs in insipid pale blues, pinks, or greens and dull blacks, brown and purples. The American buyer was still catered to with local or historical subjects, such as Henry Clay, Harrison and his log cabin, Kosciusko's tomb, the Mormon Tabernacle, and others, but pseudo-romantic, Oriental or Gothic effects were much more popular. Hand-decorated ware, the spatter and bright "Gaudy Dutch" and "King's Rose" types beloved in Pennsylvania and Ohio, and the all-over sprig designs of New England, had changed for the worse, both in body and decoration, and also were not suited to quantity production and the efficient factory methods which were coming into general use.

The old types of earthenware being outmoded, the English potters began about 1850 to introduce new ones. The most important of these is the dense, almost vitreous body, pure white in color, which was developed by several Staffordshire potteries in heavy plain ware, without decoration. It was given a variety of names, such as "White Granite," "Ironstone," or "Stone China" emphasing its strength, or "Opaque Porcelain," "English Porcelain," "Porcelaine de Terre," and similar high-flown titles introducing the idea of quality. This White Granite, as it was generally known, was cheap and durable, and immediately became popular, particularly in the United States. It is almost always undecorated, often in substantial paneled or octagonal shapes, widest at the base. Occasionally it shows designs of wheat or grapes in very low relief, small applied relief motifs colored with purple lustre or blue, or wide bands of copper lustre. Along with this new ware, a new process of decorating pottery by the use of colored decalcomania transfers was developed by Minton's about 1850, and more gradually came into general use for all cheap decorated ware, although the potters also used printed outlines filled in by hand, in the old tradition.

Another new type of ware was a very coarse earthenware with a poor color, like that known as cream-colored ware. This was produced in all-over relief designs, mainly excessively naturalistic, and covered with glazes in the appropriate bright colors, completely concealing the body. From some resemblance to a type of Italian ware with relief designs and opaque white and colored glazes or enamels to cover the dark body, this was christened "Majolica." Being cheap and attractive, it was much used for decorative pieces. Finally, a new type of porcelain appeared, a rather soft paste, so high in non-plastic materials that it could not be modeled or pressed, but must be cast in moulds. In this process, the plaster-of-Paris moulds are filled with a clay and water mixture of the consistency of cream. The porous bulk of the mould absorbs much of the water from the slip in contact with it, so that when, after a short time, the excess slip is poured out of it, a coating of clay is left on its interior surface. When this clay has dried and hardened somewhat, the mould is removed, leaving a very thin and light piece, with any relief decoration or modeling showing fine sharp outlines. This ware, developed almost simultaneously by the great English firms of Minton and Copeland about 1848, was named Parian, from the resemblance of its warm white, almost cream, color and fine texture to marble.

EARTHENWARE AND PORCELAIN (CONTINUED)

In keeping with this idea, it was used for statuettes, vases and the small *objets d'art* so much in demand for Victorian whatnots, and, to preserve the illusion of marble, was never glazed.

Of these new types, only the colored printed decoration failed to become immediately popular in the United States. The White Granite was the common tableware of the country, so that dozens of English potteries were kept busy for the next fifty years, producing it for export to "the States" exclusively, more fastidious markets declining to buy it. The American factories naturally devoted their energies to the new ware, as its simplicity solved many of their problems of manufacture and decoration. Their White Granite is almost indistinguishable from the imported ware, but often shows a blue-white color. They copied the English shapes and some of the relief decoration, especially the wheat wreath, but their sole decorative inspiration is the gold lustre bands and sparse leaves—one to a piece—used by the Mayer Pottery Company of Beaver Falls after 1881. After 1885, some decorated ware was made, but on an improved body. This is "Hotel Ware" or "Semi-Porcelain," very strong and vitrified, due to the kaolin it contains, but opaque, consequently earthenware and not porcelain, whose introduction is credited to James Pass of the Onondaga Pottery at Syracuse.

Majolica also became enormously popular as a decorative ware, E. and W. Bennett of Baltimore making some as early as 1853, and it continued to be made until the turn of the century. Of the many plants in the field, the Phoenixville Pottery of Griffin, Smith and Hill is the best known, since its ware, made between 1881 and 1892, bears the monogram of the firm, with the title "Etruscan Majolica." The American potters rarely attempted the large and complicated pieces made in England, but confined themselves to tableware, pitchers and mantel ornaments in vegetable, floral, animal or even fish forms, and many of these are impossible to distinguish from the imported ware.

Parian also became a great favorite with the American public after 1850, and with the potters as well, since it was a form of art ware requiring few if any skilled workmen, and presenting no difficulties with color and glaze. Some makers were even content to buy the moulds of others who had gone out of business, rather than attempt their own designs. But the Americans did introduce considerable change in the body, so that much of their "Parian" is not Parian at all. It is unglazed or biscuit porcelain, differing from the original in color and texture, being whiter and coarser, and was pressed, not cast, in the plaster moulds. Our potters also used designs most inappropriate to marble, particularly pitchers which, as a concession to utility, received a coat of glaze on the interior. The exterior might also be lightly glazed, and the body was sometimes colored—blue, occasionally pink, green or brown. After 1883, a modification of Parian appeared, a very thin light cast ware, lightly washed with pearly metallic lustres. This is known as "Belleek" from the pottery in Ireland where it was first made, and was introduced in this country by Ott and Brewer of Trenton.

These new departures in the whiteware field, and the general expansion of American business about 1850, brought a great many new potteries within the next few years. The most interesting of these to the collector is the United States Pottery at Bennington. The earlier firm of Norton and Fenton brought John Harrison from the Copeland factory in England early in 1846, and they experimented with Copeland's Parian for several years. When C. W. Fenton formed the new company in 1849, he put on the market his modification, the bisque porcelain, which was so like the original that he kept the name. He used the plain white of the English houses, but also an all-over fawn or buff shade, or white figures on a ground in varying shades of cobalt blue, obviously inspired by Wedgwood's Jasper ware. This was made by using a blue slip in the moulds, while the imitators of Bennington applied the blue coloring, not too carefully, to the surface of the ware. A hammered or pitted ground was also introduced, and also copied, and many pieces show a "smear glaze" on the exterior, varying from a light film like a salt glaze to a coating as

110

heavy as a dipped glaze applied directly to the ware. The "Parian" of Bennington varies widely in quality, and much of it is difficult to identify. It includes many pitchers, most of them marked, in all white, glazed or unglazed, or in the rarer blue and white or fawn figures, vases or mantel ornaments, often with grape relief, rare tableware, and occasional dogs, cow creamers and other Rockingham designs. Bennington also made some "White Granite," which is found mainly in pitchers, some few decorated in color and gold, with some ornaments from the moulds used for other ware. None of the Rockingham pitchers, however, seem to have been duplicated either in Parian or White Granite.

This period saw other new enterprises in new territory, as far west as Kaolin, Missouri, where Elihu Shepard struggled to make whiteware from 1854 to 1865. Tempest, Brockman and Company built a factory in Cincinnati, Ohio in 1862, which started the production of the first whiteware—White Granite, of course—made in the Middle West, about 1867, and continued for many years. In Peoria, Illinois, C. W. Fenton of Bennington after the closing of the factory there, built a pottery to make brown, yellow and whiteware, but was not successful, although some White Granite was made under another management after 1889. Another pottery at Kaolin, South Carolina, between Aiken and Augusta, owed its inspiration to Bennington, being organized by W. H. Farrar from that factory in 1856, with Josiah Jones from Charles Cartlidge's plant as manager. The usual White Granite and bisque porcelain or Parian were produced, the latter including copies of the pitted and blue grounds of Bennington. But the Civil War and a fire in 1864 were disastrous, and only cheaper and cruder wares were made from that date until the final closing of the factory in 1878.

The American Porcelain Works at Gloucester, New Jersey, William Bloor at East Liverpool and the American Porcelain Manufacturing Company of Charles Cartlidge at Greenpoint, New York City, all made bisque porcelain between 1854 and 1862. Cartlidge, who had been New York agent for the important English firm of William Ridgeway and Company before their failure in 1848, started to manufacture first soft-paste, then hard porcelain, in the same year. In the latter, unglazed, he made imitations of the famous Wedgwood Jasper and some busts of great Americans, including Daniel Webster, John Marshall and Zachary Taylor, about half life size. He also turned out buttons, door knobs and door-plates as staples, and some tableware, with the inevitable pitchers, including one in soft-paste porcelain decorated with an eagle in relief, and over-glaze colors and gold. Like other pioneers in this field, Cartlidge did not meet with popular support, and closed in 1856. Another New York pottery was that of Carr and Morrison. James Carr had been a potter in England, at Jersey City and in his own plant in New Jersey, and moved to New York in 1855. This factory made White Granite and majolica, including the first "cauliflower" teapot, with considerable success from 1858 until Carr retired in 1889. Again in New York—Brooklyn this time—a German, William Bloch, built the Union Porcelain Works in 1854, was succeeded in 1862 by Thomas C. Smith, who after some vicissitudes with soft porcelain, developed a true hard paste. He and his family were for many years the only American firm producing this. They made tableware with particularly fine decoration, and ornamental pieces, the best-known of these being the "Century Vase," modeled by Karl Mueller in 1876, with his "Keramos Vase" and "Liberty Cup" also fine. Before 1876, the factory rarely used marks, but adopted the printed eagle's head with an initial "S" in that year. The last and again unsuccessful attempt to produce porcelain during this period was that at New Orleans, where two wealthy Creoles, Hernandez and Saloy, built the Louisiana Porcelain Works in 1881, importing French workmen and materials to make the French hard-paste ware. They produced a few kilns of this, which was sold undecorated, but gave up the enterprise by 1890.

All these potteries represent comparatively unimportant off-shoots from the main current of the pottery industry in the United States, and almost all of them were more or less temporary. The first successful manufacturers of whiteware in the country congregated at Trenton, New Jersey, where they specialized on White Granite and the cheaper cream-colored ware. The first of the Trenton potteries was that of Taylor and Speeler. With the financial aid of William Bloor, a successful East Liverpool potter and forty-niner, they came from Ohio in 1852, and began the manufacture of the brownware and yellow-ware they had been making there. They continued with this until 1875, but by 1855 the firm, now Taylor, Speeler and Bloor, was making White Granite. William Young and Sons built another yellow-ware factory in Trenton in 1853, but they also changed almost immediately to whiteware. And Millington and Astbury, also started in 1853, made the change before 1860, issuing the "Colonel Ellsworth" pitcher (Figure 91) in White Granite to commemorate his death in 1862.

By 1859, the demand for domestic whiteware of the cheaper grade had grown so much that Rhodes and Yates fitted up especially for its production the City Pottery, which had been built as a door-knob or brownware plant by Charles Hattersley in 1853. By 1864, there were twelve potteries in Trenton, making yellow and cream-colored ware in addition to White Granite, and by 1875 these had grown to nineteen, producing around two million dollars worth of ware a year. The Trenton potters were now sufficiently established, financially and technically, to branch out into finer ware. Ott and Brewer developed after 1875 a true Parian, finer in body and workmanship than anything previously made in this country, and also made decorative ware in the Belleek body. They were followed by others, some of whom modified and simplified the type by adding color to the relief, and omitting the lustre glaze.

After 1880, many American potters made "art pottery" of one type or another, some technically interesting. The White Granite was improved by James Pass of the Onondaga Pottery at Syracuse, N. Y. into vitrified china about 1888. This was a similar body still opaque, but vitreous, in lighter and more graceful shapes. Most American tableware, usually decorated in colors, was frankly cheap and frankly imitated, at a discreet distance, finer ware. It reflected an artistic inspiration of a very low order, and since it is important neither technically, historically, nor, at the present moment, to collectors, it seems unnecessary to discuss it. It is worth noticing, however, that, as late as 1890, Mrs. Benjamin Harrison, in an access of economy rather than patriotism, wished to buy American tableware for the White House. She was unable to find any which seemed suitable, so fell back on the French porcelain of Limoges, never an especially fine product. The Ceramic Art Company of Jonathan Coxon, Jr. and Walter Scott Lenox, only a year old, was already making porcelain of the Belleek type, and as Lenox, Inc., the factory supplied the first American-made White House table service in 1918.

The development of another great whiteware producing center at East Liverpool came a few years later than that at Trenton, and thereafter parallels it very closely. William Bloor, who had been at East Liverpool in the forties, then with the pioneers Taylor and Speeler at Trenton, reappeared at East Liverpool in 1860, and took over part of an old Rockingham pottery. He made bisque porcelain or Parian, white with blue backgrounds or with colored relief, in vases, mugs, butter dishes, busts of American statesmen and other pieces, with a little glazed porcelain. His blue backgrounds, usually "hammered", however, were painted on the white body, not having the color distributed through it, as in the Bennington ware. At the outbreak of the Civil War in 1862, Bloor returned to Trenton, and it was not until ten years later that the firm of Knowles, Taylor and Knowles entered the whiteware field in East Liverpool. Taylor had begun as a glass manufacturer in nearby Steubenville, and had prospered in the Rockingham and yellow-ware business which centered at East Liverpool. Their manufacture of White Granite began in 1872, and their factory became the largest pottery in the world, making, in addition to common whiteware, small quantities of a fine porcelain of the bone china type, which they called "Lotus Ware." By 1879, twelve of the twenty-three potteries then in East Liverpool were making

White Granite or cream-colored ware, and these types gradually drove the earlier favorites from the market. Rockingham and yellow-ware were still produced in considerable amounts in 1900, but in that year, East Liverpool's production of whiteware equalled that of Trenton.

An outline of the development of white earthenware and porcelain in the United States, written from the collector's view-point, must neglect the earliest period, since it is, to the collector, almost legendary, so rare are examples of its wares. Consequently, more attention has been paid to the childhood and adolescence of this American industry, with its manifold trials and tribulations. Now, because of a dead-line set at the year 1900, since the collector is not interested in ware of more recent origin, the industry must be left at the very beginning of its full growth. This has continued steadily, with improvement in every direction, and a constantly growing support from the American public, until the present day. Now the world can send us nothing better than our own productions in the field of fine tableware. And the largest whiteware factory in the world, with a number of others, produce cheaper grades of ware which still compare very favorably with those of other countries. So that, even if the triumphant last act must be reduced to a synopsis, the many gloomy earlier passages thus fall into place as incidents in a slow but certain progress.

CHAPTER XI

Very General Remarks

A CONDENSED story of the industry in the United States, or a technical classification of pottery, can include only pertinent facts, briefly stated, and cannot attempt to give any idea of the charm of this ware, which, after all, is its truest claim on the interest of collectors. Its only claim, in fact, for the American pottery industry has produced few colorful figures to invest the things they made with a touch of romance. Instead of such flamboyant personalities as the glass-makers Stiegel, Bamper and Gallatin, there are only prosaic craftsmen, respectable but not memorable. Yet the ware they made has an elusive quality—homely, simple, naïve, unsophisticated are the adjectives commonly used, but they somehow fail to convey an accurate impression. At its best, our native pottery is an expression of folk art, with talent and even genius showing through the limitations of an undeveloped and partly understood technique, and further hampered by the stern demands of utility. But, even at its worst, it has the fascination which the household wares of the past, whether they come from Pharoah's tomb or grandmother's kitchen, hold for many of us. And it is not too ambitious to claim that a little of this pottery is as graceful in form and beautiful in color as the early Oriental and Greek wares. Much of it, on the other hand, can be nothing more than "quaint," and some of it is admittedly crude and awkward. Those who know its charm need no further elucidation, and it is an almost hopeless task to make that charm clear to those others, however reasonable they may be, who can appreciate only the productions of full-blown and sophisticated art.

The development of our pottery parallels that of other American industries. Glass, closest to it in composition and use, perhaps shows the closest similarity, but furniture, metals, fabrics, all followed the same general course. Thus the earliest pottery of this country shows its European origin closely, but distinctive American types, modified by American materials, life and customs, appear very shortly. With increasing knowledge of materials and processes, and increasing surety of technique, these reach their fullest development, at which point the potters were quite prepared to attempt the most surprising productions, from the Fenton "Monument" at Bennington to the roach traps of Pennsylvania, and often achieved really fine results. This high level, of course, did not last, but many traces of it survived in the production of the potters who followed, with more or less distinction, the traditions of their fathers even beyond the limits of the nineteenth century.

The introduction of machinery and factory methods, allowing the potter to turn out an increased quota of ware which could be "ornamental as well as useful" with no additional expenditure of time, is evident in the development of the industry. This new trend was hardly an unmixed blessing, technical progress running far ahead of artistic expression, but the designers of the early factory era were sincere and earnest, and their efforts deserve a place in the history of American applied art. The closing years of the nineteenth century, however, saw the art of design completely swamped by improvements in mechanical production, leaving it inert and paralyzed, then over-stimulated to a flood of weak and meaningless pattern. Thus our interest in the pottery of this era is confined to a very few pioneers in fine ware but mainly to the many survivals of the earlier types.

These historical, technical and artistic aspects of pottery include only part of the interest it holds for collectors, possibly a smaller part than they should. Any special type of antique which is to hold the attention of the true collector must show the property of the "closed series." This closed series has been assumed as a definition of an antique in general. The term thus means a class of objects no longer made—which can cover red plush photograph albums, Model T Fords or last year's hats. A narrower definition is that a "closed series" is a class of objects existing in a fairly definite and known number of related types and variations, to which, of course, no further additions can be made. The most perfect examples of this definition are seen in those wares which have been reproduced, wholly or partly, by mechanical means, or which bear makers' marks, and it is significant that most of these, lithographs, glass cup-plates and flasks, earthenware printed in historical designs, pewter, silver and others, have already been classified and recorded for the guidance of the collector. These lists naturally make life easier for him, and also offer him the goal of acquiring an example of each type, or of certain related ones, thus achieving a "complete collection." As applied to pottery, this "closed series" can only be seen in the later types, yellow-ware, Rockingham brownware, and bisque porcelain, and no serious attempt to classify and illustrate the various designs and pieces in which these occur has been included in this study. The other types of pottery were, as has been shown, rarely produced in duplicate, and consequently show too much individuality to be compressed into a check-list. Lists of pottery types, and of potters have been complied which will, it is hoped, serve as aids to the collector, but they should be used with some discretion. This is not entirely regrettable. Pottery as a collectors' specialty does demand more knowledge and discrimination than other types of antiques which require only a reference book or check-list and a check-book, but this fact minimizes the danger that pottery will become one of the temporary fashions in collecting which from time to time wax and wane in our midst. Those who really care for pottery can hardly regret this fact, since it assures both a clearer field for them, and a more permanent and stable value for their acquisitions.

The collector, then, is well advised to collect from his own knowledge and experience, and not by the book. Even complete and accurate check-lists of those wares for which it would be possible to compile them could not be entirely definitive, since, as has been pointed out, it is impossible to determine the provenance of so many unmarked pieces. Bennington ware attracts many and is one of the most popular and best-known types of American pottery. Yet John Spargo, the acknowledged authority on the products of this pottery, points out that only half the pieces made there are marked, while some of the most typical and interesting are indistinguishable from copies made by competitors. Other potteries used marks even less frequently, so that the collector who attempts to simplify his hobby by specializing in definitely classifiable or marked pieces finds his field limited to the point of monotony. In fact, too great an insistence on makers' marks, while it does form an easy basis for collecting, is not entirely wise. So much of the finest and most interesting ware is not marked that the emphasis on marks robs pottery of some of its interest.

There are three fetishes of present-day collecting whose unquestioned significance has been magnified to unreasonable importance. These are the check-list, the "marked piece" and "perfect condition." Certainly a fine Pennsylvania slipware platter, a Bennington deer or lion, an exceptional Ohio stoneware water-cooler would be lessened in rarity and hence in value by any defects. But these ornaments for any collection were intended to serve as ornaments, so might logically be expected to be preserved with care, and so to come down through the years without harm. On the other hand, much really beautiful and fine ware was made for hard everyday use, and, unless by some lucky accident it has escaped that use, it is bound to show some scars. This is particularly true of redware, with its soft body and glaze, and the potters who made this ware have left some of the most interesting pieces we have. So in this regard also, the collector must discriminate, avoiding both an assemblage of common and uninteresting perfect pieces, and an assortment of cracked or otherwise damaged examples of fine ware.

So much for what the pottery collector ought not to do, but it is much more difficult to suggest what he ought to do. The personal element must be considered, and certainly a hobby should suit its rider rather than anyone else. So one collection of pottery may consist only of small or miniature pieces, possibly because its owner has no room for larger ones, while another, gathered by an enthusiastic gardener, may be made up entirely of flower-pots and graceful large jars for flowers. Even without going to such extremes, every collector has his or her own preferences, which, very frequently and naturally, often take the form of specializing in the wares of one locality. Pottery, unlike many of our American antiques, often remained close to its maker's shop, making this a fairly simple hobby. The acquisition of an assortment of regional types is then made difficult for those who cannot follow them to their homes, but any collection of local ware is greatly improved in meaning and interest if a fair proportion of examples from other sections is included for comparison, while a really good one should, of course, give a complete picture, technically as well as historically, of the field, however narrow, which its owner has chosen. Possibly the clearest method of exemplifying this is to describe what might be called an ideal collection. The illustrations for this book have been chosen as carefully as possible to picture the complete history of American pottery, but a less specific choice for the same purpose might be made up of a hundred pieces, selected as follows.

Since redware is first in point of age and in the number of types in which it is found, we might start with sixteen pieces of the redware of Eastern Pennsylvania, choosing unusual but not necessarily exceptional examples. This may seem a large number, but will allow us only a few from the wide selection of graceful jars, jugs and pitchers, sugar-bowls, mugs, bottles, tea-pots, colanders, lamps and other pieces decorated with incised lines or fluted mouldings, or glazed in bright or matte black, brown or black splotches on lighter grounds, green or orange mottlings or even mica sparkles. Of course, the pottery of this section reaches its highest level in the sgraffito and fine slip-decorated plates and platters, and other pieces, and four of these should satisfy the most discriminating collector. Incidentally, he would have some difficulty in securing them. Fine examples of such ware, signed or dated or with designs of historical interest, have been procurable only occasionally, even during the past few years when so many rarities were thrown on the market. The modeled figures, cow creamers, dogs, horses, and others are also uncommon, and we should want two of these. Then the group of Pennsylvania ware could be completed by some of the commoner slip-decorated plates or bowls which, even with touches of green slip in addition to the usual yellow markings, are much less difficult to find.

The very similar slip-decorated ware of New England should also be represented by two examples, which, thoroughly authenticated, will still be difficult to distinguish from those of Pennsylvania. Six additional specimens from this territory should serve to show the common clear glaze on the red body, the black high glaze so characteristic of New England, and the colored glazes, green or mottled, again likely to resemble similar ware from Pennsylvania. The range of forms in the northern ware is more limited, but certainly the famous bean-pot must be included, as well as the wide-mouthed jugs or pitchers. Turning to the South, we should want, if possible, one piece of the slip-decorated ware made by the Moravians of North Carolina, and three pieces of the rather late and heavy but brilliantly colored and well modeled ware made in the Shenandoah valley of Virginia. Another late but interesting type, the glaze-decorated pitchers and jars made in Western Pennsylvania and Ohio, can be represented by one example. One specimen of Mid-Western hard-burned redware, with its characteristic dull and stony glazes, and one piece of salt-glazed redware for its technical interest would complete the quota of this type of pottery.

Turning to stoneware, the ownership of three marked pieces, especially good examples of form and decoration, bearing the names of the Crolius and Remmey families of New York, should content any general collector. Stoneware is marked so much more frequently than redware that we should want two jars or jugs bearing the names of New York State potters. Then there might be six examples of the very similar ware of New England, some, of course, marked, and in fine and characteristic forms or decorations, from such well-known potteries as Bennington, Norwich or Boscawen. One of these might be an outstanding piece modeled or decorated in relief. Of the stoneware made farther south, that of New Jersey is sufficiently important to be represented by a specimen with the mark of one of the early potters, and three showing characteristic and fine floral designs in blue, possibly with incised outlines, or the odd conventionalized birds. Other stoneware would include one piece from Eastern Pennsylvania, and one from Strasburg, Virginia for the sake of its unusual coloring. Then the stoneware of the South could be represented by five pieces, a number due more to the amount of this ware made than to its importance to the collector, although some pieces unknown in the other sections of the country can be found. Six examples of Mid-Western stoneware should include one early marked piece, one with the applied relief decoration made especially around Zanesville, Ohio, and one with a fine design in blue, such as the eagle pieces.

In the field of brownware, that of Bennington unquestionably deserves first place, and two of the United States Pottery's famous lions, dogs or reclining deer would stand out as high spots of the collection. Then six less rare types, including the equally famous hound-handled pitcher, some ordinary but marked soap dishes, bowls or pitchers, examples of the "Patent Flint Enamel," scroddle and possibly the "combed" ware would complete the picture. To compare with these, there should be two examples of similar ware from New Jersey, two from Baltimore, and four from the Ohio River potteries, among which it would be interesting to include several variations of the hound-handled pitcher, at least twenty-five of which are known, book flasks, and possibly the Flint Enamel, as well as such typical pieces as the Baltimore "Rebecca" tea-pot and the dog door-stops of Ohio. The cruder types of brown-ware were made in such quantities that they should be represented by ten pieces. Among these could be some from the Communistic societies at Zoar, Beaver Falls or Amana, for their historic interest, and several pieces of the salt-glazed and alkaline-glazed mottled wares of the South, for their technical interest, with some examples of either type unusual in purpose or decoration. Two pieces of yellow-ware, again better than average, could represent this rather uninteresting type.

This covers the field of "pottery" as many collectors understand it. But, to complete the picture of our American industry, a few specimens of white-ware should be included. Two pieces of porcelain from the Tucker or Hemphill factory in Philadelphia, or from another of the early makers, would, of course, be prizes to boast of, and another might be from the late but important Union Porcelain works, the Century Vase, Keramos Vase or Liberty Cup. The Bennington potters again claim an important place with their unglazed bisque porcelain or Parian, so that four examples, including the characteristic blue and white pitchers, would not be too many to include in the collection. Two pieces of similar ware from New Jersey, East Liverpool or South Carolina should be included for comparison, and one of the really fine figures modeled by Isaac Broome for Ott and Brewer of Trenton about 1876 might show the highest level of American Parian. Then one mug, plate or other printed piece from the Jersey City Pottery would exemplify American earthenware of the early period, and two pieces of plain White Granite or decorated Semi-Porcelain or Hotel Ware from one of the later makers, possibly the Colonel Ellsworth pitcher, necessarily marked to distinguish them from very similar imported ware, would with a specimen of the bright majolica of the eighties and nineties, also marked, serve to complete the collection.

These last selections are rather a compromise. Certainly few pottery collectors would include them, and yet a truly comprehensive collection should really contain a larger proportion of these types, since they have played an important place in the development of the American pottery industry to its present status. Further, there is some collecting interest in Majolica at the present time, and we may yet find American White Granite rivalling in popularity the American pressed glass made during the same period, under the same manufacturing conditions, and artistic inspiration and for the same public. It is possibly a hair-splitting distinction to admit pottery made by hand in the old work-shops and by the old methods even as late as 1900 into a collection of antiques, and then to banish the machine-made ware of the last two or three decades of the nineteenth century. It is possible, however, to class the first as survivals of an earlier manufacturing technique, and the second as "primitives" of our present methods of quantity manufacture and mechanical reproduction. A more captious distinction would be that the makers of the first were doing the best they could with the crude materials and processes at their command, while those of the latter, with infinitely superior resources, were deliberately doing a great deal less than their best.

In this connection, it is worth noting that the great majority of this later whiteware was produced "for the millions." The collector who appreciates such ware would do well to disregard a specious "antique" label, and rescue from oblivion some of the whiteware and glass which was put on the market, in comparatively limited amounts, within the last ten or fifteen years, by our great emporiums catering to the millions whose price limit is ten cents. This ware was so much superior to anything previously made in the same price range that several museums have exhibited it as fine examples of design and workmanship. So far, no one has investigated or catalogued it, but it would be an interesting field.

This, however, is venturing much too far beyond the limits of our "ideal collection." It is not, certainly, an important one, as out of the one hundred items to which it has been limited, less than one-quarter could be considered truly fine collectors' pieces, and it necessarily contains none of the unique and sometimes puzzling "freaks," or unique pieces, which are at once the collector's pride and annoyance. But it does present a possible goal for an ambitious collector, or a series of starting points for more specialized collections, and has the merit of being within the financial range of a not too plethoric pocketbook.

Although it is a temptation to dodge the difficult question of prices altogether, on the ground that a work of this sort is no place for such a discussion, it is certainly a detail which interests the collector, and so demands some mention. Actually, pottery values are not as definite, and are far from being as widely advertised as those of other types of antiques, particularly such as have attracted the attention of a large public. Consequently, pottery can offer no analogies to the forty-five hundred dollar highboy, the fifteen hundred dollar bottle or the three thousand dollar lithograph. There are a number of "high spots," certainly, and the wise seller and buyer both know their price records. But less experienced individuals may be compelled to guess, and thus set prices too high as often as too low. This vagueness is intensified by the stay-at-home quality of pottery, so that a piece seventy-five miles from the plant in which it was made is likely to be a stranger, and, as such, to be incorrectly valued. On the other hand, the same piece, in its proper locale may be a little too much appreciated. It is probably useless to advise the beginner that the safest place to look for the bulk of his specimens is in the shop of the dealer whose knowledge and honesty he knows, because he never, by any chance, can be persuaded of this. But, with some knowledge of types and values, it is possible to start the fascinating but slow process of acquiring pieces, often with interesting scraps of information attached, from the original owners. Then, too, the hours spent in looking through various unlikely spots in search of the always exciting bargain may be worthwhile.

Possibly the vexing question of reproductions commonly known as "fakes" should also be mentioned. There are at present a number of types of crude hand-made pottery on the market, especially those made at Williamsburg and Monticello, but none of them are, or could be, offered as antiques. Occasional pieces find their way into the shops of less scrupulous dealers, but the collector with a little experience should not find it difficult to avoid them. The present day potter finds it so hard to unlearn his training in rapid and exact duplication and the use of standard materials and processes, that it is difficult for him to reproduce the old ware. And, when he succeeds in this, his individual technique immediately becomes so noticeable that, once recognized, it can be thereafter avoided. The late Jacob Medinger did not reproduce the old sgraffito ware; he made it, as he and his father before him had done. Examples of his ware were offered for sale in antique shops as old pieces, but, to anyone who knew it for what it was, it fairly shrieked its origin. Again, the anxious collector will find safety in the arms of the honest and experienced dealer. And it must be said that, while there are actually very few deliberately dishonest dealers, there are many who can themselves be deceived, and possibly pass the deceptions along to their customers in all honesty.

This is, of course, a purely personal opinion, as the collection suggested, and, in fact, this entire chapter reflects the writer's preferences and prejudices, possibly at unnecessary length. But, after ten chapters of cold hard facts, set down as briefly, clearly and fully as possible, the reader may pardon the digression, placed where he can leave it unread without detracting from whatever value the book may have for him. It is impossible to be enthusiastic about and absorbed in any subject without developing fairly strong likes and dislikes, but the writer's have been allowed to color facts as little as possible. Many theories and opinions, as well as any number of enjoyable or amusing experiences and pleasant meetings which the search for pottery and information about it have brought, are deliberately omitted. These seem, somehow, much better suited to the give-and-take of conversation, with both sides able to contribute their share, than to the printed page. In the interest of brevity, the writer has been compelled to choose between attempting to be entertaining and trying to be helpful, and has deliberately chosen the latter course. He fully realizes that no reader will ever sit up until midnight to finish this book, but hopes some readers may find it worth keeping within reach for occasional reference, and ends with his best wishes for "good hunting."

POTTERY TYPES

A. Redware

THIS, Dr. Barber's "Lead-Glazed Pottery," has a comparatively soft and porous body, softer than that of any other ware within the scope of this study. In color, this body ranges from pinkish buff through red-browns to a true brown, and it is usually covered by a soft and easily scratched lead glaze, often "crazed" or covered by a network of fine surface cracks. It is the earliest type of American pottery, apparently made from local surface clays by the first potters in all sections of the country. Redware rarely shows formal makers' marks, those used being frequently names inscribed freehand in the soft clay. It may be classified as follows:

1. Redware, unglazed; flowerpots, water-coolers, chimney pots, stove-pipe collars, drain pipes, roofing tile, tobacco pipes, vases to be painted, hanging baskets for flowers, memorial wreaths and very late "art ware," pressed in relief designs; 1725-1900.

2. Redware, unglazed inside, lead glazed outside; flowerpots, hanging baskets for flowers, sand-shakers, picture frames, doorsteps and stove-rests; made occasionally in all localities; 1750-1900.

3. Redware, unglazed inside, salt-glazed outside, gray to pinkish gray or mottled in shade; jars, pitchers, etc., as in #4, an attempt to use salt glaze on a generally unsuitable body; found occasionally in Ohio, Pennsylvania, Maryland, and the South; 1825-1850.

4. Redware, glazed inside, unglazed outside; applebutter crocks, milk cups, milk pans, mixing bowls, baking pots, butter crocks, cake moulds, jelly moulds, cheese-pots, pie-plates, platters, pitch-

1. PENNSYLVANIA AND NEW ENGLAND REDWARE MUG; 6. LATE NEW ENGLAND AND MID-WESTERN REDWARE MUG; 4. LATE PENNSYLVANIA REDWARE MUG; 2. PENNSYLVANIA REDWARE MUG; 7. NEW ENGLAND REDWARE BEAN POT; 3. PENNSYLVANIA REDWARE MUG; 5. VIRGINIA REDWARE MUG; 8. PENNSYLVANIA REDWARE COOKING POT; 9. OHIO BROWNWARE BEER JAR; 10. VIRGINIA BOTTLE VASE; 11. PENNSYLVANIA VASE

129

ers, bottles and roach traps; common in all localities; 1750-1900.

5. Redware, lead-glazed inside, unglazed outside, but decorated with bright transparent high glaze, showing brown against brown or tan clay, usually in floral designs, free-hand or stencilled; jars, jugs, pitchers, bowls, cups, occasional animals; a decorative type, developed at Greensboro, Pennsylvania, possibly as early as 1800, also made in eastern Ohio, 1825-1885.

6. Redware, lead-glazed, or Albany slip-glazed, inside, salt-glazed outside; crocks, jars, etc., as in #4; an attempt to improve this type, not common, found mainly in Ohio, 1850-1880.

7. Redware lead-glazed inside and outside with uncolored glaze; crocks of all sizes, jars, jugs, pitchers, basins, mixing bowls, cake and jelly moulds, cups, shaving cups, custard cups, "porringers" or small bowls, colanders, churns, harvest or ring jugs, bottles, soap-dishes, candlesticks, grease-lamps, lamp-stands, chandeliers, sugar-bowls, soup tureens, tea-caddies, tea and coffee-pots, baking dishes, salt-cellars, egg cups, spittoons, chamber pots, bed-pans, foot-warmers, tile stoves, honey jars, tobacco jars, puzzle mugs, vases, finger vases, bean-pots, soup-plates, barber's bowls, wash-bowl and pitcher sets, tumblers, cake plates, ink-stands and water coolers; although several pieces are rare, this is the commonest type of redware, especially outside eastern Pennsylvania; made in all localities; 1750-1900.

8. Redware, "glazed inside with red lead, with underglaze manganese daubs; crocks, etc.,"; a type given by Dr. Weygandt in *The Red Hills,* which would seem to include only such pieces as bowls, platters, and plates; it is certainly uncommon.

9. Redware, lead glazed outside and inside, with daubs, splashes or splotches of manganese brown on the exterior; crocks, etc., as in #2, #4, #7; never a particularly common type, but found occasionally in all localities and periods.

10. Redware, brown lead glazed outside and inside, with splashes of manganese brown as above; crocks, etc., as in #2, #4, #7; this includes glazes containing finely ground manganese oxide, occasionally with iron salts as well, as the coloring ingredient, decorated with coarser or more concentrated manganese, which

may be finely speckled as in some New Hampshire pieces, evenly mottled in tortoiseshell or Rockingham effects, as produced by the Bells of Waynesboro, Pennsylvania, or dotted or splotched in larger areas; the type is found in many localities; 1775-1900.

11. Redware black or dark brown lead glazed outside and inside; crocks, etc., as in #2, #4, #7; black is obtained with the same ingredients as brown, used in larger amounts, so is found in all periods and localities, from early Massachusetts and Philadelphia ware including tea-pots and bowls very similar to the English "Jackfield" pottery to that of the late Ohio potteries, and in textures ranging from dull and stony mattes through satin mattes to high mirror glazes; 1750-1900.

12. Redware green or mottled green lead glazed outside, usually clear lead glazed inside; crocks, etc., as in #2, #4, #7; the effect of copper salts in the glaze; solid green examples are rare, but pieces mottled or streaked in green or olive tones are found occasionally in New England, Pennsylvania, Ohio and Virginia; see #25; 1750-1900.

13. Redware, lead glazed inside and outside with clear or brownblack glazes full of sparkling mica flakes; jars and crocks as in #2, #4, #7; found very occasionally in eastern Pennsylvania, in dull and bright glazes; 1800-1875.

14. Redware, lead glazed inside and outside with "freak" glazes; crocks, etc., as in #2, #4, and #7; these include a number of unusual effects, usually obtained by accident and not by design, such as "orange-peel" surfaces, mattes and satin mattes due to over-loading the glaze with coloring oxides, particularly blacks, or improper cooling of the burned ware, maroon or even rose shades caused by reduction of iron salts in the glaze through improper firing, occasional "crackles," where the glaze has crazed excessively but evenly, and many others; found occasionally in all localities; 1750-1900.

15. Redware, "smear" glazed; crocks, etc., as in #2, #4 and #7; a very light, evenly distributed coating, secured by placing unglazed ware in a "sagger" or clay box for firing; the interior of the box was heavily coated with glaze, which was volatilized or vaporized in burning, so that some of it was deposited on the ware; a rare

type, found mainly in some decorative pieces from eastern Pennsylvania; 1775-1850.

16. Redware, decorated in relief by means of applied modeled motifs; jars, pitchers, vases, wall pockets, water-coolers, flower-pots, etc.; this may also include those pieces having heavy fluted bands or edges, although these were actually made with wheels or rollers; found occasionally in widely separated localities, West Virginia, eastern Pennsylvania, New England Virginia and elsewhere, but never common; 1820-1900.

17. Redware decorated in relief by carving the unburned clay; flower-pots, jars, vases, etc.; a decorative type found occasionally in central Pennsylvania, but rare; 1750-1850.

18. Hand-modeled redware pieces in imitation of Staffordshire earthenware figures; horses with riders and attendants, cows, cow creamers, dogs, lions, deer, doves, peacocks, snakes, etc., occasional human figures; these are sometimes covered by simple lead glazes, and sometimes elaborately slip decorated; rare in eastern Pennsylvania, almost unknown elsewhere.

19. Redware dolls, doll heads and full figures, toys, miniature chairs, tables and other pieces, whistles in the form of birds, dogs, frogs, turtles, etc., banks in simple or quite elaborate forms; found occasionally among the products of many potteries in all localities, 1750-1900.

20. Redware decorated in relief by a simple transfer process, using a natural leaf as a resist or reserve, and lead glazed; jars, etc., as in #7; very rare in eastern Pennsylvania, unknown elsewhere.

21. Moulded or pressed redwares in imitation of Bennington, Staffordshire or other pottery; toby jugs, jars, pitchers, coffee-pots, tea-pots, sugar-bowls, picture-frames, figure bottles, plates in "Majolica" designs, door-stops in various forms, "Comforter" spaniels, lambs, figures, etc.; never common, made at Bennington in Pennsylvania and particularly in Virginia, 1800-1900.

22. Redware decorated in low relief, pressed in moulds having the design incised on their faces, and glazed; a very rare type in Eastern Pennsylvania, some octagonal pie-plates being ascribed to

Jacob Tawney of Nockamixon about 1794 by Barber; unknown elsewhere.

23. Open-work or cut-out redware in basket effect, carved from unburned clay as in #17, with brown or clear lead glaze; bowls, plates, etc.; a rare type in eastern Pennsylvania, very rare elsewhere; 1750-1850.

24. Redware coated inside and outside, or outside only, with cream or buff slip or clay, and glazed with clear lead glaze, resulting in cream, buff, straw yellow or orange shades; jars, crocks, etc., as in #7, especially, mugs, tea and coffee pots, sugar-bowls and other decorative pieces or tableware; a not uncommon and rather late type in Central Pennsylvania, Maryland and Virginia, found in darker shades in early Ohio Ware; 1825-1875.

25. Redware coated with slip as above, mottled or marbled with red-brown, sepia brown and green, either dusted on under the lead glaze or added to it; jars, crocks, etc., as in #2, #4, and #7, relief decorations as in #16, hand-modeled pieces as in #18, miniatures as in #19, and pressed pieces as in #21; this type represents an improvement on the green glazed ware of #12, the shading of which may be neutralized by the red body; it is not uncommon in Southern Pennsylvania, especially in the Bell ware of Waynesboro, and is the typical splotched effect of that made by the Bells of Strasburg, Virginia; 1825-1900.

26. Redware coated with slip as above in marbled or veined effect, the coloring being in the slip; found in occasional tableware or decorative pieces in various localities, from the yellow and green veinings of some Connecticut slipware plates to the marbled brown, red and orange pieces made in Winchester, Virginia; some thin and fine pitchers and cups having bands of gray and blue marbling are not American but English, being similar to a type of copper lustre with the metallic coating omitted; the American pieces are rare; 1780-1850.

27. Redware glazed with a manganese tan dull glaze, with sepia brown daubs of manganese; jars, crocks, etc., as in #7; this may be a hard and stony glaze, or, more probably, a porous slip which

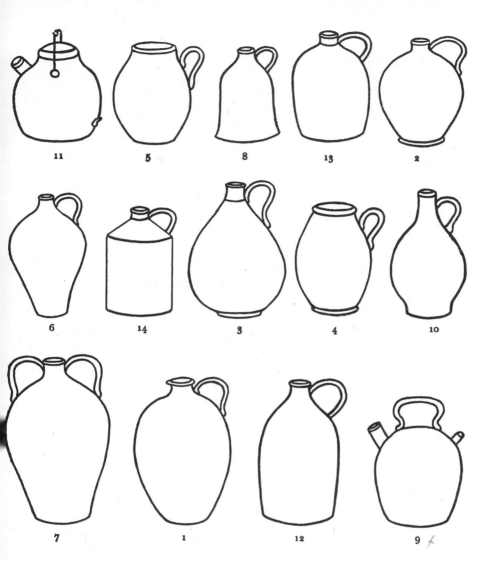

JUGS

11. Late stoneware, brownware, yellow-ware, (batter or syrup jug with tin cover and wire bail handle) all localities; 5. Early redware, New England; 8. Early stoneware, New England and New York; 13. Late stoneware, brownware, yellow-ware, all localities; 2. Early redware, Pennsylvania type (unusual); 6. Early stoneware, New England and New York; 14. Late brownware, yellow-ware; 3. Early and late redware; 4. Early redware, New England; 10. Early stoneware, New Jersey, New York, New England, (form of Bellarmine or gray-beard jugs); 7. Early and late stoneware, (large pieces) all localities; 1. Early and late redware and stoneware, common shape; 12. Late stoneware, brownware, yellow-ware, all localities; 9. Early redware, stoneware, brownware, (syrup jug) all localities

has absorbed the glaze; it is found occasionally in ware from Strasburg, Virginia, but there is a similar example from Pennsylvania in the Pennsylvania Museum; 1850-1890.

28. Redware coated with a rough cream slip outside, no glaze, no coating inside; flower-pots, sheep door-stops, some other pieces, from the potteries of Strasburg, Virginia, but unusual; 1860-1900.

29. Redware coated as above, decorated with splotches of copper green lead glaze; flowerpots, vases, etc., a Strasburg type; 1860-1900.

30. Slip-decorated redware, with underglaze designs of parallel straight or waved lines and dots in yellow cream slip tinted by the glaze—with occasional touches of green, sometimes inscribed words or names; pie-plates, platters, mixing bowls, barbers' bowls, sauce dishes, jars, crocks, flower-pots, vases, sugar-bowls, cups, mugs, pitchers, jugs, harvest jugs, bottles and animal figures as in #18; found mainly in eastern Pennsylvania, but the commoner pieces, such as pie-plates and platters were also made in New Jersey, Connecticut, Massachusetts, New York, Maryland and Ohio; 1750-1875.

31. Slip-decorated redware as above, elaborate floral, figure or scenic designs in yellow, green, chocolate brown, olive, black and blue; pieces as above; a rare type, made only in eastern Pennsylvania and North Carolina; 1750-1850.

32. Slip-decorated redware as above, but coated with one slip, almost invariably cream as in #24, and decorated as in #31 with slips in other colors; pieces as in #30; a rare eastern Pennsylvania type, many examples, particularly those on black slip grounds, probably being imported from Europe; 1750-1850.

33. Redware decorated with incised designs on the base clay under a lead glaze; crocks, jars, vases, etc., as in #7 and #30; occasional rare eastern Pennsylvania pieces show elaborate sgraffito designs, but simple parallel lines inscribed in the soft clay while the piece was on the potter's wheel are common; a few examples show more elaborate patterns, in which the deep tool marks give the effect of carving, or those obtained by the use of star

137

punches or milled rollers, as in the pottery of Boscawen, N.H., or some Pennsylvania and Virginia wares having heavy fluting as in #16; the simple ornamentation was used occasionally in all localities, 1750-1900.

34. Sgraffito redware, with decoration, usually fairly elaborate, incised through a coating of slip to show the color of the base clay; ceremonial platters, pie-plates, mixing bowls, sauce dishes, jars, etc.; the coating of slip is almost always cream, but may be green or black; an eastern Pennsylvania type, always rare; 1750-1850.

35. Sgraffito redware as in #34, with splotches of copper green under the glaze; platters, etc., as in #34; a very rare eastern Pennsylvania type; 1750-1850.

36. Sgraffito redware as in #34, with additional slip decoration as in #31, #32 and #33; platters, etc., as in #34; a very rare eastern Pennsylvania type; 1750-1850.

37. Sgraffito redware as in #34, but unglazed; platters, etc., as in #34; a very rare eastern Pennsylvania type, 1750-1850.

38. Hard-burned redware; jars, jugs, etc., as in #1, #2, #4 and #7, but with a narrower range of pieces; found throughout the South, in bodies made up of a mixture of different clays, usually covered with crude alkaline glazes, or with Albany slip or Albany slip and lead glazes; also in Ohio with the latter glazes; 1860 (1775?)-1900.

B. Stoneware

Stoneware is made from finer, denser clays than redware, which are lighter in color when burned, and the burning is carried to a much higher temperature, forming a vitreous body which is actually closer to hard-paste porcelain than to redware or earthenware in ceramic classification. The glaze is invariably a salt glaze, secured by throwing common salt into the kiln full of ware at its highest heat, the salt being vaporized and deposited on the surface of the ware to form a very thin film of glassy silicate or glaze. This is very rarely smooth or bright, usually showing a

stony lustre and considerable irregularity of surface. Since siliceous clays take this glaze best, sand was often added to those low
in silica. While the finest stoneware clays were found in northern
New Jersey and shipped to other sections, local clays, alone or in
combination, and even the redware clays of western Pennsylvania
and Ohio, were also used. This fact, with the frequent irregularity of the burning process, results in a wide color range, from
pearl to dark blue-gray, and from cream through buff, mustard
yellow and reddish brown to deep black brown. Stoneware was
made, according to tradition, at Burlington, New Jersey, in 1684,
and in New York City about 1735, but it did not begin to come
into general use until after the Revolution. Being stronger and
more durable than redware, it began to supplant this in New Jersey, New York, and New England about 1790, but both types
continued to be made there until 1900, while in Pennsylvania especially, and in other sections where the Pennsylvania German
influence was strong, stoneware never completely ousted its earlier
rival. Unlike redware, stoneware frequently bears its maker's
mark, generally his name applied with a stamp to the soft clay.
On later examples, the name, or that of the wholesaler for whom
the piece was made, may be stencilled in blue, especially in the
products of the Mid-Western potteries.

1. Plain stoneware; jars or crocks from one quart to thirty gallons capacity, "air-tight" fruit jars, butter pots or pans, water-
coolers, churns, pitchers, tobies, jugs, pancake jugs, harvest jugs,
bottles, beer-bottles, cups, mugs, bean-pots, flower-pots, hanging
baskets, pudding and cake-moulds, milk-pans, cuspidors, grease
lamps, ink-wells—"fountain" and plain, door-stops, hot-water bottles or foot-warmers, drain-pipes, chemical apparatus, etc.; while
some of these pieces are rare, this was the common type throughout the country, 1750-1900.

2. Plain stoneware, glazed inside with Albany slip (glaze) in
brown, occasionally with lead glaze, or a mixture of the two, before salt-glazing; hollow-ware as in #1, which was set in the kiln

mouth to mouth; to conserve space; the salt vapour thus failed to reach the interiors, making the additional process necessary; common in all sections, particularly New England and the Middle West, while some Southern stoneware was coated inside and outside with glaze, 1775-1900.

3. Stoneware decorated free-hand in cobalt blue, showing capacity figures, dates, names or initials, simple scrolls, conventionalized flowers and birds, rarely animal or human figures; jars, crocks, etc., as in #1 and #2, common in all localities, 1790-1900.

4. Stoneware with stencilled designs in cobalt blue, ranging from simple figures or makers' names to elaborate designs, as those showing the American eagle; jars, crocks, etc., as in #1 and #2; found in all localities, particularly in the Middle West; 1840-1900.

5. Stoneware of a dark blue-gray shade with freehand designs in purple-blue; jars, etc., as in #1 and #2; found only in the ware of Strasburg, Virginia, probably due to the use of a native cobalt ore; 1850-1890.

6. Stoneware with free-hand designs in manganese brown; crocks, etc., as in #1 and #2, rare; 1850-1890.

7. Stoneware with incised decoration; jars, crocks, etc., as in #1 and #2; simple incised lines, often combined with cobalt blue as in #3, are fairly common in all localities, but elaborate designs showing scrolls, flowers or figures, often filled in with blue, are rare; found occasionally in New England, New York, New Jersey and Ohio; 1790-1900.

8. Stoneware with applied relief decoration, often with blue ornamentation; jars, crocks, water-coolers, jugs, pitchers, etc.; found occasionally in New Jersey and Ohio, where the Tuscarawas County "clasped-hand" jugs form a local type, rare elsewhere; 1825-1875.

9. Stoneware pressed in moulds, often with blue decoration; door-stops, dogs, lions, etc., vases, water-coolers, jugs, pitchers, etc.; the Ohio dogs are not uncommon, but other pieces are rare; 1825-1900.

4. Stoneware figures, blue decoration of Staffordshire inspiration, New York State, c.1850.

35. Stoneware jar, blue decoration, Abraham Mead, Greenwich, Conn. (Courtesy of the Brooklyn Museum of Art.)

36. Stoneware jug, blue and incised decoration, Daniel Goodale, Greenwich,
Conn., 1818-1830. (Clement Collection, Brooklyn Museum.)

37. Stoneware jar, blue and incised decoration, Thomas Commeraw, Corlear's Hook, New York City, c.1790-1835. (Courtesy of the Metropolitan Museum of Art.)

38. Stonewall Inkwell, incised decoration, New York State, c.1850. (Courtesy of George S. McKearin.)

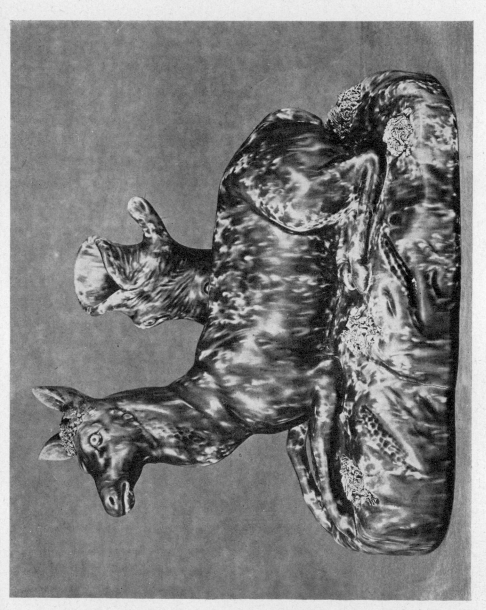

39. Flint Enamel doe figure, Bennington, Vt., 1847-1858. (Courtesy of George S. McKearin.)

40. (*Top*) Rockingham tulip vase, similar to Sandwich glass pieces; Bennington, 1847-1858. (Author's Collection.) 41. (*Bottom*) Rockingham cow creamer, Bennington, 1847-1858. (Courtesy of the Brooklyn Museum.)

42. Rockingham pitcher, immature brown glaze, probably fired only once, and experimental; Norton & Fenton, Bennington, Vt., 1845-1847. (Courtesy of the Metropolitan Museum.)

43. Rockingham lion figure, Bennington, Vt., 1847-1858. (Courtesy of J. Hasbrouk Wallace, Brooklyn Museum.)

44. Rockingham sugar-bowl, Bennington, 1847-1858. (Courtesy of the Brooklyn Museum.)

45. Redware water-cooler, applied and incised decoration light brown glaze, Ohio, c.1830-40. (Courtesy of the Ohio State Museum.)

46. (*Top*) Redware sugar-bowl, dark brown glaze, Eastern Ohio, c.1830-40. (Courtesy of Rea M. Knittle.) 47. (*Bottom*) Redware flower-pot, brown glaze decorations on unglazed clay, Greensboro, Penna., c.1890. (Courtesy of Dr. Paul R. Stewart.)

48. (*Top*) Redware platter, modeled from silver design, Eastern Ohio, c.1830-50. (Courtesy of Rea M. Knittle.) 49. (*Bottom*) Redware pitchers, red-brown glaze decoration on unglazed clay, Hamilton & Jones, Greensboro, Penna., c.1890. (Courtesy of Dr. Paul R. Stewart.)

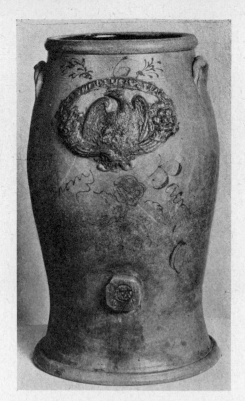

50. (*Top*) Stoneware water-cooler, applied and blue painted decoration, Eastern Ohio, c.1850. (Courtesy of Rea M. Knittle.) 51. (*Bottom*) slipware plate, Zoar, Ohio, c.1834-50, the star motif an emblem of the community. (Courtesy of the Ohio State Museum.)

52-53. (*Left & above*) Stoneware water-cooler, applied and blue painted decoration; Hamilton & Jones, Greensboro, Penna., c.1880. (Courtesy of Dr. Paul R. Stewart.)

54. Stoneware jar, 20-gallon capacity, blue stencilled decoration; James Hamilton, Greensboro, Penna., c.1875. (Courtesy of Dr. Paul R. Stewart.)

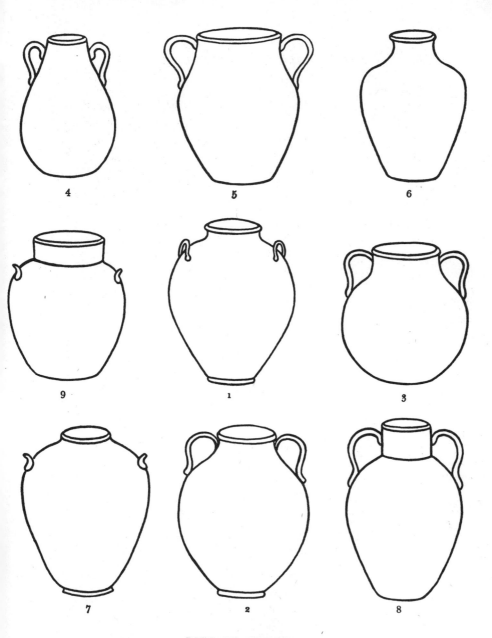

JARS OR CROCKS

4. EARLY REDWARE, UNUSUAL PENNSYLVANIA TYPE; 5. EARLY REDWARE AND STONEWARE, ALSO LATER TYPES; 6. LATER REDWARE; 9. EARLY AND LATE STONEWARE, NEW ENGLAND, NEW YORK, PENNSYLVANIA AND OHIO; 1. EARLY REDWARE AND STONEWARE OF ALL LOCALITIES, WITH NEW ENGLAND TYPE HANDLES; 3. EARLY REDWARE, RARE IN LATER PIECES, SOMETIMES UNGLAZED; 7. EARLY REDWARE AND STONEWARE, LATER REDWARE; 2. EARLY REDWARE AND STONEWARE OF ALL LOCALITIES, ALSO FOUND IN LATER TYPES; 8. EARLY STONEWARE, NEW ENGLAND AND NEW YORK

10. Stoneware figures modeled by hand, often with blue decoration; toby pitchers, heads, animals, etc.; rare but found in all localities; 1790-1900.

11. Dolls, toys, bird or animal whistles, banks and miniature pieces; found occasionally in all localities; 1790-1800.

C. Brownware

If we recognize the division of pottery types into "hand-made"—those thrown on the potter's wheel, then decorated and glazed by the same artizan, and "machine-made"—those reproduced, decoration and all, by mechanical means, brownware becomes a transitional type. It is made from clays finer in texture than many of those used for redware, and burned to a higher temperature, resulting in cream or buff bodies, actually very similar to coarse earthenware and less dense and vitreous than stoneware. These clays were used by many of the small individual potteries for thrown ware, especially in the Middle West and South after 1830, but are best known as the body which, with a lead or alkaline glaze mottled from light brown to black with manganese and iron salts, is called "Rockingham ware." This was made in factories and reproduced in quantities by pressing in moulds of plaster of Paris, so that unique pieces are rare. Being formed thus, and then burned twice, once before and again after glazing, Rockingham is fairly thin and fine as compared with other types. For this, and for the thrown ware made from the same body, a natural glaze known as "Albany Slip," which fuses to a transparent brown, was much used. On modeled or irregular surfaces, this is so transparent as to give a mottled effect, but on the cruder and less carefully burned ware, it is usually an immature opaque glaze, dull and stony. Brownware was introduced about 1830, and was made as Rockingham in New Jersey, Bennington, Vermont, Pittsburgh, Pennsylvania, Baltimore, Maryland, East Liverpool and other Ohio towns and other scattered localities. Both main divisions are rarely marked.

143

1. Unglazed Brownware, (a rather contradictory term); this may be applied to door-stops, lions, dogs, etc., and occasional other pieces made from buff-burning brownware clays, sometimes "flashed" or colored dark red by kiln gases; 1840-1875.

2. Brownware, with plain brown glazes made up entirely or largely of Albany Slip, ranging from a bright transparent high glaze, light brown to black in color, to dull stony opaque dark brown; jars, crocks, usually straight-sided cylinders thrown by hand, sometimes cast in hexagonal shapes, jugs, harvest jugs, pitchers, bottles, pancake jugs, cups, mugs, two section shaving mugs, tobies, bean-pots, flower-pots, pudding and cake moulds, milk pans, cuspidors, ink-wells, churns, drinking cups for poultry, door-stops, foot-warmers, plates, etc., (often difficult to distinguish from the hard-burned redware of A-38) ; made occasionally in the East, more commonly in the Middle West and South; 1830-1900.

3. Brownware as above, with colored bands or ornament; jars, crocks, etc., as in #2; light-colored bands, with white or clear glaze, are common on very late ware in all localities, rare Ohio pieces show green bands, secured with chromium oxide, occasional jars have capacity figures or crude scrolls in cobalt blue; 1850-1900.

4. Brownware salt-glazed over Albany clay as above; jars, etc., as in #2; an attempt to improve the glaze, but seldom clear and bright. A Southern type, unknown elsewhere; 1860-1900.

5. Brownware as above, covered with alkaline or leadless glazes, usually clear; jars, etc., as in #2; a common type in the South, especially in Georgia and North Carolina on buff or mottled bodies, merging into A-38, rare elsewhere; 1860-1900.

6. Brownware as above, with black or brown-black high glazes; jars, etc., as in #2, dog door-stops as in #8; unusual, found occasionally in the Middle West especially, 1850-1900.

7. Dolls, toys, bird or animal whistles, banks and miniature pieces or ornaments modeled by hand, not duplicated in moulds; found occasionally in all localities, particularly in the Middle West, 1830-1900.

144

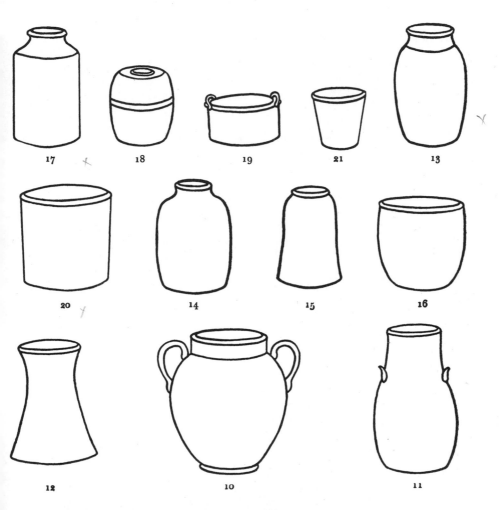

JARS OR CROCKS

17. Late redware, early and late stoneware, brownware, all localities; 18. Brownware, yellow-ware, all localities; 19. Late redware, early and late stoneware, (butter crock) all localities; 21. Late redware, stoneware, especially New England; 13. Late stoneware, brownware, yellow-ware, all localities; 20. Late stoneware, late brownware, yellow-ware, all localities; 14. Late redware, early and late stoneware, brownware and yellow-ware, all localities; 15. Late stoneware, brownware, all localities; 16. Late redware, early and late stoneware, brownware and yellow-ware; 12. Early and late stoneware, (small pieces) all localities; 10. Early stoneware, all localities; 11. Early and late stoneware, brownware, (churns, large pieces) New England and Middle West

145

8. Rockingham Brownware, or "Bennington" covered with mottled lead or alkaline glazes, ranging from light brown through rich tortoise-shell shades to black, and pressed in moulds; jars, flower-pots, pitchers in many patterns, tobies, spittoons, coffee- and tea-pots, sugar-bowls, creamers, cow creamers, tureens, covered dishes, cups, mugs, plates, cake plates, sauce-dishes, platters, bowls, soap-dishes, cake, pudding and jelly-moulds, bottles, book and other flasks, lamps, candle-sticks, picture-frames, vases, water-coolers, log cabin and other banks, foot-baths, tea-urns, foot-warmers, animal figures, dogs, lions, deer, cows, etc.; although some of the pieces mentioned are rare, Rockingham was made in quantities in many localities, the same designs frequently being repeated by several factories but it is so typical of the factory at Bennington, Vermont, that it is often known by that name; 1830-1900.

9. Rockingham Brownware as above, produced in moulds, mottled or sponged in light brown on cream; jars, etc., as in #7, especially tableware; a type intermediate between the Rockingham of #8 and yellow-ware; made in many localities, but especially in Ohio; 1850-1900.

10. "Blue Rockingham," moulded or pressed ware of the Rockingham type, covered with a mottled blue or blue-black glaze; jars, etc., as in #8; a rare type, found in Ohio, 1840-1870.

11. Flint Enamel Brown-ware, moulded or pressed as above, covered with a finely mottled brown, cream, yellow, orange and blue high glaze, the colors being suspended in the glaze itself, rendering it opaque; jars, etc., as in #8; this glaze was originated and patented at Bennington about 1850, but was copied by other potteries, the earliest Ohio pieces dated 1852, show only a yellow-brown glaze streaked with green and dark brown; 1850-1880.

12. Combed Brownware; covered by a dark slip, scratched or combed in wavy lines to show a lighter body or vice versa; jars, etc., as in #8, especially plates; a rare Bennington type; 1850-1860.

13. Scroddled Brownware, moulded or pressed as above, made by coloring the body itself, varying shades being mixed in layers to give a marbled or veined effect; jars, etc., as in #7, especially

ornamental pieces; rare, made at Bennington and elsewhere; 1845-1875.

14. Marbled brownware, covered with yellow and brown slips worked with rags or sponges into veined or marbled effects; jars, etc., as in #7; a rare Bennington type; 1850-1857.

15. Brownware door-knobs and drawer-knobs; not "collectors' pieces," but once so much in demand that several factories confined their production to these over long periods; they were made by mixing colored clays as in #13, as well as by the use of mottled or black glazes; 1840-1900.

D. Yellow-Ware

This type represents the transition from "pottery" to earthenware. The cream or buff body is finer than the first, but coarser than the second, and, like earthenware, it was produced by means of moulds in factories as distinguished from the potteries in which hand-made ware was made. The clear lead or alkaline glaze, however, intensifies the colored body to the characteristic coloring, which may vary from pale buff to deep yellow. Yellow-ware was largely made in the same factories as Rockingham type brownware, often from the same moulds, the very light-colored brownware of #8-C being a transitional type. Some of the Rockingham factories, particularly Bennington, made little or no yellow-ware, but others, as those of Trenton, specialized in this, later improving their products into coarse earthenware. Yellow-ware is rarely marked, and few designs which can be attributed to a definite factory are known.

1. Plain yellow-ware; jars, pitchers, spittoons, tea-pots, tureens, mugs, cups, plates, platters, sauce-dishes, bowls, cake-, butter-, and jelly-moulds, candlesticks, soap-dishes, bottles, etc.; although some of the pieces listed are rare, this was a common type, made in quantities in several localities and distributed throughout the country; 1830-1900.

2. Yellow-ware decorated with lines or bands of white, blue,

PITCHERS

8. EARLY AND LATE STONEWARE, BROWNWARE, ALL LOCALITIES; 3. EARLY AND
LATE REDWARE, PENNSYLVANIA; 12. MID-WESTERN STONEWARE; 5. EARLY RED-
WARE, PENNSYLVANIA; 9. LATE REDWARE, MID-WEST; 6. LATE STONEWARE AND
BROWNWARE, ALL LOCALITIES; 2. EARLY REDWARE, STONEWARE, NEW ENGLAND;
1. EARLY REDWARE, NEW ENGLAND; 4. REDWARE, EARLY STONEWARE, NEW
ENGLAND AND MID-WEST; 7. EARLY AND LATE REDWARE, ALL LOCALITIES

black or brown; bowls, mugs, pitchers, plates, etc.; very similar to the English Mocha-ware, but heavier and plainer; 1840-1900.

3. Yellow-ware with a heavy coarse pale buff body, actually very close to the Cream-Colored earthenware listed below, but heavier and coarser; jars, pitchers, etc., as in #1; a Mid-Western type, 1850-1870.

4. Yellow-ware pressed or cast in moulds in decorative forms; door-stops, candlesticks, pitchers, etc. Often from the same moulds used for Rockingham ware, found occasionally in the Middle West, 1830-1900.

WHITEWARES

A. Earthenware

This has already been defined as opaque non-vitreous and more or less porous clay ware, with a cream or, more frequently, a white body. It has always been manufactured in factories, in which each piece passed through the hands of several workmen, and has always been reproduced in moulds, since it is used largely for tableware, which requires duplication of shapes.

1. Cream-colored ware, abbreviated commercially as "C. C. Ware," a coarse body, cream or pale buff in tint, usually with a hard alkaline glaze, very close to yellow-ware in composition and appearance, and used as an improvement on it for the same un-decorated kitchen and service ware. It resembles the "Mocha Ware" of England, and was made by many potteries in this country from 1850 to 1900, but never bears makers' marks.

2. Creamware; a fine earthenware body with an alkaline or lead glaze; the cream color is very similar to that of the cream-colored ware above, but is due to unavoidable impurities in the raw materials, and not to deliberate use of impure materials for the sake of economy. It was developed in finely made and beau-tifully decorated tableware by the early English potters, particu-larly by Wedgewood, who introduced it as "Queensware" about 1760. This was the first type of earthenware to come into gen-eral use, and then went out of fashion about 1820, to be revived again in recent times. Only a very few American potters before 1850 attempted its production, none of them successfully.

3. White Earthenware; this seems the only simple and under-standable term in general use for the ware with pure white body and clear hard alkaline glaze, developed in England about 1810,

as an improvement on Queensware, and which has since been the standard type of tableware. It was also attempted by a few American potters before 1850, but its successful production in this country did not come until after 1880.

4. Ironstone china; an early improvement on the type above, a fine dense body patented by Charles James Mason of Fenton, England in 1813, and made by him and his successors until 1900, but never in America. The name was pirated by several makers of White Granite, but the two types are quite different.

5. White Granite, also known as "Ironstone China," "Semi-Porcelain," "Flint China," "Porcelain de Terre," "Stone Ware," etc.; a white earthenware body of greater hardness and density than the standard, developed about 1850 by the English potters, and made by them for the American trade, and by many American potters in heavy undecorated tableware between 1860 and 1900.

6. Semi-Porcelain, also known as "Hotel Ware," "Porcelaine Opaque," "English Porcelain"; an improvement on the above, actually vitreous but not translucent, so not a porcelain; developed about 1880, and used for decorated as well as plain tableware, lighter and more graceful than white granite, until 1900; the names, however, were sometimes applied to ware so crude as to be classed as Cream-Colored ware.

7. Earthenware decorated over the glaze; this is, of course, less durable than under-glaze decoration, so is rare, except as "art ware" and very cheap tableware, some of which was made by American factories after 1880.

8. Earthenware decorated over the glaze with metallic lustres; this lustre ware was never made commercially by American potteries; as a matter of fact, much of the early English lustre is redware.

9. Earthenware decorated under the glaze by hand; many different types and styles, made in all countries and periods.

10. Earthenware decorated under glaze by printed designs; developed by the English potters about 1750, used by them and in other countries through all the years since, the first American

printed ware being made by the American Pottery Company at Jersey City about 1840. Single color printing, first in fine lines from copper plates, then in larger areas, as in the "Old Blue" of Staffordshire, then again in finer lines after 1830, is most common. But printed designs of both early and late types were filled in by hand with colors, and decalcomania or printed transfers in varied colors have been used for many years, although rarely in this country before 1900.

11. Earthenware covered with white or colored opaque glazes containing tin; these are very early types, known as "Delft" in England and Holland, and as "Faience" or "Majolica" in France and Italy, the opaque glazes being used to mask poor body color due to crude raw materials.

12. Majolica; a term applied to ornamental ware with much modeled design, having buff or yellow bodies covered by bright-colored lead glazes applied in large areas. The type was developed in England about 1850, and made by many English and several American firms from 1875 to 1900.

13. Earthenware pressed or cast in moulds with relief designs; a type of decoration found occasionally in all localities and periods.

14. Earthenware decorated with relief designs separately pressed and applied to the moist soft ware before drying or burning. Wedgwood's Jasper merely perfected an earlier type, and the method was in use as late as 1880 for White Granite having scattered flower sprigs colored with blue or purple luster; it was never used by American whiteware potters.

15. Unglazed earthenware; most earthenware being slightly porous and also designed for use and not ornament, is glazed, the best-known exceptions being the Basalt and Jasper bodies, which are vitreous but opaque. These were originated by Wedgwood and copied by later English and Continental potters, but not by those of the United States.

16. Salt-glazed earthenware; this differs from the typical stone-

ware in its white color, and is also softer and less vitreous and much thinner and lighter; it was first made in the Staffordshire district of England about 1680, but was superseded before the full development of the industry by ware with lead or alkaline glazes, and was not made in this country.

B. Porcelain

As the subject of porcelain, with its varying types and their characteristics, must be largely academic to the collector of American ware, it may be sketched rather lightly. Oriental or hard-paste porcelain is made up of kaolin and feldspar, burned to a very high temperature. Consequently, the hard alkaline glaze is melted or fused into the body, which has itself become vitreous, retaining its shape and white or blue-white color through the presence of the more refractory or infusible kaolin, but so nearly a glass as to be translucent, or transmit light in thin sections. This body is also non-absorbent, has a glassy conchoidal or shell-like fracture, and is very close to steel in hardness. Early European attempts to duplicate this ware led to the discovery of artificial mixtures in which a large proportion of powdered glass was used to secure vitrification at a lower temperature than that used by the Oriental potters. These are known as soft-paste or artificial porcelain, as distinguished from that made up of natural raw materials. However, the German, Böttger, managed to duplicate the Chinese body at Dresden about 1710, and his discovery gradually spread through Europe, displacing the early soft paste, which is naturally excessively rare. The English porcelain factories varied this body by using some glass and calcium phosphate with the feldspar and kaolin, and Josiah Spode in 1800 introduced a new vitreous body, a soft paste containing a high proportion of the phosphate in the form of bone ash, which he called "Bone China," and which has remained the favorite porcelain body of the English manufacturers.

There is consequently much variation in porcelain bodies, making the exact identification of the type of paste difficult. On a broken surface, the fracture of hard paste will be glassy through-out, while that of soft paste will be slightly granular, with the edge showing the clearly defined coating of glaze. If the base or foot of a piece of porcelain has been left bare of glaze to prevent it from sticking to the sagger in firing, as is often the case in early ware, it will be found that a knife will leave a black mark on much, but not all, hard paste, but never on soft paste. On this bare surface, too, it will be found that hard paste is non-absorbent and soft paste slightly absorbent. This difference is apparent when the unglazed surface is touched to the tongue, or, less clearly, when a drop of ink is applied to it, which can be wiped entirely off hard paste, but, if left for a few minutes, penetrates the soft paste slightly. If no unglazed surfaces appear on a piece, the only distinction between pastes is in the color. This is not always sharply defined, but hard pastes should have bluish and soft pastes a cream tint.

The glazes used on porcelain are always alkaline, not lead, mixtures, and the decoration, except in the case of unusual "art ware," is applied over the glaze. The high temperatures to which porcelain bodies and glazes are burned alter or destroy most porcelain colors, so that these must be applied and fired separately, after body and glaze have been burned, and at a lower heat.

1. Hard porcelain; Oriental, Continental, made by Tucker, Cartlidge, the Union Porcelain Works, and in other American firms after 1880.

2. English hard-paste porcelain; varied from the above by the introduction of small amounts of glass and calcium phosphate; not made in America.

3. Early Continental soft-paste porcelain; containing a high content of glass; rare, not made in this country.

4. English soft-paste porcelain, containing calcium phosphate as bone ash, known as "Bone China"; much used by several English firms after 1800, but made only experimentally in America.

5. Parian; an unglazed hard porcelain body made up of non-

plastic feldspar and flint with no clay, which cannot be modeled or pressed, but must be cast in moulds of plaster of Paris, from which it takes fine sharp impressions. It was presumably developed simultaneously about 1848 by the great English firms of Minton and Copeland, and christened "Parian," from the resemblance of its warm white, almost cream, shade and slight texture to marble. It was used for statuettes and ornaments, and was copied by several American firms unsuccessfully until about 1875.

6. Bisque or unglazed hard porcelain; made by the United States Porcelain Company at Bennington, and copied by their competitors in pitchers and ornamental pieces as a substitute for Parian.

7. "Smear-glazed" hard porcelain; a very light film of glaze, like a salt-glaze, not secured by dipping the ware in the glaze, but vaporized from a heavy coating of glaze on the interior of the sagger or clay box which held the ware, so that a slight coating of glaze was deposited on the surface; made by many American firms from 1850 to 1875.

8. Belleek; a variation of Parian, developed at Belleek in Ireland about 1865. It is cast with very thin walls, and covered by a thin film of light-colored glazes with a pearly lustre. It was made by several American firms after 1883, and frequently varied by omitting the lustre, and coloring the relief designs in pale tints.

9. Porcelain decorated over the glaze; the common method of decorating porcelain in all periods and countries.

10. Porcelain decorated under the glaze; a method used only for unusual pieces.

PART IV

CHECK-LIST
OF
AMERICAN POTTERS

1611-1900

Note

ALL explanations, apologies and acknowledgments for this list are included in the introduction, and it must now be allowed to stand on its own merits. The arrangement, partly geographic, partly alphabetic, partly chronological, may seem rather original, if not actually absurd. But the presentation of so many potteries, whose changes of ownership and production can be extremely confusing, seemed clearest in the form given. Thus the list follows the text in its division into geographic areas, but cities and towns are listed alphabetically, as is customary. Finally, the potteries of each town are given in chronological order, but all entries covering the history of each pottery are given in order, each ownership on a separate line, before the story of the next one to be built is begun.

The numbers in parenthesis after each entry refer to the bibliography, and give the authority for each statement. Number 128, however, is used to cover a multitude of references which, if given in detail, would more than quadruple the size of the bibliography. It includes local histories, newspapers, directories, stray mentions in works on other subjects and personal recollections. Number 127 is used for makers' marks or local types known to the writer, but not mentioned elsewhere. Thus it is given as authority for including a number of potteries about which nothing is known beyond the fact that they made and marked ware.

This list certainly shows up missing names, dates and other unavoidable blanks, which are more easily glossed over in the text.

However, it also makes additions and corrections simpler. So the writer sincerely hopes that each reader will be able to add something to it. If this wish comes true, it will eventually be possible to achieve a complete and perfect list. An asterisk denotes additional information in the appendix.

Potteries of Eastern Pennsylvania,
New Jersey, Delaware, Maryland and Eastern West Virginia

Allentown, Lehigh County, Pennsylvania
  Henry Albert, c. 1816-1825; slip-decorated and plain redware; no mark. (25)
  Samuel Horn, c. 1825-1835; same; no mark. (25)
  William Fische Pot Factory, c. 1869-70; listed in directory. (119)
  George W. Bach, 1888-1900; redware, unglazed as "art ware"; no mark. (119)
Bacon Hill, Cecil County, Maryland
  Grosh Pottery, c. 1880-1900; redware; no mark. (21).
Bally, Montgomery County, Pennsylvania
  William Glaes, c. 1850; redware; no mark. (119-125)
  John Fisher, 1877-1879; same; no mark. (78)
Baltimore, Maryland
  Nicolas Auer (Ayer), c. 1796; probably redware, no examples known. (128)
  John Brown, c. 1796; same. (128)

  Thomas and Caleb Floyd, Fells Point, c. 1896; same. (128)
  Caleb Floyd, 1799-1807; same. (128)

  John Kelly, Old Town, 1796-1807; same. (128)
  James Kelly, c. 1829; same. (128)

  Maulden Perrine, Old Town, c. 1796; same. (128)
  Maulden Perrine, 1824—not listed in directory 1800-1819; stone ware and redware; no mark. (128)
  M. Perrine & Co., 1829; same; no mark (128)
  Maulden Perrine, 1834-1850; "Stone and earthenware, chemical stoneware"; no mark. (100) (1-12-25-128)

M. Perrine & Co., 1850-1900; stoneware, black glazed and Rockingham type brownware, especially dog door-stops; no mark (1-12-25-128)

James Brown, 1799-1807; probably redware; no examples known. (128)

Catherine Brown, (C. Brown & Co.), 1834-1837; redware and stoneware; no mark. (128)
Richard Wallace, 1796-1803; probably redware; no examples known. (128)
Johnson & Mason, c. 1803; same. (128)
Thomas Morgan, 1800-1837; same. (128)

David Parr, 1819-1829; same. (128)
David Parr & Co., 1829-1834; redware and stoneware; no mark. (128)
Margaret Parr (David Parr, partner), 1834-1842; same; no mark. (128)
James L. Parr, Maryland Pottery, 1842-1850; same. no mark. (128)

Henry H. Remmey (son of Henry Remney of Philadelphia) c. 1818-1835; stoneware; no mark; moved to Philadelphia (1-25-73)
Elisha Parr, 1824-1837; redware and stoneware; no mark. (128)

N. S. Jones, 1824-1832; "Tea, coffee-pot and earthenware mfr."; redware; no mark. (128)
James E. Jones, 1834-1837; same; no mark. (128)
James E. Jones and Brother, 1840; same. (128)
James E. Jones, "Queensware," 1850; no mark. (128)

William Amos, 1833-1837; "Stone Potter"; no mark. (128)

Benjamin Greble, (also Alexander Greble), 1829-1834; "tea and coffee-pot manufacturers"; redware; no mark. (128)
Benjamin Greble, 1837-1850; "stoneware, tea and coffee-pot mfrs.", no mark. (128)

William Linton, 1842-1850; stoneware and redware; no mark; former employee of Perrine. (128)

W. A. Atkinson, ca. 1850; "Earthenware, tea and coffee-pots, jugs, jars"; no mark. (128)

* Edwin Bennett, 1846-1849; stoneware, yellow-ware and Rocking-ham; moved from Pittsburgh, Penna., no mark. (1-12-25-128)

E. & W. Bennett, 1849-1856; same; William Bennett moved from Pittsburgh; mark is "E. & W. Bennett, Canton Ave., Baltimore, Md.", impressed. (1-12-25-128)

Edwin Bennett, 1856-1900; Rockingham, majolica, white-wares; marks are "E. B. "impressed, or initials or name in design, or coronet in wreath, printed, on whiteware. (1-12-25)

Edwin Bennett Pottery Co., 1890-1900; whiteware; marks similar to above. (1-12-25)

D. F. Haynes & Co., Chesapeake Pottery, 1881-1890; majolica, Parian after 1885, White Granite, Semi-porcelain; marks are monogram in frame, with name of ware and "Balto.", printed (1881-1884) or monogram alone, printed. (1-12)

Haynes, Bennett & Co., 1890-1900; whiteware; mark is monogram, printed. (12)

Barnesville, Schuylkill County, Pennsylvania

J. A. Weber, c. 1875; redware; mark is name impressed. (127)

Bedminster, Bucks County, Pennsylvania

Rudolph Drach, c. 1780-1800; slip decorated, sgraffito and plain redware; plate marked with name known. (1-25)

Bernville, Berks County, Pennsylvania (near)

Joseph Hume, c. 1850-1876; redware; no mark. (78)

Bethel, Berks County, Pennsylvania

Isaac Dubbs, 1863-1867; redware; no mark. (119-125)

Bird-in-Hand, Lancaster County, Pennsylvania

Jacob Swope, c. 1820; redware; tobacco pipes; no mark. (1)

Zuriel Swope (son), c. 1860; same; no mark; moved to Lancaster. (1-101)

Bladensburg, Prince George's County, Maryland
  George Muk, c. 1848; redware, slip-decorated and plain, marked piece known. (128)
Boonesboro, Washington County, Maryland
  ——Bothman, c. 1850; redware, similar to that made at Waynesboro, Penna., no mark. (111-127)
* Bridgeton, Cumberland County, New Jersey

  George Hamlyn, East Lake Pottery, c. 1835; redware, stoneware; mark is name and address, impressed. (18-25)
  ——Hamlyn (son?), c. 1870-1900; stoneware; no mark. (21)

Bucksville, Bucks County, Pennsylvania
  Christian Klinker, 1772, (1787)-1792; slip-decorated, sgraffito and plain redware; occasional mark is initials in slip. (1-25)
Burlington, Burlington County, New Jersey
  Daniel Coxe, c. 1684-1691; probably redware, possibly whiteware; no examples known. (1-12-25)
Caln, Chester County, Pennsylvania
  Thomas and John Vickers, 1740-1750, (1806); slip-decorated, sgraffito and plain redware; may have moved to West Whiteland, certainly moved to Lionville; marks are "T. V." or "V." inscribed. (1-25-28)
Camden, Camden County, New Jersey
  Moro Phillips, 1867-1897; stoneware, blue decorated; moved from Philadelphia; no mark. (1)
Carversville, Bucks County, Pennsylvania
  Phillip Kline, c. 1808; slip-decorated, sgraffito and plain redware; also brick; mark is name. (1-25)
  Richard Moore, 1824-1840; slip-decorated, sgraffito and plain redware; no mark; moved to Quakertown, Penna. (1-25)
  Jacob Neisser (Neizzer), 1827-1860; same; no mark. (1-3-25)
Chambersburg, Franklin County, Pennsylvania
  John Bell, 1826-1832; redware; no mark; moved to Waynesburg. (20)

Chapel, Berks County, Pennsylvania
——Frederick, c. 1840-1875; redware, some tombstones; Nathan
Weigner, owner; no mark. (78-119)

John Frederick (son), c. 1875-1893; same; no mark; (78-119);
James Stahl, 1893-1895; (successor) same; no mark. (78-119)

Cumberland, Allegheny County, Maryland
Christian Neff, 1790-c. 1810; redware; no mark. (128)
Jacob Easter, c. 1850; redware, brownware; no mark. (127-128)
Chester, Delaware County, Pennsylvania
Chester Pottery, c. 1880; redware, flower-pots; no mark. (101)
Downingtown, Chester County, Pennsylvania
Thomas Vickers & Sons, c. 1809; advertised "Queensware"; no
examples known. (1-25)
Doylestown, Bucks County, Pennsylvania
Henry C. Mercer, 1890-1900; experimental slip-decorated and
sgraffito redware, also tile, mark is monogram impressed.
(1-12)
Dryville, Berks County, Pennsylvania

——Melcher, c. 1790-1804; redware; no marks; (78); John Dry,
(successor) 1804-c. 1850; redware, slip-decorated and plain;
marks are "D" or "D. Dry," inscribed. (78)
Daniel, Nathaniel and Lewis Dry (sons), c. 1850-1880; same;
same marks; (78)

Lewis K. Tomlinson, c. 1850-1889; redware; mark is "L. K. T."
impressed or inscribed. (78)
Eagle Point, Berks County, Pennsylvania
Peter Haas, 1866-1875; redware; Nathan Dunnwolfe, potter;
no mark. (78)
Elizabeth, Union County, New Jersey

John Pruden, 1816-1879; slip-decorated, sgraffito and plain redware, stoneware, Rockingham brownware, including large
heavy pitcher with eagle and flag relief; mark on stoneware

166

is name and address, impressed; (1-12-25); succeeded by
L. S. Beerbauer & Co., 1879-1900; Rockingham and Flint
Enamel brownware, cream-colored earthenware; Beerbauer
from Phoenixville, Penna., William Leake of Bennington, Vt.,
a partner; mark is name in circle around star, impressed.
(1-12-25)

Elk Ridge Landing, Baltimore County, Maryland
Daniel Hughes and William Russel, c. 1780; probably redware;
advertised for "5 or 6 potters". (128)

Ephrata, Lancaster County, Pennsylvania
Pottery in the Kloster of the United Brethren, c. 1750-1850;
redware no mark. (128)

Exeter Township, Berks County, Pennsylvania
Mahlon Guldin, c. 1850-1875; redware; no mark. (78-119)

John Troxell, 1850-1886; redware; no mark. (17-119)
William Troxell (son), 1886-1899; same; Ferdinand Winterhalter, potter; no mark. (78-119)

Flemington, Huntington County, New Jersey
Fulper Bros., c. 1805-1900; redware, later stoneware, then art
pottery; mark on stoneware is name impressed. (22-127)

Franconia, Montgomery County, Pennsylvania

John Leidy, 1796-c. 1815; fine slip-decorated, sgraffito and
plain redware; no mark; possibly also at Soudertown, Penna.,
(1-3-25-28); succeeded by
Joseph Groff, c. 1815-1832; same; no mark. (1-3-25-28)

Frederick, Montgomery County, Pennsylvania
Enos Cope, c. 1825-1875; slip-decorated, sgraffito and plain redware; no mark; John Link, potter, c. 1870. (1-3-25-119)

Freystown, Berks County, Pennsylvania
Abraham Glaes, c. 1840-1867; plain redware; no mark; (78);
son, John G. Glaes, at Passmore, Penna.
George Frey, c. 1830-1872; same; no mark. (78)

Fritztown, Berks County, Pennsylvania
    John G. Specht, 1852-1895; redware; no mark; some pieces
    with applied decoration, from plaster moulds. (78)
    Christian Shutter, 1852-1900; redware; no mark. (78)
Gardenville, Bucks County, Pennsylvania (near)

    Abraham Stout, 1760 (1776)-1795; redware; no mark. (1-3-25)
    Isaac Stout (son), 1795-c. 1810; same; no mark. (1-3-25)

Gerysville, Bucks County, Pennsylvania

    Wendell Renninger, c. 1800-1815; redware; no mark. (119)
    John Renninger (son), 1815-1843; same; no mark. (119)
    John Renninger, Jr., (son), 1843-1873; same; no mark; worked
    pottery only intermittently. (119)

Gloucester, Camden County, New Jersey
    American Porcelain Manufacturing Co., 1854-1857; porcelain,
    mainly uncolored and unglazed as Parian of poor quality;
    mark "A. P. M. Co." impressed; (1-12-25); succeeded by
    Gloucester Porcelain Co., 1857-c. 1872; same; no mark;
    (1-12-25)
* Haddonfield, Camden County, New Jersey
    Charles Wingender & Co., c. 1890; fine decorated stoneware;
    mark "Haddonfield, N. J., C. W. & Co." impressed. (1-127)
Hagerstown, Washington County, Maryland

    Henry Adams, c. 1812; redware; no mark. (20)

    Leisinger & Bell, 1800-1813; redware; no mark; (20), succeeded
    by
    Peter Bell, 1813-1824; same; no mark; moved to Winchester,
    Va. (20)

    John Snaveley, c. 1813; same; no mark. (20)
    Daniel Reichard, c. 1813; same; no mark. (20)
    Henry Weise, son of Weise of Shepardstown, W. Va.; 1870;
    redware and stoneware; no mark. (111)

Hamburg, Berks County, Pennsylvania
Conrad Gerbrich, c. 1870; redware; no mark. (78)
Hamlin, Lebanon County, Pennsylvania
Christian Humsicker, c. 1800; redware; no mark. (119)
*Haycock Township, Montgomery County, Pennsylvania

Conrad Mumbauer, c. 1760-1800; slip-decorated, sgraffito and
plain redware; no mark; (1-25-119); succeeded by
John Mondeau (Monday) (son-in-law), 1828-1862; same; no
mark; (119) succeeded by
Simon Singer, 1862-1814; same; occasional mark is name inscribed. (28-119-125)

Harrisburg, Dauphin County, Pennsylvania
Cowden & Wilcox, c. 1880; stoneware; mark is name impressed.
(127)
Hereford, Berks County, Pennsylvania
Greiseiner Pottery, c. 1800-1865; redware; no mark. (78-119)
Hockessen, Delaware
Abner Marshall, 1860-1866; yellow-ware, Rockingham Brown-
ware; no mark. (1-22-25)
Honeybrook, Chester County, Pennsylvania
William Schofield, 1825-1900; slip-decorated, sgraffito and plain
redware; no mark; formerly at Vickers pottery, Lieoville. (28-
125)
Jackson Township, Lebanon County, Pennsylvania
——Weidle, c. 1880-1900; redware; no mark. (119)
Jonestown, Lebanon County, Pennsylvania
Zach Gingerich, c. 1875; redware; no mark. (119)
Jersey City, Hudson County, New Jersey

Jersey Porcelain and Earthenware Co., 1825-1828; some hard-
paste porcelain; no mark; (125); succeeded by
D. & J. Henderson, 1829-1833; fine stoneware, yellow-ware;
Rockingham brownware; marks are "Henderson's Flint Stone-
ware Manufactory, Jersey City" or "D. & J. Henderson, Jersey
City", in circle, impressed. (1-12-25-127)

American Pottery Manufacturing Co., 1833-1840; yellow-ware, Rockingham brownware, white earthenware; mark is "American Pottery Manufg. Co." in flag, printed, on whiteware; same as above on brownware; (1-12-25); name changed to

American Pottery Co., 1840-1845; same as above; marks are "American Pottery Co., Jersey City" in circle, impressed, on brownware, same, in curved line or in design with "Canova", printed, on whiteware; (1-12-25); succeeded by

Rhodes, Strong & McGeron, Jersey City Pottery, 1845-1854; white and cream-colored earthenware; no mark; (12); succeeded by

Rouse & Turner, 1859-1892; same as above, also Parian; mark is "R. & T." with British coat-of-arms, printed; (12)

Krausdale, Lehigh County, Pennsylvania
    John Kraus, c. 1800; redware; no mark. (77)
Langhorne, (Attleboro), Plumstead County, Pennsylvania
    Joseph Johnson, 1830-1865; slip-decorated, sgraffito and plain redware; no mark. (25)
Lancaster, Lancaster County, Pennsylvania
    Henry Gast, 1825-1890; redware, tobacco pipes; mark is name inscribed. (1-101)
    George A. Swope, c. 1880-1900; redware, flower-pots; moved from Bird-in-Hand; no mark. (1-101)
    Edward W. Hardy, c. 1890-1900; same; no mark. (101)
Leesport, Berks County, Pennsylvania
    John George Buehler, 1843-1887; redware; no mark. (78)
Lewistown, Mifflin County, Pennsylvania
    A. G. Curtin Dipple, c. 1885-1900; redware, flower-pots, stoneware; mark is name and address, impressed. (101-127)
Lebanon, Lebanon County, Pennsylvania
    Ludwig Ginguich, c. 1860-1886; redware; no mark. (119)
    ——Weaver, c. 1850-1870; same; no mark. (119)
Lincoln University, Chester County, Pennsylvania

    Thomas Cope, c. 1874-1890; redware, flower-pots; former workman at Vickers pottery; mark is name impressed. (28-125)
    Cope, Witmer & Bros., 1890-1900; same; no mark. (101)

Lionville, Chester County, Pennsylvania

Thomas and John Vickers, 1750-1822; (1821-22) ; moved from Caln or West Whiteland; slip-decorated, sgraffito and plain redware; marks are "T. V." or "V." Inscribed. (1-3-5-25-28)
John Vickers & Son, 1822-c. 1850; same; no mark. (1-3-25-28)
Paxton Vickers (son), c. 1850-1878; same; no mark. (28-125)

Lititz, Lancaster County, Pennsylvania
Samuel Sturgis, 1840-1893; redware, tobacco pipes; no mark. (1)

Manheim, Lancaster County, Pennsylvania
John Gibble, c. 1865; redware, Indian-head tobacco pipes; no mark. (1)

Martinsburg, Berkley County, West Virginia
James Weise, c. 1870, son of Weise of Shepardstown; redware, stoneware; no mark. (111)

Mercersburg, Pennsylvania
Hugh McConnell, c. 1826-1870; Point (Madison) Middlesex County, New Jersey (See MaHewan); stoneware and redware; no mark. (111) (12B)

Middletown Point, Middlesex County, New Jersey—see Mahewan.

Mohrsville, Berks County, Pennsylvania

John Snyder, c. 1835-1873; redware; no mark. (119)
John Snyder, Jr., 1873-1876; same; no mark; (119); succeeded by
Daniel Egoff, 1876-1896; same; no mark; came from Virginsville, Penna. (78-119)

Moselem, Berks County, Pennsylvania

Abraham Reiser, 1832-1859; redware; no mark; owner, employed several potters. (78)
Peter S. Reiser (son), 1859-1898; same; no mark. (78)

Mt. Etna, Berks County, Pennsylvania

Henry Fair, c. 1870-1891; redware; no mark. (78-119)
Michael B. Fisher, 1891-1900; same; no mark. (78-119)

Myerstown, Lebanon County, Pennsylvania
Henry McQuate (near), 1845-1859; slip-decorated and plain
redware; no mark. (25-62)
* Neiffer, Montgomery County, Pennsylvania
——Spies, c. 1850; redware; no mark (119)

Jacob Neiffer, c. 1830-1850; slip-decorated, sgraffito and plain
redware; no mark; (119); succeeded by
William Medinger, 1850-c. 1880; same; no mark. (76-119-125)
Jacob Medinger, c. 1880-1900; same; favorite glazes mottled olive
and satin black; operated until 1930; occasional mark is name
inscribed. (76-119-125-127)

J. U. Adams, 1855-1891; plain redware; no mark. (119)
Newark, Essex County, New Jersey
Baltazar J. Krumeich, c. 1845-1860; stoneware; mark is name
and address, impressed. (127)
New Berlin, Union County, Pennsylvania
Phillip Seebold, 1820 (or 1825)-1845; redware, tobacco pipes;
no mark. (1)
Adam Maize (Mouze), 1810-1845; sgraffito and plain redware;
no mark. (1-3-5)
New Britain, Bucks County, Pennsylvania
Christian Miller, c. 1845-1850; slip-decorated, sgraffito and plain
redware; no mark. (1-25)
* New Brunswick, Middlesex County, New Jersey
Horner & Shiveley, c. 1831-1841; "Flint Stoneware"; no mark;
(66-128)
A. J. Butler & Co., c. 1850; stoneware; mark is name and
address, impressed; (127)
Newmanstown, Lebanon County, Pennsylvania
Johann Theobald Schultz, c. 1790; slip-decorated, sgraffito and
plain redware; no mark. (119)
Newtown, Bucks County, Pennsylvania
Frank C. Lock, c. 1880-1900; redware; no mark. (101)
Newtown Pottery, c. 1870-1900; same; no mark. (101)

Niantic, Montgomery County, Pennsylvania
  Huber Pottery, 1842-1876; redware; no mark; Huber was not a potter, various lessees or foremen operated plant. (77-83) (77-119)
Nockamixon, Bucks County, Pennsylvania

  Cornelius Herstine, 1785-c. 1810; slip-decorated, sgraffito and plain redware; no mark. (1-3-5-25-28)
  Daniel Herstine (son), c. 1810-1844; same; no mark. (1-3-28)
  David Herstine (son), c. 1844-1875; same; no mark. (28-119)
  Daniel Herstine (son), 1875-1900; same; no mark; operated until 1910; (28-119)

  Jacob Kintner, c. 1780-1840; same; no mark. (1-3-25-28)
  Jacob Tawney, c. 1794; same; mark is name. (1-25)

  John Herring (Harring), c. 1818-1826; same; no mark. (1-5-25-28)
  David Harring (son), 1826-1866; same; no marks. (1-25-28)
  ——McKentee, c. 1840; same; no mark. (125)

Norristown, Montgomery County, Pennsylvania
  Keller Pottery Co., c. 1880-1900; redware; no mark. (101-119)
Noxatawney Township, Berks County, Pennsylvania
  Peter Haas, 1866-1875; redware; no mark. (119)
* Old Bridge, Middlesex County, New Jersey
  ——Van Winckle, (Wickle), 1800-   ; stoneware; no mark. (1-25)
Ono, Lebanon County, Pennsylvania

  Martin Wiley, c. 1850-1875; redware; no mark. (119)
  Solomon Hook (son-in-law), 1875-1882; same; no mark. (119)

Passmore, Berks County, Pennsylvania
  John G. Glaes, 1870-1900; redware; no mark; operated until 1911. (78-119)
Pfeiffer's Corner (near Weissport), Carbon County, Pennsylvania
  George A. Wagner, 1875-1896; redware, yellow-ware; no mark. (119)

Pennsburg, Montgomery County, Pennsylvania

Richard Bitting, 1847-1880; slip-decorated, sgraffito and plain redware; no mark; not a potter, leasees were John Renninger, William Roudebusch and Jacob Schauer. (25-119)

Perkiomenville, Montgomery County, Pennsylvania

John Link, 1873-1898; moved from Frederick; redware; no mark. (77-119)

Lewis Johnson Pottery, c. 1870-1900; sgraffito, slip-decorated and plain redware; Jacob Stofflet, potter, 1874-1877; other leasees; marked sgraffito plate by Stofflet known, otherwise no mark. (77-119-127)

* Perth Amboy, Middlesex County, New Jersey

——, c. 1800; stoneware; no mark. (22)

J. R. Watson, c. 1833-1840; stoneware, firebrick; no mark. (128)

T. W. Whiteman, c. 1863; stoneware; mark is name impressed (127)

A. Hall & Sons c. 1866; Rockingham and "scroddle" brownware; no mark; first architectural terra cotta in the United States. (1-66)

* Philadelphia, Pennsylvania

Joshua Tittery, c. 1683; probably redware. (19)

William Creus, c. 1690-1695; tobacco pipes, probably redware. (19)

Anthony Duche, 1700-1762; probably redware. (55)

Gousse Bonin and George A. Morris, 1769-1772, (1774); white earthenware decorated in blue; see p. 000; rare mark is small script "p" in blue under glaze. (1-19-25-98)

Jeremiah Warder, c. 1780-1784; sold pottery and equipment, 1784, including busts of Washington. (19)

William Stradley, c. 1785; probably redware. (19)

Andrew Miller, 1785-1810; slip-decorated, probably slip-coated and plain redware; red and black teapots; no mark. (1-19-25)

Abraham Miller, 1810-1858; same, also white earthenware or queensware; some silver lustre about 1824, Rockingham type brownware, yellow-ware, white earthenware, biscuit and glazed figures, "Tam o' Shanter" Rockingham pitcher about 1843, refractory ware, stove linings, first floor and wall in the United States in 1845, refractory ware, stove linings, (1-22-25-128); succeeded by

Charles J. Boulter, 1858-1900; Tucker & Hemphill workman, later with Miller; refractory ware, experimental soft-paste porcelain; no mark. (1-25)

Mordecai Gilbert, c. 1788; redware; no mark. (128)

John Curtis, 1790-1811; slip-decorated, sgraffito and plain redware, cream-colored earthenware; no mark. (1-25)

Christian Piercey, c. 1788-1794; redware; no mark. (128)

Binney & Ronaldson, c. 1809; redware, black glazed or slip-covered, teapots, etc., no mark. (1-25)

Alexander Trotter, Columbian Pottery, 1810-1812; cream-colored earthenware or queensware; no examples known; moved to Pittsburgh. (1-25-128)

"Captain" Mullowney, Washington Pottery, 1810-1817 (or 1829-1850), redware, sgraffito, slip-decorated, black-glazed, plain; no mark. (1-25)

Daniel Freytag, 1810-c. 1830; white earthenware; no examples known. (1-25)

Thomas Haig, 1812-1833; slip-decorated, sgraffito and plain redware; no mark. (1-25)

James and Thomas Haig (sons), 1833-1890; same, also Rockingham brownware, including cow creamer, log cabin bank, O'Connell head and Washington-Masonic pitchers; stoneware after 1858; no mark. (1-25)

David G. Seixas, 1816-1822; cream-colored earthenware similar to Liverpool type; no examples known. (1-25)

Branch Green, c. 1820; stoneware; no mark. (73) moved from Old Bridge.

Henry Remmey, 1810-1835; grandson of John Remmey I of New York; stoneware; no mark. (1-25-73)

Henry H. Remmey (son), 1835-1859; moved from Baltimore; same; no mark. (73)

Richard C. Remmey (son of above), 1859-1900; same; mark is initials impressed. (1-25-73-127)

Burnet & Remney (Henry H. Remney), c. 1840; stoneware; no mark. (73)

William Ellis Tucker, American China Manufactory, 1826-1828. (1-25-51-95)
Tucker & Hulme, 1828-1829. (1-25-51-95)
William Ellis Tucker, 1829-1832. (1-25-51-95)
Tucker & Hemphill, 1832. (1-25-51-95)
Joseph Hemphill, 1833-1837. (1-25-51-95)
Thomas Tucker, 1837-1838; all made porcelain, see pp. 102-4; rare marks are current name of firm and "Philadelphia" or "Philad." Inscribed in red, brown, etc., over glaze, also inscribed workmen's marks. (1-25-51-95)
Smith, Fife & Co., c. 1830-1831; hand-paste porcelain, very similar to that of Tucker and Hemphill; rare mark is name. (1-25-98)

Isaac Spiegel, 1837-1858; Tucker & Hemphill workman; slip-decorated, sgraffito and plain redware, Rockingham brownware mantel ornaments, etc., no mark. (1-25)
Isaac Spiegel (son), 1858-1879; same; no marks. (1-25)
John Spiegel (brother), 1879-c. 1890; biscuit redware art ware; no mark. (12)

Peter Kelley, c. 1840; redware, log cabin banks; mark is name impressed. (125)
Bagaly & Ford, c. 1843; porcelain; no mark. (1)
Ralph Bagnall Beech, (1846-1852); redware, Rockingham brownware, O'Connell head pitcher, possibly Taylor head some porcelain; rare mark on porcelain, name impressed, none on other ware. (1-12-25)
——English, Frankford, c. 1850; redware; no mark. (125)
Moro Phillips, 1853-1867; stoneware; moved from Wilson's Landing, Va., moved to Camden, N. J.; no mark. (1)
Kurbaum & Schwartz, c. 1853; porcelain; mark "K. & S" impressed. (1-25)
George Allen, 1859-c. 1863; whiteware; bought equipment of Beech pottery; no mark. (128)

J. E. Jeffords & Co., Port Richmond Pottery, 1868-1890; Rockingham brown-ware, toby pitcher, cow creamer, printed and painted white earthenware; Stephen Theiss of Bennington, designer; mark is "J. E. J. & Co." in diamond. "Warranted Fireproof" outside, printed, on whiteware. (1-12-22)

Galloway & Graff, Philadelphia City Pottery, 1868-1900; brown-ware jars, impressed "Galloway's Everlasting Jar, Pat. 1875" (127-128)

*Phoenixville, Chester County, Pennsylvania

Schrieber & Betz, Phoenixville Pottery, 1867 (1870)-1877; terra-cotta; no mark; succeeded by (1-25)

Beerbauer & Griffin, 1877-1879; white granite, bisque porcelain or Parian; no mark; succeeded by (1)

Griffin, Smith & Hill, 1879-1900; Parian, majolica; mark is monogram of "G. S. & H.", or monogram with "Etruscan Majolica" in circle around it. (1-25)

Pittston, Luzerne County, Pennsylvania
Evan B. Jones, c. 1880; stoneware; mark is name and address; impressed. (127)

Plumstead, Bucks County, Pennsylvania
Helfreich Toomey, 1830-1860; slip-decorated, sgraffito and plain redware; no mark. (1-3-25)
——Schrum, 1845-1850; same; no mark. (25)
——Bartleman, c. 1840-1850; same; no mark. (25)

Powder Valley, Lehigh County, Pennsylvania

Charles Stahl, 1847-1896; slip-decorated, sgraffito and plain redware; no mark. (77-119)

Isaac Stahl (son), 1896-1898; same; no marks; Isaac and Thomas Stahl still operating. (77-119)

Quakertown, Bucks County, Pennsylvania
Moore & Kinzie, c. 1840-1850; slip-decorated, sgraffito and plain redware; succeeded Richard Moore of Carversville; no mark (1-25)

Rahway, New Jersey

John Mann, c. 1830-1900; redware, black glazed tea-pots; mark is name and address impressed (1-18-25)

Reading, Berks County, Pennsylvania

Conrad Kuch, 1767-1784; redware; no mark. (78)

Henry Krimler, c. 1767; redware; no mark. (78)

John Fry, 1768-1784; redware; no mark. (78)

Godfrey Leaman, c. 1780; redware; no mark. (78)

Daniel P. Schenefelder, 1869-1900; slip-decorated and plain redware stoneware, stoneware marked with name and address in oval, impressed, no mark on redware (78). Mary Schenefelder, daughter, decorator.

Fox, Haag & Co., 1869-1900; unglazed redware, (terra-cotta) vases; no mark. (119)

Rich Valley, Montgomery County, Pennsylvania

Nunemacher Pottery, c. 1850; redware; no mark. (119)

Rock Hill, Bucks County, Pennsylvania

John Headman, 1800-1830; slip-decorated, sgraffito and plain redware, rather coarse body, heavy slip decoration; no mark. (1-3-25-28)

Peter Headman (son), 1830-1870; same; no mark. (1-3-25-28)

John Headman (son), 1870-1900; same; no mark. (28)

Andrew Headman (brother of John I), 1806-c. 1840; same; no mark. (1-3-25-28)

Charles Headman (son), c. 1840-1890; same; occasional mark is name or initials inscribed. (28)

George Diehl (near), 1832-c. 1860; same; no mark. (1-3-25-28)

William Diehl (son), c. 1860-c. 1885; same; no mark. (1-25-28)

Rockland Township, Berks County, Pennsylvania

Christian Rieff, c. 1767; redware; no mark. (78)

Heinrich Stofflet, c. 1814-1830; redware; no marked plate known (24-67-83) (25-78-119)

Jacob Stofflet (son), 1830-1845; redware; no mark; later worked in other potteries. (78-119)

Ronk, Lancaster County, Pennsylvania
   Ganse Pottery, c. 1870; redware; mark is name. (125)
* Sayreville, (Roundabout), Middlesex County, New Jersey
   Xerxes Price, c. 1802; stoneware; mark is name and address
      "Roundabout," or initials, impressed. (1-12-25)
   ——c. 1850; stoneware; no mark. (128)
Seidersville, Northampton County, Pennsylvania
   John Renninger I, 1849-1851; redware; no marks; moved from
      Gerysville. (119)
Shartlesville, Berks County, Pennsylvania

   Daniel P. Henne, c. 1860-1870; redware, especially toys and
      modeled pieces; no mark. (78-119)
   Joseph K. Henne (son), c. 1870-1880; same; no mark. (78-
      119)

Shepardstown, Jefferson County, West Virginia

   ——Weise, c. 1850; redware; no mark. (111)
   Wm. Weise (son) c. 1860; same; no mark. (111)
   ——Happel, c. 1880; same; no mark. (111)

Shoemakersville, Berks County, Pennsylvania

   Henry Moll, c. 1840-1850; redware; no mark. (78-119)
   Benjamin Franklin Moll (son), c. 1850-1865; same, also deco-
      rated flower-pots; no mark. (78-119)
   Franklin B. Moll (son), c. 1865-1885; same; no mark. (78-
      119)

Silvertown, Lebanon County, Pennsylvania
   John Thierwaechter, c. 1875; redware; no mark. (119)
Somerset, Mercer County, New Jersey
   Somerset Pottery Works, c. 1875; stoneware; mark is name im-
      pressed. (127)
Soudertown, Montgomery County, Pennsylvania
   John Leidy, c. 1790; possibly located here, see Franconia. (28)
* South Amboy, Middlesex County, New Jersey

Warne & Letts, or J. Letts, c. 1778-c. 1820; stoneware; mark is
name in full or "T.W.J.L" or "J.L.," impressed. (1-12-25-73)
  succeeded by
Joseph Henry Remney (great-grandson of John Remney I of
New York), c. 1820-1823; stoneware; no mark. (1-73)

Humiston & Walker, 1826-1835; stoneware; no mark. (1)
John Hancock, 1829-1840; stoneware and yellow-ware; no mark.
  (1-12-25)

C. Fish, Swan Hill Pottery, 1849-1850; stoneware; no mark;
  (1-11-25) succeeded by
James Carr (Carr & Locker), 1852-1854; Daniel Greatbach and
  Enoch Moore also partners; yellow-ware and Rockingham
  brownware, covered posset pitcher, hound-handled pitcher,
  "druggists' ware"; mark, "Swan Hill Pottery" impressed;
  plant burned, moved to New York City (1-12-23)

A. Cadmus, Congress Pottery, c. 1850; Rockingham brownware;
  rare mark is name and address, impressed; (1-25-127) succeeded by
William Allen, c. 1855; same; no mark. (1)

Spring Mills, Montgomery County, Pennsylvania
  Moorehead & Wilson (Morehead Clay Works), c. 1866-1900;
  unglazed redware, (terracotta), flower-pots, etc.; no mark.
  (1-25)
Stonetown, Berks County, Pennsylvania
  Christian Link, c. 1870-1900; redware, stoneware; redware with
    dark brown glaze, some large vases and picture frames from
    plaster moulds; marks on redware, "C.Link" or "C.Link,
    Exeter," in oval, impressed; on stoneware, "Christian Link,
    Stonetown," with eagle, impressed. (78)
St. Mary's, St. Mary's County, Maryland
  Thomas Baker, "Pot House," c. 1750; redware, plain and slip
    decorated. (128)
Thurmont, Frederick County, Maryland

J. W. Baecher, 1853-1880; redware, similar to that of Waynesboro, Pennsylvania; no mark. (20)

James C. Markley, 1880-1882; same; no mark. (20)

Adam Kern, 1880-1892; same; no mark. (20)

* Trenton, New Jersey

John McCully, 1799-1752; redware; no mark. (22)

Speeler & Taylor, Trenton Pottery, 1852-1856; Taylor formerly at Jersey City, both at East Liverpool; yellow-ware, Rockingham brownware; no mark. (1-12-25)

Taylor, Speeler & Bloor, 1856-1859; same, also White Granite; Bloor went to East Liverpool, O.; no mark. (1-12-25)

Speeler & Taylor (John F. Houdayer), 1859-1865; White Granite; no mark. (12)

Taylor & Co., Trenton Pottery Co., 1865-1870; same; no mark. (12)

Taylor & Goodwin, Trenton Pottery Co., 1870-1872; same; no mark. (1-25)

Isaac Davis, 1872-1879; same; no mark. (12)

Millington & Astbury, 1853-1859; Rockingham brownware, large cow creamer, hound-handled pitcher, yellow-ware; no mark. (1-12-25)

Millington, Astbury & Poulson, 1859-1870; same, also White Granite; including "Col. Ellsworth" pitcher; mark is "M.A.P." in oval, impressed. (1-12-25)

Millington, Astbury & Maddock, 1872-1875; White Granite, sanitary ware; no mark. (1-12)

Astbury & Maddock, 1875-1882; sanitary ware. (1-12-25)

Thomas Maddock & Son, 1882-1900; sanitary ware, white earthenware; mark is "T.M. & S.," with anchor, printed. (12)

Charles Hattersley, City Pottery, 1853-1856; redware, brownware door knobs; no marks. (1-12-22-25) succeeded by

James and Thomas Lynch, 1856-1858; drain-tile; succeeded by (12-25)

Rhodes & Yates, 1858-1865; Rhodes came from Jersey City Pottery; White Granite and cream-colored ware; no mark. (1-12-22-25)

Rhodes & Titus, 1865-1870; same; no mark. (12)

Yates, Bennett & Allen, 1870-1875; same; no mark; succeeded by (12)

City Pottery Co., 1875-1900; same; no mark. (12)

William Young & Sons, 1853-1879; Rockingham brownware, yellow-ware, some porcelain; no marks; succeeded by (1-12-25)

Willetts Manufacturing Co., 1879-1900; White Granite; marks are name under knot design, "W.M.Co." on globe or with imitation of British arms, or "W.M.Co., Semi-Porcelain," printed. (12)

Trenton China Co., 1859-1891; White Granite, some decorated in gold and colors; no mark. (22-25)

Henry Speeler (of Speeler & Taylor), 1860-1879; White Granite; no mark; (1-25) succeeded by

Carr & Clark, 1879; same; no marks; succeeded by (12)

Burgess & Campbell, International Pottery Co., 1879-1900; White Granite, white earthenware with "flowing blue" underglaze decoration, porcelain until 1888; marks are name or initials, printed. (12)

John Moses & Sons, Glasgow Pottery, 1860-1890; Rockingham brownware, yellow-ware, cream-colored ware, White Granite; marks are name in initials with "Glasgow Pottery," or "J.M." with eagle, printed. (12-25)

Brearley, Stephens & Tams, Greenwood Pottery, 1861-1865; White Granite; no mark. (12)

Stephens & Tams, Greenwood Pottery, 1865-1900; same, porcelain after 1876; marks are arms of New Jersey with "G.P." to 1876, then "Greenwood Pottery," printed. (12-25)

Coxon & Co., Empire Pottery, 1863-c. 1875; White Granite, cream-colored ware; no mark. (1-12-25)

Coxon & Thompson, c. 1875-1880; same; no mark; (12) succeeded by

Alpaugh & McGowan, 1880-1883; same Bone china; no marks; succeeded by (12)

Trenton Potteries Co., 1883-1900; same; no mark. (12)

Bloor, Ott & Booth, City Pottery, 1863-1867; Bloor from East Liverpool; White Granite; no mark. (1-12-25)

Ott & Brewer, 1867-1892; White Granite and cream-colored ware to 1875, then fine true Parian and Belleek; (Bloor returned to East Liverpool): marks are name in circle, or "O. & B. Belleek," with crown and scroll or with crescent, printed. (1-11)

Cook Pottery Co., 1892-1900; whiteware: no mark. (22)

Trenton Pottery Co., see Taylor & Co.

Mercer Pottery Co., 1869-1900; White Granite, art ware; mark is name of "M.P.Co." in design, printed. (12-25)

New Jersey Pottery Co. c. 1869-1883; White Granite; no mark. (25)

James Mayer, Arsenal Pottery, c. 1869; white Granite; no mark. (22)

Union Pottery Co., 1869-1889; same; no marks. (12)

Morris & Wilmore, Columbia Art Pottery, 1876 (1891)-1900; Belleek; mark is monogram in shield with "Belleek, Trenton, N.J." printed. (12-22) New pottery 1892

American Crockery Co., c. 1875-1879; White Granite; no mark. (12)

Burroughs & Montfort, 1879-1882; art ware; mark is "B. & M. Co." with crown, printed. (12)

Eagle Pottery Co., 1882-1895; white Granite; semi-porcelain; no marks. (12-22)

J. Cook Pottery Co., 1895-1900; same; no marks. (22) (12)

Rittenhouse, Evans & Co. c. 1880-1890; Belleek; no mark. (12)

Anchor Pottery, c. 1894-1900; whiteware; marks are anchor and name, name alone, or "A.P.," with two lions, on name with initials "J.E.N.," all printed. (12)

Ceramic Art Co., 1889-1900; fine hard-paste porcelain; mark is monogram in circle with pallette, or in wreath, printed; (9); succeeded by Lenox, Inc. (12)

Tulpehocken Township, Berks County, Pennsylvania

Christian Brichdel, c. 1767; redware. (78)

Isaac Frantz, 1870-1873; tobacco-pipes only. (78)
Henry Frantz (brother), c. 1865-1886; redware; no mark. (78)

Tylersport, Montgomery County, Pennsylvania

Johannes Nessz (Neesz), 1798-1829; workman at Spinner pottery, Willow Creek; slip-decorated, sgraffito and plain redware; especially plates with equestrian designs in sgraffito, elaborate slip-decorated pieces with designs in dot of slip, some smear-glazed pieces and toys; no marks. (1-3-25-28)
John Nase (son), 1829-1850; same; no marks. (1-3-25)

Michael Scholl (Sholl), 1818-1826; slip-decorated, sgraffito and plain redware; mark is conventional flower motif, impressed. (1-3-25-28)
Frederick Hildebrand, c. 1825-1845; same as above; unusual type of sgraffito with design pricked in dots and smear glazed; no mark. (1-3-25-28)

Upper Berne Township, Berks County, Pennsylvania
Daniel Herme, c. 1860-1880; redware; no mark. (78-119)

Upper Hanover, Montgomery County, Pennsylvania
Samuel Troxell, c. 1823-1835; slip-decorated, sgraffito and plain redware; pieces marked with name known. (1-3-25)
——Greber, 1848-1855; same; no marks. (25)

Vincent, Chester County, Pennsylvania
George Huebner, 1783-1798; moved from Montgomery Co.; slip-decorated, very fine sgraffito, with double borders of inscriptions and characteristic motifs, plain redware; occasional mark is initials. (1-3-25)

Virginsville, Berks County, Pennsylvania
Daniel Egoff, c. 1860-1876; redware; no marks; moved to Mohrsville. (78-119)

Waynesboro, Franklin County, Pennsylvania

John Bell, 1833-1881; moved from Chambersburg; large pottery little slip-decorated, no sgraffito, much slip-coated redware, unusual glazes mottled or splotched in bright orange or olive tones; and a brown mottled glaze resembling Rockingham, on redware; much of ware marked with name, or name and address, impressed. (20-25)

John W. Bell (son), 1881-1895), same; mark is name and address, impressed. (20)

Upton Bell (son of above), 1895-1900; same; mark is name and address, impressed. (20)

West Whiteland, Chester County, Pennsylvania

Thomas and John Vickers may have been located here, 1806-1821; see Caln. (28)

Willow Creek, Melford, Bucks County, Pennsylvania

David Spinner, 1800-1811; sgraffito; especially equestrian designs, slip-decorated and plain redware; rare mark is name. (1-3-25)

Womelsdorf, see Wrightstown

Wrightstown (near Womelsdorf), Berks County, Pennsylvania

Joseph Smith, 1763-c. 1800; slip-decorated, sgraffito and plain redware; no mark. (1-3-25)

Thomas Smith, c. 1800-   ; same; no marks. (1-3-25)

Feege & Feege,   -1862; same; no marks; (78) sold to Willoughby Smith (no relation of above), 1862-1900; same, also stoneware; marks are "W. Smith," "Smith" or "Womelsdorf," impressed. (78-119)

Jesse Beck, c. 1850; redware; no mark. (78-119)

Wilmington, Delaware

William Reiss, c. 1851; redware, stoneware; no marks. (1-25)

York, York County, Pennsylvania.

Pfaltzgraff Pottery, c. 1840-1900; redware; stoneware mark on stoneware "Pfaltzgraff Pottery," impressed. (127-128)

* Exact location unknown, and workmen using marks

George Huebner, Montgomery County, Pennsylvania; redware; no mark; moved to Vincent, Penna., 1783; (1-25)

Henry Roudebuth, Montgomery County, Pennsylvania, c. 1810-1820; slip-decorated, sgraffito and plain redware; mark is initials. (25-127)

Michael Fillman, c. 1815; workman at Scholl pottery, Tylersport; slip-decorated and sgraffito pieces marked with name known. (125-127)

Johannes Lehman, c. 1830; workman at Hildebrand and other potteries in Tylersport; sgraffito pieces marked with name known. (125-127)

Benjamin Berge (Bergey), Montgomery County, Pennsylvania, c. 1835-45; slip-decorated and plain redware; no marks. (1-5-25)

Solomon Miller, c. 1849-1880; workman at Bell Pottery, Waynesboro; redware pieces marked with name incised known. (125-127)

C. Gerlach,   , Penna.; redware pieces marked with name known. (127)

Jacob Ditzler, Adams County, Pennsylvania, c. 1840; redware; no mark. (125)

Samuel Paul,   , Pennsylvania; marked sgraffito piece known; (127)

——Miller, York County, Pennsylvania, c. 1850; slip-decorated and plain redware; no mark. (125)

W. Marteen,   , Penna., c. 1870-1880; redware; mark is name impressed. (127)

Conrad Ranninger (Renninger), Montgomery County, Pennsylvania, 1835-1845; redware; no mark. (15)

Potteries of New England and New York

*Albany, Albany County, New York

Paul Cushman, 1805-1825; stoneware; mark is name impressed or incised; (22-25)

Israel Seymour, 1806-1810; stoneware; no mark; moved to Troy. (22)

——Orcutt, c. 1843; stoneware; no mark; mined Albany slip clay in 1846. (22)

Amesbury, Essex County, Massachusetts
Phineas Chase, c. 1850; redware; no mark. (118)
Ashfield, Franklin County, Massachusetts

Walter Orcutt, 1847. (92)
Orcutt, Guilford & Co., 1848-1850; stoneware, brownware; marks are "Orcutt, Guilford & Co., Ashfield, Mass." "Orcutt, Belding & Co.," "Walter Orcutt & Co." (92) succeeded by
Hastings & Belding, 1850-1854; same; mark is name and address, or "Ashfield," impressed; (92); succeeded by
Van Horn & Boyden, 1854-1856; same; mark is name and address, impressed. (92)

* Athens, Greene County, New York

Nathan Clark, c. 1820-1840; redware, later stoneware; mark is name impressed. (22-127)
Clark & Fox, 1840-1850; same; mark is name impressed. (22-127)
Nathan Clark, c. 1850-1890; stoneware; also at Lyons and Mt. Morris; mark is name impressed. (22-127)

Barnstable, Barnstable County, Massachusetts
——, c. 1825; redware, fine green glaze; no mark. (128)
Bennington, Bennington County, Vermont

Captain John Norton, 1793-1823; redware; stoneware c. 1800; no mark. (22-24-25)
Luman Norton (son) & Co., 1823-1833; stoneware; mark is "L. Norton & Co., Bennington, Vt.", impressed. (22-24-25)
L. Norton & Son, 1833-1840; same; mark is name and "Bennington" or "East Bennington," impressed. (22-24-25)
Julius Norton (son), 1841-1844; same; mark is "J. Norton" or "Julius Norton," "Bennington" or "East Bennington" impressed. (24-25)
Norton & Fenton, 1844-1847; stoneware, Rockingham brownware, yellow-ware; marks are name and "Bennington" or "East Bennington," impressed. (22-24-25)
Julius Norton, 1847-1850; stoneware; mark same as above. (24-25)

J. & E. Norton, 1850-1859; same; mark is name and address, impressed. (24-25)

J. & E. Norton & Co., 1859-1861; same; mark similar to above. (24-25)

E. & L. P. Norton (sons), 1861-1881; same; similar mark. (24-25)

E. Norton, 1881-1883; same; similar mark. (24-25)

Edward Norton & Co., 1883-1894; same; similar mark. (24-25)

Christopher Weber Fenton, 1847-1849; succeeded Norton & Fenton; Rockingham, bisque porcelain as "Parian" etc., see pp. 61, 63, 110; mark is "Fenton's Works, Bennington, Vermont" in scrolled square in raised relief, on Rockingham and Parian; redware "Paul and Virginia" pitcher. (1-24-25)

Fenton, Hall & Co., Lyman, Fenton & Park, Lyman, Fenton & Co., 1849-1852; same; marks are occasionally same as above, or "Lyman, Fenton & Co., Fenton's ENAMEL, PATENTED 1849, BENNINGTON, VT." on Flint Enamel and some Rockingham ware; (1-12-24-25)

United States Pottery Co., (O. A. Gager & Co.), 1852-1859; same; marks are occasionally as above, or ribbon in relief, inscribed "U.S.P." on Parian, (1852-c. 1855), or "UNITED STATES POTTERY CO., BENNINGTON, VT." in oval or scrolled frame, impressed, on Parian or White Granite, (1853-1858). (1-12-24-25)

Jacob Merz, 1859-c. 1865; slip-decorated and plain redware; no mark. (25)

Enos Adams, c. 1859; Rockingham Brownware; no mark. (25)

Bergholtz, Niagara County, New York

Charles A. Mehweldt., 1851-c. 1860; slip-decorated, sgraffito and plain modeled redware; no mark. (25)

Beverley, Essex County, Massachusetts

William Tarbell, c. 1790-1816; redware; no mark. (110)

William Tarbell, Jr. (son), c. 1816-1819; same; no mark. (110)

Robert A. Herrick, c. 1833-1860; same; no mark. (110)

Binghampton, Broome County, New York

White & Wood, c. 1850-1860; stoneware; mark is name impressed. (22-127)

Boston, Massachusetts

——, c. 1769; redware; no examples known. (25)

Frederick Mear, Boston Earthenware Factory, 1852-1858; Rockingham brownware, light in color; mark is name impressed. (53)

Plympton & Robertson Pottery Co. 1824-1866; Rockingham and yellowware; no mark, James Robertson, manager; Homer, owner. (87)

William A. Homer (formerly agent for above), 1865-1875; same as above, also White Granite; no mark; Robertson went to Chelsea 1872: (25-53) ; succeeded by

New England Pottery Co., (Gray & Clark), 1875-1900; White Granite, porcelain after 1880, art ware after 1890; marks are "N.E.P.Co.," under design of Indian, "Ironstone China" over, or monogram of "N.E.P." and "Stone China" in frame, printed, on earthenware, (1883-1886), "Rieti" in design, (1886-1889) or "N.E.P." in scrolled frame, (1889-1895) on art ware. (1-12-25-53)

Boston Pottery Co., c. 1895; Rockingham brownware, yellowware; no marks; owned by Akron, Ohio firm. (1)

Boscawen, Merrimack County, New Hampshire

Jeremiah Burpee, 1804-c. 1835; reddish stoneware, fine incised decoration; no mark. (25)

Braintree, Massachusetts (see Germantown)

Peter Clark, c. 1745-1774; redware; no marks; moved to Lyndeboro, N.H. (36)

Brooklyn, New York (see New York City)

Burlington, Chittenden County, Vermont

Jacob Fenton, 1801-c. 1820; redware and stoneware; no mark. (25)

Norman L. Judd, 1806-1809; redware and stoneware; no mark; moved to Rome, N.Y. (25)

Nichols & Alford, c. 1850; stoneware and Rockingham brownware; no mark. (25)

Nichols & Boynton, c. 1853; same; mark is name impressed; (25) succeeded by
Ballard Bros,   ; same; no mark. (25)
A. K. Ballard & Co.,   ; same; no mark; (25) succeeded by
F. Woodworth & Co.,   ; same; no mark; (25)

Cambridge, Middlesex County, Massachusetts
Boston Porcelain and Glass Manufacturing Co., 1787-1788; attempted to make glass and porcelain; no examples known. (1-25-30)

A. H. & Horatio Hews, 1872-1875; redware; no marks; moved from Weston, Mass. (38)
A. H. Hews & Co., 1875-1900; unglazed redware flower-pots and art ware; no mark. (38)

Canterbury, Orange County, New York; stoneware; no mark; c. 1850. (21)
Charlestown, Suffolk County, Massachusetts
——, c. 1800; stoneware; mark is "Charlestown" impressed. (127)
Barnabas Edmunds & Co., c. 1856; stoneware; mark is name and address, impressed. (18)
Chelsea, Suffolk County, Massachusetts

A. W. Robertson, 1866-1868; brownware, redware; no mark. (1-12-25-87) (A-13) Hughe.
A. W. & C. H. Robertson, Chelsea Keramic Art Works, 1868-1872, brownware, flower-pots, no mark. (1-12-25-87)
James Robertson & Sons, Chelsea Keramic Art Works, 1872-1884; unglazed redware, art ware; marks are "Robertson & Sons, Chelsea Keramic Art Works, C.K.A.W.," or "C.K.A.W." in form of square, impressed, (1880-1884). (1-12-87) A-13)
H. C. Robertson, 1884-1888; same; mark is "C.K.A.W." impressed, (1-12-87)
Chelsea Pottery, 1891-1892; same; moved to Dedham, Mass. Mark "C.P.U.S." in clover-leaf. (12-87) (A-13)

Chittenago, Madison County, New York
Chittenago Pottery, c. 1880-1900; White Granite; no mark. (12)

Cortland, Cortland County, New York

Sylvester Blair, c. 1829-1837; stoneware; mark is "S. Blair" impressed (80)

Thomas D. Chollar, 1837-1849; same; mark is name and address, impressed; also at Homer, N.Y. (80)

Madison Woodruff, 1849-c. 1870; same; mark is "M. Woodruff, Cortland, N.Y.," impressed. (80-127)

J. Sage & Co., c. 1870; stoneware; mark is name and address, impressed. (80)

Mason-Russel, c. 1870; stoneware; mark is name impressed.

Danvers, Essex County, Massachusetts (see Peabody)

Dedham, Norfolk County, Massachusetts

Chelsea Pottery, 1892-1900; unglazed redware flower-pots and art ware; moved from Chelsea; mark is conventionalized rabbit, impressed or printed. (12-87) (A-13)

Dorset, Bennington County, Vermont

Jonathan Fenton, 1801-1834; redware and stoneware; no mark; son, C. W. Fenton, at Bennington. (25)

Dundee, Yates County, New York

——, c. 1850; stoneware; no mark. (22)

East Greenwich, Washington County, New York

——Upton, c. 1775; redware; no examples known. (25)

Ellenville, Ulster County, New York

——, c. 1850; stoneware; no mark. (22)

Exeter, Rockingham County, New Hampshire

Jabesh Dodge, 1800-1806; redware; no marks. (68)

Samuel Dodge (son), 1806-1819; same; no mark. (68)

Asa Dodge (son of Samuel), 1819-c. 1849; same; no mark. (68)

Rufus Dodge (son), c. 1849-1870; same; no mark; (68) succeeded by

Asa Lamson, c. 1870-1900; same; no mark. (68)

Fairfax, (and North Fairfax), Franklin County, Vermont

E. L. Farrar, 1831-1850; redware and stoneware; no mark. (25)

Farrar & Stearns, North Fairfax, 1850-1856; stoneware; no mark. (25)

S. H. Farrar, 1856-1863; Rockingham and Flint Enamel brownware; no mark. (25)

* Fort Edward, Washington County, New York

Haxtun & Co., c. 1875-1900; stoneware; mark is name impressed. (21-127)

Germantown (Braintree), Norfolk County, Massachusetts

Joseph Palmer and Richard Cranch, 1853-1870; built factory for glass and porcelain, but were unsuccessful; no examples known, stoneware fragments found on site. (1-25)

Goshen, Litchfield County, Connecticut-See Litchfield.

Captain John Norton, c. 1780; redware; no examples known; probably moved to Bennington, Vt. (18)

Gonic, Stratford County, New Hampshire

Elijah Osborne, c. 1839-1845; redware; no marks; same family as Osbornes of Peabody, Mass. (69)

James and John Osborne (sons), c. 1845-1875; same; no mark. (69)

James and William Osborne (son), 1875-1885; same; no mark. (69)

Gorham, Maine

Hezekiah Smith, 1782-1797; stoneware; no mark. (128) 1797-

Greenport, Kings County, New York

——, c. 1850; stoneware; no mark. (21)

Greenwich, Fairfield County, Connecticut

——, c. 1740-1760; redware and stoneware; no examples known; (86a)

"Deacon" Abraham Meade, 1760-1791; redware, stoneware; no marks. (86a)

Hardwick, Caledonia County, Vermont

Charles Bailey, c. 1800; redware; no mark. (125)

Hartford, Hartford County, Conn.

Nathaniel Seymour, 1790-1825; slip-decorated and plain red-ware; no mark. (1-18-22-25)

"Major" Seymour (son), 1825-1849; same, unglazed redware flower-pots after 1840; no mark; moved to Ravenna, O. (1-18-22-25)

John Souter, 1790-1805; slip-decorated and plain redware; no mark; (1-18-22-25); succeeded by

Peter Cross, 1805-c. 1808; same, also stoneware; sold to Goodwin & Webster; built new pottery. (1-18-22-25)

Peter Cross, new pottery, c. 1808-1810; same; no mark; (18) sold to

Benton & Stewart, (owners, retired sea-captains), c. 1810-1818; Daniel Goodale, Jr. of Whateley, Mass., manager, same; no mark. (18)

Daniel Goodale, 1818-1830; redware and stoneware; mark is "D.Goodale" impressed; sold to Goodwin & Webster. (1-22)

Isaac Hanford, c. 1796-1800; stoneware; no mark. (25)

Seth Goodwin, c. 1795-1828; redware; no mark. (1-18-25)

Thomas O'Hara Goodwin (son), c. 1828-1880; redware and stoneware; no mark. (1-18)

Horace Goodwin (brother of Seth), c. 1800-1810; redware; no mark. (18)

Goodwin & Webster, 1808-1850; redware and stoneware; bought Peter Cross pottery and second Cross or Goodale pottery; mark on stoneware is name impressed. (1-18-25)

C. Webster & Son, 1850-1857; stoneware; sold old Cross pottery; mark is name impressed. (1-18)

Webster & Seymour, 1857-1873; same; mark is name impressed. (1-18)

Seymour & Bosworth, 1873-1883 or later; same. (18)

J. C. Fisher, 1805-c. 1812; redware and stoneware; mark on stoneware is "J.Fisher" impressed. (1-25)

T. Harrington, c. 1825; stoneware; no mark. (25)

Harvey Goodwin (nephew of Seth), 1827, (1832)-1870, West Hartford; stoneware; no mark. (18)

Goodwin Bros. (H. W. and W. E. Goodwin, sons), 1870-1900; Rockingham brownware, yellow-ware, cream-colored ware; no mark. (1-18-21)

Homer, Cortland County, New York

Thomas O. Chollar, 1832-1842; redware and stoneware; no mark. (80)

Chollar & Bennett, 1842-1844; stoneware; mark is name impressed. (80)

Chollar & Darby, 1844-1849; stoneware; mark is name impressed (80)

Huntington, Suffolk County, New York

Adam States, 1751-c. 1774; slip-decorated and plain redware, stoneware, possibly as early as 1761; moved to Stonington, Conn., no mark; (1-25-79) ; succeeded by

Jonathan Titus, c. 1784-1805; same; no mark; (1-24-79); succeeded by

Samuel J. Wetmore & Co., 1805-c. 1810; slip-decorated and plain redware; (1-25-79); succeeded by

Moses Scudder, c. 1810-1825; slip-decorated, sgraffito and plain redware; no mark; (1-25-79); succeeded by

Benjamin Keeler, 1825-1827; slip-decorated and plain redware; no mark; (1-25-79); succeeded by

Lewis & Gardner, 1827-1854; redware; mark is name, impressed; (1-25-79)

Lewis & Lewis, Henry Lewis, Ketchum & Hoyt; 1854-1863; redware; marks are names impressed; Frederick J. Caire of Poughkeepsie, manager; (79); succeeded by

Brown Brothers, 1863-1900; redware; flower-pots; no mark. (79)

Jaffrey, Chesire County, New Hampshire
——; c. 1817; redware; no mark. (25)

Keene, Chesire County, New Hampshire
J. S. Taft & Co., Hampshire Pottery, 1871-1900; stoneware, redware, majolica; mark is "Hampshire Pottery" in circle with "J.S.Taft" in script, printed. (12-44)

Lee, Berkshire County, Massachusetts
—; c. 1800-1829; redware; no mark. (21)
* Litchfield, Litchfield County, Conn.
Hervey Brooks, c. 1753; redware; no examples known. (25)
John Pierce, c. 1753; same. (25)
Jesse Wadhams, c. 1753; same. (25)
Louden, Merrimack County, New Hampshire
Elijah Osborne, c. 1830-1831; redware; no marks; moved to
Gonic, N.H. (69)
Lyndeboro, Hillsboro County, New Hampshire

Peter Clark, c. 1775-1826; redware; no mark. (36)
William Clark (son) and John Southwick, c. 1826-1855; same;
no marks. (36)
Peter Clark III and Benjamin Clark (sons of William), 1850-
1879 same; no marks. (36)

Peter Clark II (son of Peter I), c. 1800-1820; redware; no
mark. (36)
Ebenezer Hutchinson, c. 1815; redware; no examples known;
moved to Vermont. (36)
Lyons, Wayne County, New York

J. Fisher & Co., c. 1840-1860; stoneware; no marks; (21); succeeded by
Lyons Stoneware Co., c. 1860-1880; same; no mark. (22)

Nathan Clark, c. 1860; stoneware, brownware; mark is name
and address, impressed; branch of Athens. (22-127)
* Manchester, Hillsboro County, New Hampshire
Thomas Ingles, c. 1844-1860; art ware, not for sale; no mark.
(1)
Middlebury, Addison County, Vermont

Caleb Farrar, 1815-1850; redware, some glazed in green, stoneware after 1820; no mark; (25) ; succeeded by
James Mitchell, 1850-c. 1870; stoneware; no marks. (25)

Monkton, Vermont
——c. 1810; unsuccessful attempt to produce porcelain from
local materials. (128)

Mount Morris, Livingston County, New York
Nathan Clark, c. 1860; stoneware; no mark; branch of Athens.
(22)

Moultonboro, Carroll County, New Hampshire
James S. Bennett, 1824-1856; redware, some with rose shaded
lead glaze, with fine black speckle; occasional mark is name.
(125)

Nashua, Hillsboro County, New Hampshire
Martin Crafts (son of Thomas Crafts of Whateley, Mass.),
1838-1850 (1844); stoneware; marks are "T. Crafts & Son,
Nashua" or "Martin Crafts, Nashua," impressed. (67)

Newbury, Essex County, Massachusetts

Joseph Bailey, c. 1734-1760; redware; no examples known. (6)
Daniel and Nathaniel Bailey (sons), 1760-1799; redware; no
mark. (6)

Newburyport, Essex County, Massachusetts
Ebenezer Morrison, c. 1750-1813; redware; no mark. (6)

* New York City (and Brooklyn) New York
Dirick Claesen, c. 1657; probably redware; no examples known.
(25)

Dirick Bensing, 1698; same. (25)
Henry Benson (possibly son), c. 1732; same. (25)

William Croylas, 1698; probably redware; no examples known.
(25-85)
William and Peter Crolius (probably sons), 1732-1762; prob-
ably redware, possibly stoneware; no examples known. (25-
85-91)
John Crolius (son of William), 1762-c.1790; stoneware; mark,
"I.C." attributed to him. (25-85-91)
Clarkson Crolius I, (son), c.1790-1830; slip-decorated and plain

redware, stoneware; mark "C. Crolius, Manhattan Wells" on stoneware attributed to him. (76) (25-85-91)

Clarkson Crolius II (son), c.1830-1848, (1870?); brown stoneware; mark "C. Crolius, Manufacturer, New York" attributed to him; John, William, and George Crolius, probably cousins, also potters. (76) (12-25-91)

John Remmey I (Johannes Remy), 1735-1762; probably redware; no examples known; (1-25-73)

John Remmey II (son) 1762-1793; stoneware; mark is initials impressed; (1-25-73)

John Remmey III (son), 1793-1820; same, especially brown stoneware; same mark; Henry Remney (brother), moved to Philadelphia, c.1810; Joseph Henry Remney (son), moved to South Amboy, N.J., 1820. (1-25-91)

John Eutatse, c.1728; probably redware: no examples known. (128)

Johnathan Durrell, 1753-1774, or later); slip-decorated and plain redware; no examples known. (25)

Thomas Campbell, c.1769; possibly redware; no examples known. (25)

—— Wilson, c.1782; same. (8)

Thomas Commeraw, c. 1790-1835; stoneware; marks are "Commeraws" or "Corlear's Hook," impressed or inscribed. (93-A4)

D. Morgan, c.1806; stoneware; occasional mark is name inscribed. (93)

Dr. Mead, c. 1816-1819; white porcelain; no mark. (1-25-128)

Hudson River Pottery, 1838-1900; stoneware and redware to 1878, then art ware; no mark. (12)

William Marshall, c.1840; "earthenware" in directory; no examples known. (128)

Salamander Work, 1848-   ; see Woodbridge, New Jersey.

Charles Cartlidge & Co., 1848-1855; door-knobs and plates, soft-paste porcelain, later bisque hard porcelain, Parian and imitation Wedgewood Jasper in 1854, lion and dog mantel ornaments; no mark. (1-4-12-25)

American Porcelain Manufacturing Co., 1855-1856; same; no mark. (1-4-12-25)

William Bloch, Union Porcelain Works, Brooklyn, 1850-1862; soft-paste porcelain; no mark. (12-25-11-12-25); succeeded by

William Smith, Union Porcelain Works, 1862-c.1870; hard-paste porcelain; no mark. (1-12-25)

Thomas C. Smith & Sons, c.1870-1900; hard-paste porcelain table and art ware, some with under-glaze decoration; no marks to 1876, then eagle's head with "S" in beak, impressed, (1876), then printed, (1876-1900). (1-12)

Carr & Morrison, New York City Pottery, 1853, (1856?)-1871; James Carr from South Amboy, N.J.; Rockingham brown-ware and yellow-ware to 1858, then majolica, 1858-1860, including the first cauliflower tea-pot, and White Granite, 1858-1871; marks are (1) arms of Great Britain, "J.C." in center, "Stone China" below, (2) shields of Great Britain and the United States joined, (3) "stone Porcelain, J.C." in rectangle, (4) clasped hands and "N.Y.C.P.," all printed, on White Granite. (1-12-25)

James Carr, 1871-1888; White Granite; marks same as above. (1-12)

Washington I. Smith & Co., Greenwich Pottery, c.1860; "Vitrified Ironstone and double-glazed drain-pipe." (7)

John Rogers, 1860-1890; terra-cotta figures, painted, "Rogers Groups," Parian; mark is name impressed; (22) (22-127-128)

Faience Manufacturing Co., Greenpoint, 1880-1892; art ware; marks are "F.M.Co." or monogram of same initials; printed or impressed. (12)

North Fairfax, Vermont (see Fairfax)

Norwalk, Fairfield County, Connecticut

Asa Smith, 1780-c.1830; slip-decorated and plain redware, stoneware; no mark (1-25)

A. E. Smith & Sons Pottery Co., c.1830-1865; stoneware; no mark (1)

Norwalk Pottery Co., c.1865-1900; same; no mark. (1)

Asa Hill and L. D. Wheeler, South Norwalk, 1850-1853; Rockingham buttons; (1-24); succeeded by

L. D. Wheeler, Wheeler & Wood, c.1853-1856; door-knobs; (1-25)

Enoch Wood, 1856-1865; Wood from Bennington, Vt., Stoneware; no marks. (1-25)

Norwich, New London County Connecticut

Christopher Leffingwell, Bean Hill Pottery, c. 1779-1792; redware; no mark; (90); succeeded by

Charles Lathrop (son-in-law), 1792-1796; slip-decorated, black glazed and plain redware; mark "Norwich" on ware of period attributed to him (1-25-90) ; succeeded by

C. Potts & Son, 1796-1816; stoneware; no mark. (1-25-90)

Andrew Tracy, c.1790-1798; not a potter, part owner; redware and stoneware; no mark; (90); succeeded by

Capt. Joseph Hosmer, 1798-1805; same; no mark; (90); succeeded by

William Cleveland, 1805-1812; stoneware; no mark; (90) ; succeeded by

Armstrong & Wentworth, 1812-1834; stoneware; marks are name and address, or "A. & W." impressed. (90)

Sidney Risley, 1836-1875; stoneware; rare mark is name and address, impressed; (1-25-32)

George L. Risley, 1875-1881; same; no marks; (32) ; succeeded by

B. C. Chace, Norwich Pottery Works, 1881-1884; same; nomarks; (32) succeeded by

C. B. Chamberlin, 1885-1887; same; no marks; (32); succeeded by

Otto N. Sudenberg, 1887-1895; same; no mark. (32)

Smith & Day, c. 1872; stoneware; mark name impressed. (22-127)

Olean, Cattaragus County, New York

199

I. H. Wands, c.1852-1870; stoneware; mark is name, impressed. (22-127)

Peabody (and Danvers), Essex County, Massachusetts

Lawrence Southwick, 1639; no record of operations. (6-110)
William Southwick, c.1735-1759; redware; no examples known. (6-25)
Joseph A. Southwick, (son), c.1759-1785; same. (6)
William Southwick, 1785-1828; redware no mark. (6)

Ananias Conklin, 1639; no record of operations. (6-110)
Obediah Holmes, 1639; no record of operations. (6-110)
William Osborne, 1639; no record of operations. (6-25-38)
Joseph Osborne, c. 1736-1759; redware, black glazed and plain; no mark. (6-38)
Joseph Osborne, (son), c.1759-1800; same; no mark. (6-38)
John Osborne, (son), c. 1800-1866; same; no mark; (38); succeeded by
Rufus Lamson, 1866-1875; moved from Exeter, N. H., redware, flowerpots, no mark; (38), succeeded by
M. P. Paige Pottery, 1875-1900; same; no mark; (38)

Johnathan Kettle, c. 1730; probably redware; no examples known. (25)
Miles Kendall, c.1740; same. (25)

Joseph Whittemore, c. 1750; same. (24) (6-25)
Daniel Whittemore (son), c.1780-1825; redware; no mark. (6)

Johnathan Osborne (son of Joseph, Jr., above), c.1780-1833; redware, black glazed and plain; no mark. (6-110)
Richard Osborne (son), c.1833-1850; same; no mark. (110)

Amos Osborne (son of Joseph, Jr., above), c.1790-1836; redware; no mark. (6-110)
Amos, Jr. and Phillip Osborne (sons), c.1836-1850; same; no mark. (110)

William Goldthwaite, c.1763-1808; redware; no mark. (6-110)

Job Wilson, c.1780-1791; redware; no mark. (6-110)
Robert Wilson (son), c.1791-1803; same; no mark. (6)

Robert Stone, c.1780-1811; redware; no mark. (6-110)
Joseph Trask, c.1790-1813; redware; no mark. (6-110)
——Tewksbury, c.1800; redware; no mark. (110)
    (other Essex County, Mass., potters listed in Henry W.
    Belknaps's *Artists and Craftsmen of Essex County*, Salem,
    1929)
Penn Yan, Yates County, New York
    Mantelly, c. 1830-1850; stoneware; no mark. (22-127)
Thomas Plymouth, Grafton County, New Hampshire
    ——Webster, c.1860-1875; redware no mark. (125)
    ——Gill, c. 1860; redware, some black glazed; no mark. (125)
* Portland, Cumberland County, Maine
    Caleb Crafts (son of Thomas Crafts of Whateley, Mass.), 1837-
       1841; stoneware; mark is name impressed. (67)
    Benjamin Dodge (son of Jabesh Dodge of Exeter), 1847-1868;
       stoneware; no mark. (67)
    Portland Stoneware Co., 1846-c.1880; stoneware and terracotta;
       no mark. (12)
    J. T. Winslow, c.1857; stoneware; no mark. (128)
    Lamson & Swazey, c.1875; stoneware; no mark. (67)
Portsmouth, Rockingham County, New Hampshire
    Jabez Dodge (son of Samuel Dodge of Exeter), c.1851; stone-
       ware; no mark. (67)
Poughkeepsie, Dutchess County, New York
    ——c.1780; redware; no examples known. (70)

John P. Caire, 1840-1842; redware, stoneware and Rockingham;
    mark is name impressed. (70-A4)
Jacob Caire, 1842-1852; same; mark is name impressed. (70)
    succeeded by
Louis Lehman, Lehman & Rudinger, 1852-1856; same; marks
    are names impressed. (70)
Rudinger and Adam Caire, 1856-1896; stoneware; mark is
    "Rudinger & Caire", impressed. (70)

Gideon Crisbaum & Co., 1853-1854; stoneware; no mark. (70)

Orcutt & Thompson, c.1860-1870; stoneware; mark is name and address, impressed; possibly wholesalers not potters (70)

Providence, Rhode Island

James Wilson, c.1767; redware, some with green glaze; no mark. (46)

Poulteney, Rutland County, Vermont

Samuel Woodman, 1800-1820; redware and stoneware; no mark. (25)

Rochester, Monroe County, New York

—— c.1836-1850; stoneware; no mark. (22)

Rome. Onieda County, New York

Norman L. Judd, 1810-1850; stoneware; no mark; moved from Burlington, Vt. (25)

Rondout, Ulster County, New York

J. M. Madden, c.1870; stoneware; mark is name and address, impressed. (127)

Salem, Essex County, Massachusetts

John Pride, c.1641; no record of operations. (6-25)

William Vinson, c.1641; same. (6)

Nathaniel Symonds, Sr., c.1740-1790; redware; no mark. (6)

Nathaniel Symonds, Jr. (son), 1790-1803; same; no mark. (110)

Nathaniel Symonds, (son), 1803-c.1850; same; no mark. (110)

Sherburne, Chenago County, New York

—— c.1850; redware and stoneware; no mark. (22)

Somerville, Middlesex County, Massachusetts

McCarthy Bros., c.1870; stoneware; mark is name and address, impressed. (127)

Somerset, Bristol County, Massachusetts

L. and B. C. Chace, c.1850; redware; mark is name and address, impressed; moved to Norwalk, Conn. (18-128)

South Norwalk, Connecticut (see Norwalk)

South Ashfield, Massachusetts (see Ashfield)

Stillwater, New York

—— c.1850; stoneware; no mark. (22)
Stonington, New London County, Connecticut

Adam States, 1796-1804; redware and stoneware; no mark; moved from Huntington, N. Y. (25-79)

Adam, Jr. and Joseph States (sons), 1804-1884; stoneware; no mark. (25-79)

St. Johnsbury, Caledonia County, Vermont

Richard Weber Fenton (brother of Johnathan Fenton of Dorset), 1808-c.1825; redware and stoneware; no mark. (25)

Leander W. Fenton (son), 1829-1859; stoneware; mark is "L. W. Fenton, St. Johnsbury, Vt.", impressed. (25)

Fenton & Hancock, 1859-c.1870; same; mark is name and address, impressed. (25)

William Hutchinson, c.1815; redware; no examples known. (25)
* Syracuse, Onondaga County, New York

Empire Pottery Co., c. 1865-1871; White Granite; no mark. (11) (12)

Onondaga Pottery Co., 1871-1900; White Granite to 1886, then Semi-Granite or hotel ware; James Pass, manager; mark is name and address, alone or in design, impressed or printed. (127-128)

* Troy, Rennselaer County, New York

Israel Seymour, 1819-1865; slip-decorated and plain redware, stoneware; mark on stoneware is name impressed; moved from Albany, N. Y. (22-25)

Orcutt, Humiston & Co., c.1850-1860; stoneware; mark is name and address, impressed; Orcutt moved from Ashfield, Mass. (92)

C. Boynton & Co.; 1860; stoneware; mark is name impressed.
Utica, Onieda County, New York

——Nash, Central New York Pottery, 1819-1820, (1828?), slip-decorated and plain redware, stone; no marks; (1-22-25); succeeded by

Noah White, 1820 (1828?)-1840; stoneware; no mark; (1-22-25)
Noah White & Sons, 1840-1853; same; no marks. (1)
Noah White, Son and Co., 1853-1865; same; no mark. (1)
N. A. White, (son of Noah), & Son, 1865-c.1875; same; no mark "White Utica, N. Y." impressed. (1-187)
Central New York Pottery Co., c. 1875-1900; same; no mark. (1)

Brayton, Kellogg & Doolittle, 1827-c.1840; stoneware, possibly redware; no mark. (25)
Justin Campbell, 1826-c.1840; stoneware; no mark. (25)
L. F. Field, c.1860-1870; stoneware; mark is name and address. (127)

Volney, Oswego County, New York
—— c.1850; stoneware; no mark. (22)

Whateley, Franklin County, Massachusetts
Stephen Orcutt, 1777-c.1800; redware; no mark. (92)

Thomas Crafts, 1802-c.1820; redware; no mark. (1-25-77) (1-25-92)
Elbridge Gerry Crafts (son), c.1820-1848; redware, black glazed, teapots, etc., to 1831, then stoneware; mark is "T. Crafts & Son., Whateley", impressed. (1-24-77) (1-25-92)

Daniel Goodale, c.1815; redware; no mark; moved to Hartford, Conn. (1-25)
David Belding, 1830-c.1840; stoneware; mark is name impressed; moved to Ashfield, Mass. (92)

Weston, Middlesex County, Massachusetts

Abraham Hews, 1765, (1769?)-c.1810; redware; no examples known. (1-38)
Abraham Hews (son) & Son, c.1810-1840; redware, stoneware; no mark. (1-38)
Abraham Hews & Sons, c.1840-1865; same; no mark. (1)
A. H. & Horatio Hews (sons), 1865-1872; same; no mark; moved to Cambridge, Mass. (1)

West Troy, Rensselaer County, New York

55. A ceramic business card, buff body, blue relief lettering, Flint Enamel Frame; 1851-1854. (Courtesy of the East Liverpool Historical Society.)

56. Rockingham type pitcher, two eagles in relief each panel, immature solid-color brown glaze, probably burned only once and experimental, probably East Liverpool, c.1840. (Author's Collection.)

57. Stoneware jar, incised decoration touched with blue, inscribed "Hurra for Van Buren," Western Pennsylvania or Ohio, c.1836. (Courtesy of the Massillon, Museum.)

58. Brownware flower-pot, incised decoration, semi-mat glaze, Ohio, c.1850-60. (Courtesy of Rea M. Knittle.)

59-60. Stoneware water-cooler, applied and impressed decoration, inscribed "Buck and Breck, 1856," commemorating the Presidential campaign of James Buchanan; E. Hall, Tuscarawas Co., Ohio, 1856. (Courtesy of Rea M. Knittle.)

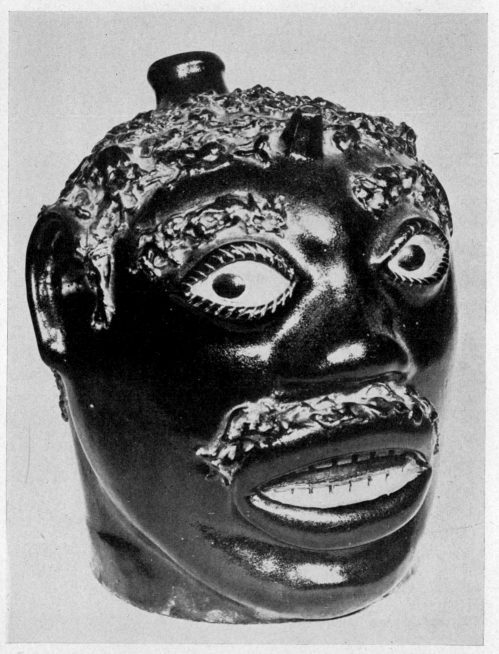

61. Brownware "Voodoo Jug," black semi-mat glaze touched with paint, Zanesville, Ohio, c.1850. (Courtesy of the Ohio State Museum.)

62. Brownware dog dorr-stop, unglazed, George Bagnall, Newcomerstown, Ohio, c.1870-75. (Author's Collection.)

63. Brownware ink-well, unglazed, Ohio, c.1850. (Courtesy of Rea M. Knittle.)

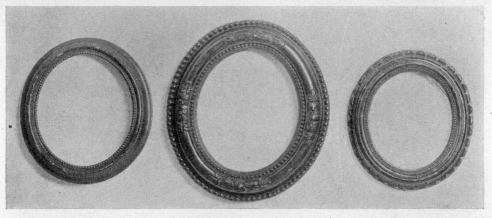

64. (*Top left*) Brownware covered jar, relief decoration, bird finial, brown glaze, John N. Stout, Ripley, Ill., c.1866-1880. (Courtesy of Rea M. Knittle.)
65. (*Top right*) Redware jug, dark streaked glaze, Galena, Ill., c.1860. (Courtesy of Mrs. W. D. Hurm). 66. (*Center*) Brownware picture-frames, semi-matte glaze, Summit County, Ohio, c.1860. (Courtesy of Rea M. Knittle.)
67. (*Lower*) Brownware fat-lamp, mat glaze, Wayne County, Ohio, c.1860. (Courtesy of Rea M. Knittle.)

68. (*Top*) Stoneware jug, applied decoration, rattlesnake and Civil War soldiers, and brownware mug, Cornwall Kirkpatrick, Anna, Ill., c.1860-1900. (Courtesy of Mrs. W. D. Hurm.) 69. (*Bottom*) Rockingham sugar-bowl, shallow bowl, relief scrolled rim, swan inkwell, all copied from Staffordshire earthenware, Liverpool, c.1850-60. (Courtesy of the Ohio State Museum.) 70. (*Next page, top left*) Flint Enamel water-cooler, green and brown glaze, Salt & Mear, East Liverpool, Ohio, 1841-1853. (Courtesy of the Ohio State Museum.) 71. (*Top right*) Redware jar, unglazed, from early Virginia Pottery, 18th Century. (Courtesy of Mr. Walter J. Sparks.) 72. (*Center*) Rockingham pitcher, green and tan Flint enamel type glaze; sugar-bowl, similar in form to Ohio blown glass bowls and tea-pot, shaded brown glaze, Shallow bowl, cake-mold and pie-plate, mottled glazes, East Liverpool, O., c.1840-1890. 73. (*Lower*) Rockingham Pitcher, relief of seated hunter, "Daniel Boone," light tan mottled glaze, octagonal deep platter, copying Staffordshire ware, seated spaniel dorr-stop, and shoe flask by Knowles, Taylor & Knowles, dark mottled glazes, deep dish and paneled pitcher; East Liverpool, c.1850-1890. (Both Author's Collection.)

74. Redware, slip decorated bowl, flask and plate, from the Moravian potteries of North Carolina, 1756-1830. (Courtesy of Joe Kindig, Jr.)

75. Stoneware water-cooler, applied and blue painted decoration, Solomon Bell, Strasburg, Va., c.1845. (Courtesy of the Metropolitan Museum of Art.)

76. Redware, slip decorated bowl, flask and plate, from the Moravian potteries of North Carolina, 1756-1830. (Courtesy of Joe Kindig, Jr.)

77. (*Top*) White earthenware sauce-boat, blue decoration, Bonnin & Morris, Philadelphia, 1771-1772. (Clement Collection, Brooklyn Museum). 78. (*Center*) Redware flower-pot, bowl and jar, shaded or mottled bright green, orange and cream glaze, Bell pottery, Strasburg, Va., 1843-1900. 79. (*Lower*) Redware vases, shaded cream, orange and green glaze, redware jar, tan glaze with brown decoration. (Both Courtesy of George S. McKearin.)

80. Stoneware jug, olive green streaked glaze, Odom & Turnlee, Knox Hill, Fla., 1859-1860.

81. Stoneware "voodoo" jug, olive green glaze, Odom & Turnlee, Knox Hill, Fla., 1859-1860.

82. Stoneware jar, light olive green glaze, Odom & Turnlee, Knox Hill, Fla., 1859-1860.

83. Stoneware jar, dark brown glaze, J. B. Long, Byron, Ga., c.1830-1850. (All Courtesy of the Florida State Museum.)

84. (*Top left*) Porcelain pitcher, decorated in color and gold with a portrait of Washington, Tucker & Hemphill, Philadelphia, 1832-1838. (Courtesy of the Philadelphia Museum of Art.) 85. (*Top right*) Porcelain vase, Dr. Henry Mead, New York, 1816. (Owned by the Philadelphia Museum of Art.) 86. (*Lower*) White earthenware sweetmeat dish, blue decoration, Bonnin & Morris, Philadelphia, 1771-1772. (Clement Collection, Brooklyn Museum.)

87. Porcelain pitcher, decorated in color and gold, Tucker & Hemphill, Philadelphia, 1832-1838. (Courtesy of the Metropolitan Museum of Art.)

88. Majolica "Sunflower" compote, Griffin, Smith & Hill, Phoenixville, Penna., 1879-1890. (Author's Collection.)

89. Porcelain Pitcher, decorated in color and gold, Thomas Tucker, Philadelphia, 1826-1828.

90. Design for porcelain vase, Thomas Tucker or Tucker & Hemphill, Philadelphia, 1826-1838. (Both Courtesy of the Philadelphia Museum of Art.)

91. White earthenware pitcher, printed decoration with title "Landing of Gen. LaFayette at Castle Garden, New York, 16th of August, 1824," and gold bands; American Pottery Co., Jersey City, 1843. (Courtesy of George S. McKearin.)

92. Light tan stoneware pitcher, relief decoration of hunting scene, D. & J. Henderson, Jersey City, N. J., 1829-1833. (Courtesy of George S. McKearin.)

93. Parian pitchers, white relief on blue "hammered" grounds, large two United States Pottery, Bennington, Vt., 1852-1858, center probably Bennington. (Courtesy of George S. McKearin.)

94. (*Top left*) Parian vase, blue and white, United States Pottery, Bennington, Vt., 1852-1858. (Clement Collection, Brooklyn Museum.) 95. (*Top right*) Parian pitchers, white relief, United States Pottery, Bennington, Vt., 1852-1858. (Clement Collection, Brooklyn Museum.) 96. (*Lower*) Yellowware mug, blue and white bands, Jabez Vodrey, East Liverpool, O., c.1850; White earthenware plate, Vodrey & Frost, Louisville, Ky., 1839-46. (Courtesy of the East Liverpool Historical Society.)

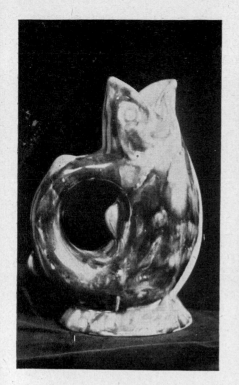

97. (*Top left*) Majolica pitcher, George Morley, East Liverpool, O., 1884-1890. (Courtesy of the East Liverpool Historical Society.) 98. (*Top right*) White earthenware pitcher relief of the "Murder of Col. Ellsworth" (1862), Millington, Astbury & Poulson, Trenton, N. J. (Clement Collection, Brooklyn Museum.) 99. (*Lower*) White earthenware, "Moss Rose" pitcher, and porcelain "Lotus-Ware" vase, Knowles, Taylor & Knowles, East Liverpool, O., 1870-1890. (Courtesy of the East Liverpool Historical Society.)

100. White Earthenware platter, blue decoration, "Pickett's Charge at Gettysburg," Edwin Bennett Pottery Co., Balti-

Sanford S. Perry, 1831-c.1865; stoneware; no mark; (25); succeeded by

Shepley & Smith, c.1865-1895; stoneware, bottles, etc; mark is name and address, impressed. (25)

George Walker, Temperance Hill Pottery, 1860-1880; Rockingham brownware; no mark. (25)

William E. Warner, c. 1833-1860; stoneware, Rockingham brownware, including hound-handled pitcher; mark is name and address, impressed. Moved from Perth Amboy, N. J. (23-A3)

Williamson, Berkshire County, Massachusetts

——, c.1800-1830; redware; no mark. (22)

Wiscassett, Lincoln County, Maine

Benjamin Porter, c.1790-1805; redware; no mark. (25)

——Porter (son), 1805-c.1860; same; no mark. (25)

Worcester, Worcester County, Massachusetts

Norton & Hancock, 1858-1877; stoneware; no marks; Norton from Bennington, Vt. (25-82)

F. H. Norton, 1877-1885; same; no mark. (25)

Norton Abrasive Co., 1885-1900; grinding wheels, etc. (128)

Potteries of Western Pennsylvania, West Virginia and the Middle West

* Akron (including Middlebury), Summit County, Ohio

Edwin and Calvin Merrill, 1847-1861; yellowish stoneware, jugs, bottles, moulded and hand-made, tobacco-pipes; no mark; moved from Springfield; (25-26-127)

Edwin and Henry E. Merrill, Akron Pottery Co., 1861-1888; same; no mark; large plant. (26-128)

E. H. Merrill & Co., 1888-1894; same; beer and ink bottles; no mark. (26-)

Hill, Foster & Co., 1849-1851; stoneware; no mark. (25-26)

Hill, Merrill & Co., 1851-1855; same; no mark. (26)

Merrill, Powers & Co., 1855-1858; same; no mark. (26)

Hill, Powers & Co., 1859-1868; same; no mark. (26)
Hill & Adams, 1868-　　; sewer-pipe. (26)

Rowley & Baker, 1850-1857; yellow and Rockingham ware; no
　　mark; (25-26); succeeded by
Johnson, Whitmore & Co., 1857-1860; stoneware, yellowware;
　　no mark. (25-26)
Johnson & Dewey, 1860-c.1875; same; no mark. (25-26)

Johnson & Baldwin, 1860-c.1865; stoneware; no mark. (26)
Peter Bodenbuhl, c.1863-1870; same; no mark. (25-26)
Beecher & Lantz, 1863-c. 1883; same no mark. (25-26)
F. K. Knapp, 1858-1885; same; no mark. (25-26) ; succeeded by
United States Stoneware Co., 1885-1900; same; no mark. (26-
　　127)
Cook & Richardson, 1869-ca.1880; same; no mark; (25-26)
Cook, Fairbanks & Co., ca.1880-1887; same; no mark. (128)

Whitman, Robinson & Co., c.1862-1886; Rockingham brown-
　　ware and yellowware, stoneware after 1870; no mark. Imita-
　　tion white granite, buff body with opaque white glaze. (26-128)
W. H. Rockwell & Co., 1860-1890; stoneware; no mark. (26)

W. B. Allison & Co., Middlebury, c.1865-1875; stoneware, bot-
　　tles, etc.; no mark. (128)
Allison & Hart, c.1875-1880; same; no mark. (26-128)

A. Royer, c. 1865-1875; stoneware; no mark. (128)
Markel, Immon & Co., c.1869; stoneware; occasional mark is
　　name and address, impressed; (25-26-127-128)
Viall & Markell, 1869-1890; same; no mark. (25-26-128)
Camp & Thompson, c.1870-1880; brownware, stoneware; mark
　　is name, impressed. (127-128)

William Schenkle, Excelsior Pottery, 1870-1875; stoneware, no
　　mark. (128)
Schenkle Bros. & Mann, 1875-c.1885; same; no mark. (26)
William Schenkle, Ohio Stoneware Co., c. 1890; same. (128)

Spafford & Richards, 1870-1895; brownware, stoneware; no mark. (26)

William Rowley, c. 1874-1881; same; no mark. (128)

Boss Bros. c.1874; stoneware, ink and beer bottles; mark is name and address, impressed. (127-128)

Weeks, Cook & Weeks, 1882-1900; stoneware; occasional mark is name and address in raised relief on bottom of piece. (26-127)

Samuel Dyke & Co., 1889-1891; stoneware, toys miniature jugs and marbles; no mark. (26)

A. L. Dyke & Co., 1884-1891; same; no mark. (26)

Summit China Co., c.1890-1900; White Granite, decorated white earthenware; mark is "S.C.C. Akron" in shield, printed; (127-128)

Ohio Stoneware Co., c.1887; stoneware; no mark. (26)

Amana, Iowa County, Iowa

Shaker Pottery, 1856-1900; redware, some cream-colored earthenware; no mark. (128) John Fritz, Potter.

Anderson's Landing, Washington County, Pennsylvania

Wm. A. Anderson, c.1870-1880; stoneware; mark is name and address, stencilled in blue; possibly dealer. (127)

* Anna (see Lowell, Ill.)

Annapolis, Parke County, Indiana

H. S. Atcheson, 1841-1900; stoneware; no mark. (22)

Ann Arbor, Washtenau County, Michigan

——, c.1838; redware; no mark. (128)

* Atwater, Summit County (and Atwater Station, Portage Co.), Ohio

Caleb and Joshua Atwater, c.1830-1840; stoneware; no mark. (115)

Solomon Purdy, c.1850; stoneware; marks are "S. Purdy", with or without "Portage Co." or "Atwater", impressed. (127-128)

Gordon B. Purdy 1860,1870; (son) ; same; occasional mark is name, impressed. (26-115)

Fitzhugh Purdy, Purdy & Loomis; same, possibly brownware; mark is name, impressed. (26-115)

I. M. Mead & Co., c.1840-60; stoneware; mark is name impressed.

W. F. Burns, Atwater Station, 1850-1874; stoneware; no mark. (128)

George Stroup, c. 1871-1881; same; no mark. (128)

Avon, Lorain County, Ohio

——, c.1832; redware; drain-title; no mark. (26)

* Beaver Falls, Beaver County, Pennsylvania

Economy Society Pottery, c.1834-1881; redware, stoneware; no mark; (12-128); succeeded by

Mayer Pottery Co., 1881-1900; White Granite; mark is "J. & E. Mayer" in design, printed. (12-128)

Isaac A. Harvey, 1859-1869; Rockingham brownware; mark name impressed; moved from East Liverpool, O.; (22) (127); succeeded by

Thomas & Webster, 1869-1873; door-knobs; moved to East Liverpool. (22-26)

J.Graff, 1873-c.1880; yellow-ware; no mark; (22); succeeded by Beaver Falls Art Tile Co., 1888-1900; tile. (22)

Berlin, Somerset County, Pennsylvania

Eval & Zom, c.1830; redware, tobacco pipes, no mark. (1)

Boonville, Cooper County, Missouri

——, c.1840; stoneware; no mark. (22)

Brazil, Clay County, Indiana

Tourpet & Becker, 1859-1900; stoneware; no mark. (22-102)

Isaac Cordrey, c.1869; same; no mark. (22-102)

Bridgeport, Harrison County, West Virginia

West Virginia Pottery Co., 1880-1900; stoneware; no mark. (103)

Bridgewater, Beaver County, Pennsylvania

W. L. Hamilton, c.1837; probably stoneware; no mark. (108)

Burlington, Des Moines County, Iowa

Turley Bros., 1870-1900; stoneware; no mark. (104)

* Canton, Stark County, Ohio

John Shorb, Jr., 1817-1824; stoneware; no mark. (25-128)
Adam A. Shorb (son), 1824-c.1850; same; no mark. (25-128)

George Binkley, 1826-c. 1840; redware and stoneware; mark "B" impressed; moved from Kendall (Massillon), O. (128)

Adam L. Shorb, (cousin of above), 1840-c. 1860; stoneware; no mark; Daniel Grace, potter and manager. (25-115-128)

David Sherrick, c.1840-1850; redware; no mark. (128)

Cape Girardeau, Cape Girardeau County, Missouri

James Pass, 1880-1883; whiteware, Rockingham brownware; no mark; unsuccessful, went to Syracuse, N. Y. (12-128)

Caldwell, Calloway County, Missouri

——, 1827-1891; stoneware; no mark. (22)

Calhoun, Henry County, Missouri

Mrs.Robbins and Son, c.1873; stoneware; no mark. (22)

Carbon Cliff, Rock Island County, Illinois

——, c.1870-1900; large pottery, employing eighty men; stoneware, brownware, garden ornaments; no mark. (105)

Cassville, Huntinngton County, Pennsylvania

C. B. Hyssong, c. 1870-1900; stoneware; no mark. (101)

N. W. Greenland, c.1885-1900; same; no mark. (101)

Charleston, Brooke County, West Virginia

Wm. McLuney, c. 1809; stoneware and redware; no mark. (128)

——, c.1813; same; no mark. (128)

Chatfield Corners, Fulton County, Ohio

Eben French, c.1837-1845; stoneware; no mark. (26-115)

Chicago, Cook County, Illinois

——, c. 1864; probably stoneware; no mark. (7)

American Terra-Cotta Co., 1886-1900; art pottery; no mark. (12-22)

Chillicothe, Ross County, Ohio

——, c. 1811; redware; no examples known. (26)

——, c. 1850; crude yellow-ware; no mark. (128)

* Cincinnati, Hamilton County, Ohio

William McFarland, 1799-1801; redware; no examples known; moved from Kentucky; (25); joined or succeeded by

James and Robert Caldwell, 1810-c.1820; same; also from Kentucky. (25-26)

William Iler, c.1819-1831; same. (26)

William Saunders, c. 1819; same. (26)

Joseph Stevens, c.1825-1829; same. (26-115)

James K. Ogden, c.1825-1829; redware; no mark. (26-115)

Isaac Clark, c.1831-1837; same. (26)

James F. Francisco, Cincinnati Pottery, c.1831-1837; redware; no mark. (26)

Nelson Ball, c.1831-1837; ware made unknown. (26)

Israel Thompson, c.1831-1837; same. (26)

James and Alexander Vance, c. 1831-1837; redware; no mark; moved from Greensboro, Penna. (26-115)

James Doane, c.1831-1837; yellow-ware; no examples known. (26-115)

S. Quigley, c.1834; stoneware; mark is "S. Quigley, Franklin Factory, Cincinnati, O.", impressed. possibly user, not maker. (127)

Uriah Kendall, 1834-1846; stoneware; no mark. (25-26)

Kendall & Sons, 1846-1850; Rockingham, brownware and yellow-ware; no mark. (25-26)

William Bromley, 1843-1860; stoneware, Rockingham and yellow-ware, no mark. (25-26)

Bromley & Son, 1860-c.1870; same; no mark. (25-26)

Peter Lessel, 1848-1852; same; no mark. (25-26)

Peter Lessel & Bro., 1852-1879; same; no mark. (26)

George Lessel (son), 1879-1899; same; no mark. (26)

George Scott, 1846-1889; stoneware, brownware, Rockingham, yellow-ware; no mark. (25-26)

George Scott & Sons, 1889-1900; same, also White Granite; no mark. (25-26)

George Pyatt, 1853-1859; Rockingham and yellow-ware; no mark; moved from Zanesville, O., went to Kaolin, Mo., (25-26-115)

Hamlet Greatbach, 1854-1856; yellow-ware; no mark. (25-26)
Skinner, Greatbach & Co., 1856-1857; same, no mark; succeeded by
Bromley & Bailey, 1857-1860; same; no mark. (26)
William Bromley, 1860-c.1865; same; no mark. (26)

Valentine Eichenlaub, 1855-1857; stoneware, yellow-ware; no mark. (26)

Brewer & Tempest, c.1854; yellow-ware; no mark. (25-26)
Tunis Brewer, 1856-1859; Rockingham and yellow-ware; no mark. (25-26)
J. A. Brewer, 1859-1869; no mark. (25-26)

Andrew Behn, 1857-1877; same; no mark. (25-26)
George Peter Behn (son), 1857-1900; same; no mark. (26)

Michael and Nimrod Tempest. Hamilton Street Pottery, 1857-1865; yellow-ware, brownware fruit jars, some bisque porcelain; no mark. (25-26); succeeded by
Frederick Dallas, 1865-1882; same; White Granite after 1869; no mark. (25-26)
Dallas Pottery Co., 1882-1900; White Granite; no mark (26)

John Ochsle, Findlay Street Pottery, 1857-1877; stoneware, brownware; no mark. (26)
Phillip T. Ochsle (son), 1877-1887; same; no mark. (26)

Queen City Terra-Cotta Co., 1859-c.1870; ornaments in unglazed redware or terra-cotta; no mark. (26)

Samuel Pollock, Dayton Street Pottery, 1859-1874; yellow-ware, Rockingham; no mark; (26) succeeded by
P. L. Coultry, 1874-1900; same, also art ware; no mark. (26)

Tempest, Brockmann & Co., 1862-1881; cream-colored earthenware, first White Granite in Middle West in 1867; no mark; (12-25-26); succeeded by
Tempest, Brockmann & Sampson Pottery Co., 1881-1888; same; no mark. (12-26)
C. E. Brockmann, 1888-1900; same; no mark. (12-26)

August Miller, 1865-1900; Rockingham, yellow-ware; no mark. (26)

John Fisher, Berlin Street Pottery, 1871-1895; Rockingham, yellow-ware, garden ornaments; no mark. (26)

H. Mappes, Vine Street Pottery, 1859-1880; Rockingham and yellow-ware; no mark. (25-26)

Mappes Bros., 1880-1900; same; no mark. (26)

Thomas Wheatley, 1880-1884, 1899-1900; art ware; no mark. (12-26)

Rookwood Pottery Co., 1880-1900; art ware; marks are name, initials or monogram, usually impressed. (12-26)

Clay City, Clay County, Indiana

——, 1846-1900; stoneware; no mark. (102)

Cleveland, Cuyahoga County, Ohio

A. D. Higgins, c.1837-1850; stoneware; occasional mark is name and address, impressed. (26-127-128)

Columbus, Franklin County, Ohio

Frederick Abbe, c.1848-1850; stoneware; no mark. (128)

A. Jenkins, c.1840-1850; same. (128)

Thomas Buchanan, c.1850; same. (128)

Crooksville, Muskingum County, Ohio

Lazalier Burley, c.1846; stoneware; no mark. (26)

Burley & Winters, c. 1850-1890; stoneware and brownware; mark on brownware is name and address in circle, impressed on bottom. (127-128)

* Cuyahoga Falls, Summit County, Ohio

Camp, Cook & Co., 1863-c.1880; stoneware; no marks; later brick manufacturers. (26-128)

Thomas Harris, 1863-1900; stoneware; mark is name impressed; (127-128)

J. R. Thomas, 1857-1887; same; no mark. (128)

Thomas Bros., 1887-1900; same; no mark. (128)
Dalton, Wayne County, Ohio

Curtis Houghton & Co., 1842-1864; brownware, stoneware; no
mark. Houghton from Bennington, Vt. (114)
Edwin Houghton, 1864-1890; same; occasional mark is "Dalton
Pottery" impressed. (114-127)
Eugene Houghton, 1890-1900; same; no marks; still in existence.
(114)

Danville, Des Moines County, Iowa
—— c.1858; stoneware; no mark. (22)
—— c.1858; stoneware; no mark. (22)
Dayton, Montgomery County, Ohio
—— Wood, c.1870; brownware; mark is "Wood, Potter, Dayton,
Ohio" impressed. (127)
—— Getz, c.1880-1900; stoneware; no mark; moved from Canton,
O. (114)
Broome & Morgan, 1882-c.1900; stoneware; art ware; no marks.
(9-26)
Detroit, Michigan
—— c.1820; redware; no mark. (22)
——, c.1864; stoneware; no mark. (7)
——, c.1864; stoneware; no mark. (7)
Doylestown, Wayne County, Ohio
S. Routson, 1835-1846; brownware, stoneware; occasional mark
is name impressed; moved to Wooster, O. (25-115)
Dover, Tuscarawas County, Ohio
H. Wores c.1825-1846; stoneware; mark is name impressed.
(115-127)
Eagle Springs, (near Hillsboro), Highland County, Ohio
Richard Iliff, c.1806; stoneware; no mark; moved to Hillsboro.
(25)
* Edgerton, Rock County, Wisconsin
Pauline Pottery, 1883-1900; art ware; mark is "C" in crown,
impressed. (12)

*East Liverpool, Colmbiana County, Ohio
    John Koontz (near), c.1807; redware; no examples known. (128)

James Bennett, 1839-1841; yellow-ware and Rockingham brown-
    ware; no marks; came from Jersey City and Troy, Ind. (12-
    25-26)
Bennett Bros., 1841-1844; same, some poor Flint Enamel, pan-
    eled pitchers in this and Rockingham; no mark; James joined
    by William and Edwin; succeeded by Croxall Bros; James
    and Edwin moved to Pittsburgh. (12-25-26-127-128)

Benjamin Harker, Sr., 1840-c. 1844; same ware, probably Rock-
    ingham hound-handled pitcher; no mark. (25-26)
Benjamin and George Harker (sons), Etruria Pottery, c.1844-
    1849; same; no mark. (25)
Harker, Taylor & Co. (George Harker and James Taylor),
    1849-1851; same; small hound-handled pitcher with boar,
    dog and grape relief; rare mark is name and address in relief
    on raised oval. (25-127-128)
George S. Harker & Co., 1851-1890; same; white Granite after
    1879; no mark. (26)
Harker Pottery Co., 1890-1900; White Granite; mark is mono-
    gram of "H-P Co." with bow and arrow and "Semi-Porcelain",
    printed. (12-26)
Salt & Mear (with James Ogden and John Hancock), latter from
    South Amboy, N. J., 1841-c.1853; Mansion Pottery; yellow-
    ware; mark name and address on raised oval; (25-26); suc-
    ceeded by
Benjamin Harker, Sr., and William G. Smith, c.1853-1857;
    yellow-ware and Rockingham; no mark; (25-26); succeeded
    by
Foster & Garner, 1857-1863; same; no mark; (25-26); succeeded
    by Croxall Bros.

Thomas Croxall & Bros., 1844-1856; mocha-type, yellow-ware
    and Rockingham; no mark; succeeded Bennett Bros., pottery
    destroyed by fire, 1852 built new plant. (25-26)
Croxall & Cartwright, 1856-1898; same; "Rebecca-at-the-Well"
    Rockingham teapot, with the flower finial like Baltimore type,
    but with lighter glaze; no mark; (25-26-127); succeeded by
    Foster & Garner, Ball & Morris.

John W. Croxall & Sons, 1898-1900; same; no mark. (26)

John Goodwin, 1844-1853; yellow-ware and Rockingham, also
   door-knobs; went to Trenton, N. J., (25-26); succeeded by
S. & W. Baggott, 1853-c.1895; same, including small Gothic
   paneled pitcher; no mark; built Eagle Pottery. (25-26-127)

William Brunt, Sr., 1847-c.1856; (William Bloor) yellow-ware
   and Rockingham; new factory for door-knobs, 1850; no mark.
   (26-128)
Henry Brunt (son) & Son, c.1856-1895; same; no mark. (26)
Brunt & Thompson (W. H. Brunt, son of Henry), 1895-1900;
   same; no mark. (26-128)

John Henderson, c.1847-1857; yellow-ware and Rockingham,
   also bird whistles and toys in Rockingham; no mark; (26-
   127) ; succeeded by
Morley, Goodwin & Flentke, 1857-1878; same, White Granite
   after 1874; no mark; (26); succeeded by
Goodwin & Flentke, 1878-1879; White Granite (26); succeeded
   by
Standard Co-Operative Pottery Co., 1879-1886; same; no mark.
   (26)
Standard Pottery Co., 1886-1900; same; no mark. (26)

Wylie Bros., c.1848-1854; yellow-ware and Rockingham; no
   mark; moved to Pittsburgh, Penna. (25-26)
Woodward & Vodrey, 1849; yellow-ware and Rockingham, also
   terra-cotta; no mark. (25-26)
Woodward, Blakely & Co., 1849-1857; same; no mark; (26);
   succeeded by Wm. Brunt, Jr., West, Hardwick & Co. and
Vodrey Bros. (sons of Jabez Vodrey), 1857-1885; same; including yellow-ware with colored bands like English Mocha-ware,
   to 1879, then White Granite; rare mark on Rockingham is
   name, impressed, on whiteware, monogram "V-B" in design,
   printed. (12-25-26-127)

Ball & Morris, Union Pottery, c.1850-1856; yellow-ware and
   Rockingham; no mark; (26); succeeded by Croxall & Cartwright.

Henry Speeler, c.1850-1852; yellow-ware and Rockingham; no mark; former workman for John Goodwin; moved to Trenton, N. J. (128)

Isaac W. Knowles, and Isaac Harvey, 1853-c.1856; yellow-ware; no mark. (25-26)
Isaac W. Knowles, c.1856-1870; yellow-ware and Rockingham, fruit jars, pie plates, Rockingham half-pint cornucopia flask; no mark. (26-127)
Knowles, Taylor & Knowles, 1870-1890; same to 1872, then White Granite, some porcelain as Lotus Ware; marks show name or initials, usually with ornament, printed. (12-25-26)

Knowles, Taylor & Knowles Co., 1890-1900; same, also Semi-Porcelain or Hotel China; similar marks. (9-26)

N. U. Walker, 1852-1890; terra-cotta and Rockingham ornaments, crouching lion door-stops; no mark. (26-127)
Adams Bros., 1856-1872; brownware and stoneware "novelties"; no mark. (128)

Foster & Rigby, 1857-1860; yellow-ware and Rockingham; no marks; (26); succeeded by
T. Rigby & Co., 1860-1872; same; no mark; (26); succeeded by
John Goodwin, 1872-1876; same; no mark; in East Liverpool 1844-1853, in Trenton 1853-1863, out of business 1865-1872; (25-26-)
Goodwin Bros, (sons), 1876-1893; cream-colored earthenware; mark shows name, printed. (12-26)
Goodwin Pottery Co., 1893-1900; whiteware; similar mark. (12-26)

Booth Bros., c. 1858-1865; brownware; and stoneware "novelties and heating stoves"; no mark. (128)

William Bloor, 1859-1862; porcelain, as blue and white Parian or glazed; blue mottled glaze on Rockingham body; no mark; (25-26-115) ; succeeded by

William Brunt, Jr. (son of William Brunt above), Phoenix
Pottery, 1862-1866; yellow-ware and Rockingham; no mark;
sold to West, Hardwick & Co.; built new plant. (26)
William Brunt, Jr., 1866-1878; same; no mark; (26)
Wm.Brunt, Son & Co., 1878-1894; White Granite; no mark. (26)

Elijah Webster, 1859-1864; stoneware; no mark; moved from
Beaver Falls, Penna.; (25-26); succeeded by
Manley & Cartwright, 1864-1872; yellow-ware and Rockingham;
no mark. (25-26)
Manley, Cartwright & Co., 1872-1880; same; no mark.
Cartwright Bros., 1880-1900; "Garfield Drape" plates in mottled
blue and light green glazes copied from pressed glass; White
Granite after 1887; no mark. (26-127-128)

John Goodwin, Novelty Pottery, 1863-1865; yellow-ware and
Rockingham; no mark; moved from Trenton, N. J. (see
above); (26); succeeded by
Marks, Farmer, Manley & Riley, 1865-1869; same; no mark.
(25-26)
A. H. Marks, 1869-1870; same; no mark; (128); succeeded by
McNichol, Burton & Co., 1870-1892; same; no mark. (26)
D. E. McNichol Pottery Co., 1892-1900; Rockingham, yellow-
ware and cream-colored earthenware; mark on latter is "semi-
Granite" and initials around shield, printed. (12-26)

William McCullough, 1865-1895; yellow-ware and Rockingham;
no mark. (26)

West, Hardwick & Co., Phoenix Pottery, 1866-1868; Rocking-
ham, yellow-ware and White Granite; no mark; succeeded
Wm. Brunt, Jr.; (26-128); succeeded by
George Morley, Phoenix Pottery, 1868-1884; same; no mark;
built new pottery, 1884. (26)
George Morley & Co., Lincoln Pottery, 1884-1890; same, also
majolica, owl pitchers, etc., no mark. (26-127) also Wellsville,
W. Va.
East Liverpool Potteries Co., 1890-1900; same; no mark. (128)
Simms & Starkey, c.1866-1869; yellow-ware and Rockingham;
no mark. (26)

Simms & Laughlin, c.1869-1872; no mark. (26)

Simms & Ferguson, 1872-1875; same; no mark; (26); succeeded by

Brunt, Bloor, Martin & Co., Dresden Pottery, 1875-1892; White Granite; mark is "Dresden China" in design, printed; (12-26) ; succeeded by

Potters' Co-Operative Co., 1892-1900; same; same mark. (12-26)

Agner, Fouts & Co., 1862-1884; yellow-ware and Rockingham; no mark. (26)

Agner & Gaston, 1884-1887; same; no mark; (26); succeeded by

Sebring Pottery Co., 1887-1900; White Granite, Semi-Porcelain; mark, "Sebring's Semi-Vitreous Porcelain", with crown, impressed. (12-26)

Brunt & Hill, 1867-1874; yellow-ware and Rockingham; no mark; (26); succeeded by

John Wylie, Great Western Pottery, 1874-1900; White Granite; no mark; of Wylie Bros., above; returned from Pittsburgh, Penna. (26)

James McDevitt (and others), California Pottery, 1867-1871; yellow-ware and Rockingham; no mark. (25-26)

McDevitt & Moore, 1871-1900; same; no mark. (25-26)

Burgess, Webster & Viney, 1867-1869; stoneware; no mark; (26); succeeded by

N. M. Simms, 1869-1870; same; no mark; (128); succeeded by

Starkey & Curbey (Ourbey), 1870-1872; yellow-ware and Rockingham; no mark; (26-128); succeeded by

Samuel Worcester, 1872-1875; same; no mark. (26)

Bulger & Worcester, 1875-1888; same; no mark. (26)

Thompson & Herbert, 1868-1870; yellow-ware and Rockingham; no mark. (25-26)

C. C. Thompson & Co., same, much yellow-ware including melon-shaped covered dish, largest producers of yellow-ware and Rockingham in the country in 1895, also White Granite and cream-colored earthenware; mark on white-ware is initials over griffin, printed. (12-26-127)

Samuel and Elias Jackson, 1868-1879; bisque porcelain ornaments; no mark. (26)

William Burton, 1870-c.1875; yellow-ware and Rockingham; no mark. (26)

John Leith, c. 1870; brownware, lion doorsteps. (128)

Laughlin Bros., 1873-1879; White Granite, under-glaze decorated whiteware; no mark. (12-26-128)

Homer Laughlin, 1879-1897; same also porcelain 1885-1889; mark is name, printed. (12-26)

Laughlin China Co., 1897-1900; Semi-Porcelain; similar mark. (12-26)

R. Thomas & Sons Co., 1873-1900; door-knobs; moved from Beaver Falls, Penna. (26)

Harrison, Flentke & Co., 1874-1881; yellow-ware and Rockingham; no mark; succeeded by Knowles, Taylor & Knowles. (26)

William Colclough, c.1875; Rockingham, pig banks, etc., and clay pipes. (26-127)

Joseph Morton, c.1875; clay pipes. (26)

Burford Bros., 1879-1900; floor and wall tile to 1881, then cream-colored earthenware and Semi-Porcelain; no mark. (128)

Benjamin Harker, Jr., & Sons, Wedgewood Pottery, 1877-1881; White Granite; no mark; (26) succeeded by

Wallace & Chetwynd, 1881-1900; same; no mark. (26)

Frederick, Schenkle, Allen & Co., 1881-1888; yellow-ware, some with colored relief floral decoration, Rockingham; no mark; (12-26-127) ; succeeded by

Globe Pottery Co., 1888-1900; same, also White Granite; no mark. (12)

East River, Harrison County, West Virginia
  Brown & McKenzie, c.1870-1890; stoneware; no mark. (103)
Evansville, Vanderburg County, Indiana

  A. M. Beck, 1882-1884; majolica; no mark; (12-102); succeeded by

Benninghoff, Uhl & Co., 1884-1891; White Granite; no mark; (12-102); succeeded by

Crown Pottery Co., 1891-1900; same; mark is "C. P. Coy" with crown, printed. (12-102)

Bockting Bros., 1885-1900; stoneware; no mark; also at Huntingburg. (22)

Fallston, Beaver County, Pennsylvania

Fallston Pottery Co., c.1875-1900; stoneware; no mark. (101)

Enterprise Pottery Co., c.1880-1900; same; no mark. (101)

Fieldon, Jersey County, Illinois

——, c.1868; stoneware; no mark. (105)

Fort Scott, Kansas

——, c.1890; brownware; no mark. (22)

Franklin, Warren County, Ohio

Franklin Porcelain Co., 1880-1884; White Granite, soft-paste porcelain; mark is "F. P. Co. P." impressed. (12)

Frazeesburg Road, Muskingum County, Ohio

John Vandemark, c.1840-1850; stoneware; no mark. (115)

Freeman's Landing, Jefferson County, West Virginia

Carlyle & McFadden, 1850-1853; stoneware; no mark; moved to Toronto, O., and made draintile. (26)

Fultonham, Muskingum County, Ohio

Samuel Weller, 1873-1900; stoneware, art ware; no mark. (26)

Gamesville, Ozark County, Missouri

H. S. Smith, c.1890; stoneware; no mark. (29)

Geneseo, Kansas

——, c.1890; brownware; no mark. (104)

* Greensboro, Greene County, Pennsylvania

Alexander and James Vance, c.1800-1810; redware; no mark; later at Cincinnati, O. (25-31-115)

Vance & Boughner, c.1810-1812; same; no mark. (25-31)

Alexander Boughner, c.1812-1850; redware, some decorated with glaze, some salt-glazed, and stoneware; mark on stoneware is name and address, stencilled in blue. (25-31-127)

A. & W. Boughner, 1850-c.1890; same; similar mark. (31-127)

James Hamilton, Eagle Pottery, 1844-c.1890; stoneware, 40-50 gallon jars; some pieces show eagle design stencilled in blue; mark is name and address, or "Eagle Pottery", stencilled in blue or impressed. (31-127)

Hamilton & Jones, c.1870; stoneware; mark is name and address, impressed or stencilled in blue. (127-128)

Williams & Reppert, c.1875; same; mark is name and address, impressed or stencilled in blue. (127-128)

Greensburg, Westmorland County, Pennsylvania
Michael Straw c.1837; stoneware; no mark. (128)

Hamilton, Butler County, Ohio

—— Sims, Royal Pottery Co., 1880-1883; art ware; no mark. (12-26) succeeded by
Adolph Metzner, 1884-1900; stoneware; no mark. (128)

Harmony, Beaver County, Pennsylvania
Economy Society, 1810-1820; redware; no mark; two potters employed in 1810. (128)

Harmony, Clay County, Indiana
S. H. Brown, c.1869-1900; stoneware; no mark. (102)

Hillsboro, Highland County, Ohio
Richard Iliff, 1806-c.1820; stoneware; no mark; moved from Eagle Springs, O. (25)
Fisher & McLain, c.1810-1840; stoneware; no mark. (25)
Amariah Gossett, c.1810-1840; same; no mark. (25)

Hue, Vinton County, Ohio
Edward Gaffney, c. 1875-1900; stoneware; no mark. (26)

Huntingburg, Dubois County, Indiana
Beckting Bros. c.1870-1900; stoneware; no mark; also at Evansville. (22)

Huntington, Huntington County, Pennsylvania
——, c.1870; stoneware; no mark. (128)

Johnstown, Cambria County, Pennsylvania
Hiram Swank & Sons, c.1865-1900; stoneware; mark is name and address, impressed or stencilled in blue. (127-128)

Jonathan Creek, Muskingum County, Ohio
  Joseph Rosier, c.1815; stoneware; no mark. (25)
  A. Emsinger, c.1828-1840; slip-decorated and plain redware, stoneware; no mark. (25)
Jugtown, Grundy County, Illinois
  ——, c.1870; stoneware; no mark. (105)
Kaolin, Jefferson County, Missouri
  Elihu H. Shepard, 1852-1863; yellow-ware, some cream-colored earthenware; no mark; George Pyatt of Zanesville, O., manager. (1-25)
Kendall, (Massillon), Stark County, Ohio
  George Binckley, c.1825; redware; mark "G.B." impressed; moved to Canton, O. (128)
Lakenan, Shelby County, Missouri
  Huggins & Co., c.1870-1880; stoneware; no mark. (22)
Ledgedale, Pike County, Pennsylvania
  T. Bells, c.1880-1900; redware; no mark. (101)
* Limaville, Stark County, Ohio
  Limaville Terra-Cotta and Stoneware Works, A. Stockburger, C. Hehr, c.1865-1895; brownware, some black glazed, stoneware, large terracotta figures and vases; no mark. (127-128)
Lisbon, Columbiana County, Ohio
  Phillip Brown, Oliver Griffith, Samuel Wilson, (not known which was owner), c.1820; redware; no mark. (128)
Logotee, Martin County, Indiana
  ——, c.1842-1900; stoneware; no mark; B. Griffith, potter, c.1890-1900. (22)
London, Madison County, Ohio
  ——, c.1840-1850; stoneware; no mark. (128)
Louisville, Stark County, Ohio
  Stoneware and Tile Co., (Empire Clay Co.); 1880-1900; stoneware; no mark; moved to Brazil, Ind. (128)
Lowell, LaSalle County, Illinois—see Anna
  Wallace and Cornwall—modeled jugs; mark: "Anna Pottery"
  ——Kirkpatrick, c. 1866-1900; stoneware; no mark. (105-126)

Mankato, Blue Earth County, Minnesota
——, c.1875-1895; stoneware; no mark. (22)
Martin's Ferry, Belmont County, Ohio

William Callahan, c.1837; redware; stoneware; no mark. (26-128) succeeded by
Joseph P. Stevens, James Harris, John Danas, c.1840; stoneware, no marks; (128); succeeded by
Samuel Young, c.1850; same; no mark. (128)

Macomb, McDonough County, Illinois
Eagle Pottery Co., c.1880-1891; stoneware; no mark. (22)
Macomb Pottery Co., c.1880-1900; same; no mark. (22)
Massillon, Stark County, Ohio
Adam Welker, c.1860-1885; stoneware, brownware; no mark. (128)
Boerner, Shapley & Vogt, Massillon Stoneware Co., 1882-1900; stoneware; no mark. (128)
Menasha, Winnebago County, Wisconsin
Batchelder Pottery, c.1850-1880; stoneware; no mark. (33)
Morgantown, Monongalia County, West Virginia

——Foulke, c.1784-1800 slip-decorated, slip-coated and plain redware; no mark; (1-11-25-96-108); succeeded by
John W. Thompson, 1800-c.1840; no mark; (1-11-25-96-108)
Greenland Thompson, (son), c.1840-1890; same, some with applied floral relief, stoneware; no mark. (11-96-108)
Thompson, Williams & Co., c.1870-1890; same; no mark. (128)
Middlebury, Summit County, Ohio (see Akron.)
Milford Center, Union County, Ohio
—— Canfield, 1857-1869; stoneware and drain tile; no mark; came from Connecticut. (26)
Millersburg, Holmes County, Ohio
Henry Snyder, c.1875-1885; stoneware and tile; no mark. (128)
Milton, Wood County, Ohio
——, c.1838-1840; stoneware; no mark. (22)
* Mogadore, Portage County, Ohio

J. H. Fenton, c.1854-1875; stoneware; brownware; no mark. (128)

S. L. Stoll & Co., 1864-c.1880; brownware, stoneware, toys, whistles, minature jugs, etc.; no mark. (26-127-128)

N. Fossbender, 1860-1875; same; no mark. (26-127-128)

J. S. and E. D. Monroe, 1845-1880; same; no mark. (26-127-128)

F. L. Sheldon, 1845-1878; same; no mark. (26-127-128)

J. C. Smith, c.1862; stoneware; mark is name and address, impressed; (127-128)

E. W. Myers, c.1870; stoneware; no mark. (128)

Myers and Hall, c.1872; stoneware; occasional mark is name and address, impressed. (26-127)

Myers, Baird & Hall, c.1874-1880; same; no mark. (128)

Merrill, Earl & Ford, c.1880-1900; stoneware; tobacco pipes, no mark. (26-128)

Monmouth, Warren County, Illinois

Western Stoneware Co., 1870-1890; stoneware; no mark. (22)

Monmouth Pottery Co., 1890-1900; stoneware, Rockingham; no mark. (22-105)

Mound City, Pulaski County, Illinois

—— Koch, c.1866; stoneware; no mark. (105)

Mount Sterling, Muskingum County, Ohio

John Burley, c.1840-1850; stoneware; no mark. (26)

Moorefield, Hardy County, West Virginia

——, c.1870-1880; stoneware; no mark. (103)

Navarre, Stark County, Ohio

Navarre Stoneware Co., c.1880-1900; stoneware, some brownware, large flowerpots "sponged in blue and cream"; no mark. (127-128)

New Cumberland, West Virginia

Chelsea China Co., 1888-1893; white earthenware; mark is crescent and star, printed. (12)

* New Brighton, Beaver County, Pennsylvania

Thomas Jackson, 1843-1847; probably redware; no examples known. (108)

Thomas Elverson, 1862-1880; yellow-ware and Rockingham brownware; no mark. (108)

A. F. Smith, c.1880-1900; same; no mark. (21-108)

Elverson & Sherwood, c.1870; stoneware; no mark. (108)

Sherwood Bros. Co., 1877-1900; same; capacity two carloads of ware a day; no mark. (108)

D. G. Schofield & Co., c.1877-1893; stoneware; no mark. (108)

Newcomerstown, Tuscarawas County, Ohio

Harmon and Gustavus Fox, 1840-c.1860; stoneware; no mark. (128)

George Bagnall, c.1870-1875; same; no mark; unusual unglazed "pug" dog door-stops. (127-128)

New Geneva, Fayette County, Pennsylvania

——, c.1854-1900; redware, stoneware, similar to that of Greensboro; no mark. (128)

New Philadelphia, Tuscarawas County, Ohio

Andrew McChesney, 1840-1850; stoneware; no mark; (128); succeeded by

Thomas Read; c.1850-1865; same; mark, "T. Read" impressed; (127-128) succeeded by

Nelson Tracy, ca.1865-1875; same; no mark. (128)

John B. Tracy (son), c. 1875-1890; same; no mark. (128)

Laban H. Works, c.1845; stoneware; mark is "L. H. Works", impressed; (127-128); succeeded by

Joseph Figley, c. 1850; same; mark is "J. Figley" impressed; (127-128); succeeded by

Thomas Read, c.1855; same; operated both potteries; mark as above; (127-128) ; succeeded by

Nelson Tracy; same; no mark; operated both potteries. (128)

T. A. Packer, c.1875-1885; same; no mark. (128)

Lambright & Westhope, c.1885-1895; same; no mark. (128)

Newtown Township, Tuscarawas County, Ohio
  W. P. Harris, c.1828-1856; stoneware; E. Hall, potter; applied relief decoration, especially "clasped hands"; mark is "E. Hall" and address, impressed. (63)
New Ulm, Brown County, Minnesota
  ——, c.1870-1880; stoneware; no mark. (22)
Orrville, Wayne County Ohio

  Amos Hall and Robert Cochran, 1862-1877; stoneware; no mark; (128); succeeded by
  Peter Eichert and Jacob Fleckinger, 1877-1900; same; no mark. (128)

Owensboro, Greene County, Indiana
  —— Reynolds, c.1869; stoneware; no mark. (102)
Palatine, Marion County, West Virginia
  Knotts, Sunderland & Co., c.1870-1900; stoneware; no mark. (103)
  Richey & Hamilton, c.1875; stoneware; mark is name and address, stencilled in blue. (127)
Paris, Stark County Ohio
  Joel Smyth, Smyth & Harmell, c.1840; stoneware; no mark. (115)
Parkersburg, Wood County, West Virginia

  ——, 1866-1874; stoneware; no mark. (21)
  Donahue Pottery, (Donagno), 1874-1900; same; mark is name and address; moved from Fredericktown. (21-103)
Peoria, Peoria County, Illinois
  Fenton & Clark, 1859-1865; yellow-ware and white or cream-colored earthenware; no mark; Fenton from Bennington, Vt., Daniel Greatback, designer, 1859. (1-25); succeeded by
  American Pottery Co., 1865-1873; same, also brownware; no mark. (1-25)
  Peoria Pottery Co., 1873-1894; Rockingham stoneware to 1889, then White Granite; mark on stoneware is "Peoria, Illinois," impressed, on whiteware, monogram of "P. P. Co.", printed, (12)

Perry, Ralls County, Missouri

    R. Winfel, c. 1876; stoneware; no mark; (22)

* Pittsburgh, Allegheny County, Pennsylvania

Bracken & James, c.1800-1803; probably redware; no examples known. (128)

Thomas Bracken, 1803-1825; probably same; none known. (128)

Thomas R. James, 1803-1807; probably same; none known. (128)

William Price, 1805-c.1820; "Delft-ware" in directory, probably redware, no examples known. (128)

Griffith Bros. c.1815; probably redware, none known. (128)

James Barr, c.1815-1847; redware, stoneware; no mark. (128)

Thomas Freeman, c.1825; probably redware; no mark. (128)

Trotter & Co., c.1813-1815; "Queensware, pitchers, coffee and teapots, etc., similar to those of Philadelphia", probably white earthenware, probably moved from Philadelphia. (128)

Jacob Hocusweiler, 1815-1856; redware, probably stoneware; no mark. (128)

Vodrey & Frost, 1827-1830; stoneware, yellow-ware; no mark; no examples known; moved to Louisville, Ky. (1-25-128)

F. Bauders, c.1841; stoneware; no mark; (128)

Hugh Donaldson, c. 1839; probably stoneware; no mark. (128)

P. Auber, Birmingham, c. 1860; stoneware; no mark. (128)

A. N. Burchfield c. 1860; stoneware; no mark. (128)

Euler & Sunshine, c.1860; stoneware; no mark; (128)

Foel & Ault, E. Birmingham, c.1860; stoneware; no mark. (128)

Bennett Bros., (Daniel, William, James and Edwin), Pennsylvania Pottery, Birmingham, 1844-1849; yellow-ware and Rockingham brownware, octagonal pitcher with mask spout; no mark; moved from East Liverpool, O.; Edwin Bennett moved to Baltimore, 1846, William, in 1849; James died in Pittsburgh, 1862; (1-12-25-128)

Daniel Bennett, 1849-1866; Rockingham and yellow-ware; no mark. (128)

John Frell & Co. c. 1860; stoneware; no mark. (128)

S. M. Kier, 1867-1900; stoneware, cream-colored earthenware, fire-brick; no mark. (25-128)

Henry Pettie & Co., c.1860; stoneware; no mark. (128)

John Wylie, 1870-1874; White Granite; no mark; moved to East Liverpool, O. (25-128)

Price's Landing, Washington County, Pennsylvania

Isaac Hewett, Excelsior Works, c.1870-1880; stoneware, mark is name and address, stencilled in blue. (127)

Putnam, Muskingum County, Ohio

Solomon Purdy, c.1820; slip-decorated and plain redware; no examples known; possibly moved to Zoar, then to Atwater. (25-54-117)

——Mootz (near), c. 1825-1840; stoneware; no mark. (25-54)

J. Bodine (near), c. 1836-1845; same; no mark. (25-64)

Samuel Havens (near), c. 1836-1846; same; no mark. (25-64)

Prosper Rice (near), 1827-1850; stoneware, Rockingham brownware; mark on former is name impressed. (25-64)

Joseph Bell (near), 1827-1850; stoneware; mark is name impressed. (25-64)

Ravenna, Portage County, Ohio

Seymour & Stedman, c. 1850; stoneware; mark is name and address impressed; Seymour from Hartford, Conn. (18)

Misler Bros., c. 1880-1900; stoneware; no mark. (128)

Red Oak, Stephenson County, Illinois

—— c. 1864; stoneware; no mark. (21)

* Red Wing, Goodhue County, Minnesota

Joseph Pohl, c. 1858-1870; stoneware; no mark. (21)

——Boynton, 1870-1872; same; no mark. (21)

—— Philles, 1872-1877; same; no mark. (21)

Red Wing Stoneware Co., 1877-1900; same; no mark; (21); largest stoneware plant in the United States in 1888.

David Hallam, 1870-1872; stoneware; no mark. (21)

Red Wing Stoneware Co., 1872-1900; same; no mark. (21)

Richmond, Wayne County, Indiana

Bott, Hammersley & Co., c. 1875; brownware, yellow-ware, flower-pots, etc., no mark. (102)

Ripley, Brown County, Illinois

John N. Stout, c. 1866-1880; brownware; rare mark is name inscribed. (127-128)

(12 potteries in Ripley in 1880, making brownware and stoneware). (105)

Roscoe, Muskingum County, Ohio

—— Rich, c. 1870; brownware, stoneware; mark is name impressed. (115)

Rock House, Hocking County, Ohio

—— c. 1884 stoneware; no mark. (21)

Roseville, Muskingum County, Ohio

W. Bullock, c. 1870-1885; stoneware; mark is name and address, impressed. (127-128)

W. S. Mayers, c.1870-1880; stoneware; mark is name and address stencilled in blue. (127)

J. B. Owens, 1885-1892; flower-pots; no mark; moved to Zanesville. (26)

Balderson & Pace, c.1875; brownware, stoneware; no mark. (25-26)

H. H. Melleck, c.1875; stoneware; mark is name and address, impressed. (127)

W. B. Lowry, 1882-1900; cooking ware; no marks. (128)

Lowry Bros., 1890-1900; same; no mark. (128)

James L. Weaver, c.1887; stoneware; no mark. (128)

Williams & McCoy, 1886-1900; same; no mark. (26)

H. Sowers, c.1887; brownware and stoneware; no mark. (128)

Kildow, Dugan & Co., 1885-1890; cooking ware; no mark. (128)

Kildow, Withers & McCoy, 1890-1900; same; no mark. (26)

John Burton, c.1887; stoneware; no mark. (128)

Salem, Columbiana County, Ohio

Thomas Hughes, 1812-c.1825; redware and stoneware; no examples known; (26) succeeded by
Christian Harmon, c.1825-1840; stoneware; no mark. (26)

Salem Cross Roads, Westmoreland County, Pennsylvania
——, c. 1837; stoneware; no examples known. (128)
——, c.1837; same. (128)
Sandyville, Tuscarawas County, Ohio
Wesley Riggs, c. 1820-1830; redware, stoneware; no mark. (117-128)
Salina, Illinois
——c.1875; stoneware; no mark. (21)
Santa Fe, Alexander County, Illinois
Charles Crock, c.1880; stoneware; no mark. (105)
Sargent's Bluff, Iowa
——, 1838-1900; stoneware; no mark. (21)
Shoals, Martin County, Indiana
Devol & Catterson, c.1870; stoneware; no mark. (102)
Somerset, Perry County, Ohio
S. E. Heighshoe, c.1850; stoneware, brownware; occasional mark is name impressed. (115-127)
* Springfield (now part of Akron), Summit County, Ohio
Fiske & Smith, c.1822-1830; stoneware; no examples known. (25-26)
Edwin H. Merrill, 1835-1847; stoneware, especially beer bottles; occasional mark is name and address, impressed; moved to Akron. (25-26-127)
A. Smith, c.1870; stoneware; no mark. (128)
Wait & Ricketts, c.1870; stoneware; occasional mark is name and address, impressed. (127-128)
St. Clairsville, Jefferson County, Ohio
Samuel Sharpless, 1808-1830; redware; no mark. (25-26)
St. Louis, Missouri
St. Louis Stoneware Co., 1865-1900; stoneware and drain-tile; no mark. (21)

Steubenville, Jefferson County, Ohio
  Peter Cross, c.1805; slip-decorated and plain redware; no examples known. (25-26)

  J. C. Fisher, 1787-1808; same; no examples known. (25-26-128)
  Thomas Fisher (son), 1808-c.1825; same; also stoneware; no mark. (25-26-128)
  Fisher & Tarr (Thos. Fisher), c.1820; stoneware; no mark. (128)
  Jesse Holden c.1830; stoneware; no mark. (128)

  Steubenville Pottery Co., c.1879-1900; "decorated ware" in directory, white Granite; large pottery; (12-128)
Symmes Creek, Butler County, Ohio
  William Miner, 1869-1883; stoneware; mark is "Miner" impressed. (25-127)
Tallmadge, Summit County, Ohio
  Alvin S. Moore, 1850-1870; stoneware; no mark. (128)
  T. H. Fenton, c.1850-1880; stoneware, brownware; no mark. (128)
  Tyron, Wright & Co., 1868-1875; stoneware; no mark (128)
Tiltonville, Jefferson County, Ohio
  Vance Faience Co., c.1880-1900; owned moulds of Bennington hound-handled pitcher, and reproduced it in art glaze and Rockingham; mark is name in circle, impressed. (12-128)
Upper Alton, Madison County, Illinois
  ——, 1856-c.1866; stoneware; no mark. (105)
Urbana, Campaign County, Ohio
  Frederick Ambrose, 1811-   ; redware; no examples known. (25)
Troy, Perry County, Indiana

  James Clews, Indiana Pottery, 1837-1838; attempted the manufacture of whiteware; (1-25-102); succeeded by
  Jabez Vodrey, 1839-1847; yellow-ware, Rockingham brownware, cream-colored earthenware; no mark; moved from Louisville, Ky., went to East Liverpool, O. (1-25-102)

John Saunders and Samuel Wilson, 1851-1863; Clews' pottery
 burned, new one built; Rockingham brownware; no mark.
 (1-22); succeeded by
Benjamin Hinchco, 1865-c.1885; same; no mark. (1-25)

Vanport, Beaver County, Pennsylvania

 McKenzie Bros., c.1840-1870; stoneware; no mark. (21-108)
 Fowler & McKenzie, 1870-1900; same; no mark. (21)

 Wagoner Bros., c.1860-1870; stoneware, brownware, some black
  glazed; mark is name and address, impressed. (127-128)
Vernon, Crawford County, Iowa
 ——, c.1841-1865; stoneware; no mark. (21)
Wellsville, Columbiana County, Ohio

 Joseph Wells, 1826-c.1835; redware and stoneware; no mark.
  (26-128)
 S. Wells (son) c.1835-1856; stoneware; no mark. (128)

 ——, c.1850-1852; yellow and Rockingham brownware; no mark.
  (26)
 George Jones, Wellsville Terra-Cotta Works, 1867-1900; bisque
  redware ornamental pieces; large pottery; no mark. (128)

 Morley & Co., 1879-1885; White Granite and majolica; mark is
  name printed. (26); succeeded by
 Pioneer Pottery Co., 1885-1896; White Granite; mark is "Aurora
  China" in circle around monogram, printed. (12-26)
 J. Patterson & Son, c. 1887; yellow-ware, Rockingham; mark is
  name impressed. (128)
 J. H. Baum, c.1880-1895; white Granite; mark shows name in
  design. (12)
Wellsburg, Brooke County, West Virginia
 R. Brown, c1841-1846; redware, stoneware; no mark. (128)
 H. N. Bakewell, c.1831-1846; stoneware; no mark. (128)
Washington, Franklin County, Missouri
 —— Walford, c.1848; attempted production of whiteware. (22)

Glassir & Co., c.1872; stoneware; no mark. (22)

Washington Stoneware Co., c.1897; same; no mark. (22)

West Boone, Boone County, Iowa

——, c.1865; stoneware; no mark. (22)

West Bridgewater, Beaver County, Pennsylvania

Hamilton Bros., c.1840; stoneware; no mark. (108)

Wheeling, Ohio County, West Virginia

——ca. 1810; redware; no mark. (108)

J. Miller, c.1869-1880; stoneware; mark is name and address, impressed. (127-128)

Wheeling Pottery Co., 1879-1900; White Granite, semi-porcelain; art ware; marks are (1) name in wreath, (2) name with flags, (3) monogram with " Stone China," (4) "LaBelle China," alone, all printed. (12)

West Virginia China Co., 1880-1891; white-wares; no marks. (128)

Ohio Valley China Co., 1890-1895; art ware; mark is initials in scrolled square. (21-128)

Warwick China Co., 1887-1900; White Granite, semi-porcelain; mark is helmet and crossed swords with "W. C. Co.," on scroll, printed. (12)

Willoughby, Lake County, Ohio

Mattice & Penfield, c.1857; draintile and pottery; no mark. (128)

* Wooster, Wayne County, Ohio

——, c.1817; redware; no examples known. (128)

S. Routson, 1846-1886; brownware, plain and slip-decorated stoneware; no marks; moved from Doylestown. (25-128)

Zalia, (East Toronto), Hancock County, West Virginia

——, c.1870; stoneware; no mark. (22)

Zanesville, Muskingum County, Ohio

Samuel Sullivan, 1808-   ; slip-decorated, slip-coated and plain redware; no mark. (25-26)

Bernard Howson, John Hallan, George Wheaton, 1840-1846; yellow-ware and Rockingham; no mark. (25-63)

Bernard and John Howson (son), 1846-1853; same; no mark. (63)
John Howson, 1863-1874; same; no mark. succeeded by
Fisher & Lansing, 1874-1879; floor-tile; no mark. (63)

George Pyatt, 1846-1851; yellow-ware and Rockingham; no mark. (25-63)
Pyatt & Getz, 1851-1852; same; no mark; Pyatt moved to Cincinnati, O., later to Kaolin, Mo. (63)

Joseph Rambo (near), 1863-c.1870; same; no mark. (63)

George Pyatt, 1866-1879; same; no mark; moved from Kaolin, Mo. (63)
J. G. Pyatt (son), Tremont Pottery, 1879-1900; same; no mark. (63)

Alfred Wilbur, Ninth Ward Pottery, 1873-1878; same; no mark. (63); succeeded by
Calvin Bombaugh, Star Pottery, 1873-1900; same; no mark. (63)

Daniel Hanelsack, 1874-c.1880; same; no mark. (63)
H. K. Smiley, 1878-   ; same; no mark. (63)
Key & Swope, 1879-1900; same; no mark. (63)
R. H. Bodine, 1878-1900; patent cooking ware. (63)
Zanesville Stoneware Co., 1887-1900; stoneware; no mark. (26)
J. B. Owens, 1887-1900; "decorated flower-pots," in brownware; no mark; also Roseville; (128)

Zoar Tuscarawas County, Ohio
Pottery of the Separatist Society of Zoar, c.1834-1850; buff-glazed redware, brownware; S. Purdy, potter moved from Putnam, later at Atwater; rare marks are "Zoar" or "S. Purdy, Zoar," impressed. (117-127-128)

* Exact Location Unknown
Jacob Dick, Tuscarawas Co., O., c.1830-1840; stoneware; mark is name and county, impressed. (25-115)
John Hopkins, Seneca Co., O., c.1834-1840; stoneware; mark is name, impressed. (115)

S. Meade, Medina Co., O., c.1860; stoneware; (115)
C. Tupper, Portage Co., O., c.1870; stoneware; mark is name impressed. (127)
Clem Hamilton, Tuscarawas Co., O., c.1870; brownware; mark is name impressed. (127)
George Morley & Bros., Madison Co., Ill., c.1870; "earthenware"; no mark. (25)
—— Nicomb, Saline Co., Ill., c.1880; stoneware; no mark. (105)
John Fisher, Cambria Co., Penna., c.1879; stoneware; no mark. (21)

Potteries of the South

Arab, Marshall County, Alabama
   ——, c.1870-1900; stoneware; no mark. (21)
Bath, Beaufort County, South Carolina
   Thomas J. Davies, 1861-1865; coarse brownware, black or brown glazed, some "voodoo Head" jugs; no mark. (1-25)
Baxter, Putnam County, Tennessee
   Lafever Pottery, 1840-1900; stoneware, brownware, some salt glazed over Albany slip; no mark. (99)
   William Hedicaugh, c.1870-1900; same; no mark. (99)
   Monroe Vickers, c.1880-1900; same; no mark. (99)
Bedford, Lamar County, Alabama

   Peter Cribbs (brother of Daniel Cribbs of Tuscaloosa), c.1865-1875; stoneware; no mark. (22)
   —— Cribbs (widow), c.1875-1890; same; no mark. (22)

Bell City, Groves County, Kentucky
   Howard & Son, c.1870-1900; brownware, stoneware; no mark. (106)
   D. W. Russell, c.1870-1900; same; no mark. (106)
Betharaba, Montgomery County, South Carolina

Moravian Pottery, 1756-1777; Brother Aust, potter, redware, slip-decorated and plain; no mark. (61)
Big Spring Gap, Wise County, Virginia
William Wolfe, 1875-1881; brownware; stoneware; no mark; moved from Blountsville, Tenn. (1-22-25)
Biloxi, Harrison County, Mississippi

—— Mayer, c.1856-1890; redware; no mark. (12)
Joseph F. Mayer (son), c.1890-1900; same; no mark. (12)

George Ohr, 1890-1900; artware of scroddle type; mark is name, inscribed. (12)
Blackburn, Catawba County, North Carolina
——, c.1875-1900; stoneware, alkaline-glazed ware; no mark. (21)
Blountsville, Sullivan County, Tennessee
William Wolfe, 1848-1875; slip-decorated, sgraffito and plain redware; no mark; moved to Big Spring Gap, Va. (1-25)
Bolton, Fulton County, Georgia
Brown Pottery, c.1890-1900; stoneware, some over Albany slip, alkaline glazed ware; no mark. (81-121-126)
Bogart, Oconee County, Georgia
J. D. Brewer, c.1870-1900; stoneware, alkaline-glazed ware; no mark. (81-107-122)
Brandon, Rankin County, Mississippi
——, c.1854; stoneware; no mark. (22)
Byron, Crawford County, Georgia

James Long, c.1820-1830; probably redware; no mark. (123)
James B. Long (son), c.1830-1850; same, stoneware, alkaline-glazed ware; mark "J.B.L." impressed, often on handle. (123-127)
Jasper Long (son of above), c.1850-1865; stoneware; alkaline-glazed ware; no mark. (123)
John S. Long (son of above), 1865-c.1890; same; no mark. (123)
John N. Long, c.1890-1900; alkaline-glazed ware; no mark. (107-121-123)

Camden, Kershaw County, South Carolina
Richard Champion, 1784-1791; possibly experimental hard-paste porcelain; no examples known. (124)
Cartersville, Bartow County, Georgia
Gordy Pottery, c.1865-1900; stoneware, alkaline-glazed ware; no mark. (113)
Charleston, Charleston County, South Carolina
John Bartlam, c.1765-1771; white earthenware; no examples known. (1-19-25)
Chattanooga, Hamilton County, Tennessee
Montague Pottery, c.1875-1900; stoneware, some over Albany slip; no mark. (99)
Cleveland (Walkerville), Waite County, Georgia
Meaders Pottery, c.1830-1900; alkaline-glazed ware with distinctive pitted glaze, large jars; no mark; pottery at Leo, Ga., operated by same family. (22-60-121-126)
Columbus, Muscogee County, Georgia
J. M. Matthews, c.1880-1900; alkaline-glazed ware; no mark. (21-107)
Columbus, Hickman County, Kentucky
Schenk & Rocker, c.1870-1900; stoneware, some with Albany slip, brownware; no mark. (106)
——, c.1880-1890; same; no mark. (106)
Coosada, Bedford County, Alabama
McLean Pottery, c.1880-1900; brownware; no mark. (21)
Daisy, Hamilton County, Tennessee
C. L. Krager, 1870-1900; stoneware; no mark. (99)
Dent, Crawford County, Georgia
Beecham Pottery, c.1850-1900; three potteries operated by members of the family in 1900; alkaline-glazed ware; no mark. (21-81-121-125)
Edgefield, Edgefield County, South Carolina
——, c.1826; probably redware; no mark. (22)
Eldorado, Union County, Arkansas
——, c.1850-1860; stoneware; no mark. (22)

Galliards, Crawford County, Georgia
  Thomas Dickson, c.1870-1900; alkaline-glazed ware; no mark. (121)
  H. N. Long, c.1880-1900; same; no mark. (121)
  H. D. Marshall, c.1880-1900; same; no mark. (121)
Gillsville, Hall County, Georgia
  Hewell Pottery, c.1830-1900; stoneware; alkaline-glazed ware; no mark. (116-121)
  Halcombe Pottery, c.1830-1900; same; no mark. (121)
  Colbert Pottery, c.1870-1900; same; no mark. (121)
Grand Junction, Hardeman County, Tennessee
  ——, c.1890-1900; stoneware; no mark. (21)
Hart, Marion County, Mississippi
  ——, c.1859; stoneware; no mark. (22)
Hickman, Fulton County, Kentucky
  A. Cable, c.1859; redware, salt-glazed, or with black lead glaze; no mark. (22) Later at Sulphur Fork, Tenn. (22-100)
Hickory, Catawba County, North Carolina
  Hilton Pottery, c.1890-1900; stoneware; no mark; first potter at Hickory a Moravian, c.1780. (10-112)
Hopewell, Prince George County, Virginia
  ——, c.1880-1900; stoneware; tobacco pipes; no mark. (21)
Jamestown, James City County, Virginia
  ——, c.1610; probably redware; no examples known. (71-120)
Jugtown (near Sterrett), St. Clair County, Alabama
  ——, c.1890; probably redware. (121)
Jugtown (Thomasville), Hall County, Georgia
  Rogers Pottery, c.1830-1900; stoneware, alkaline-glazed ware; no mark. (81-121)
Jugtown, North Carolina (see Steeds)
* Kaolin, Mitchell County, South Carolina
  Southern Porcelain Co., 1856-1876; H. W. Farrar of Bennington and Jersey City, manager; bisque porcelain, etc., to 1862, then brownware; see p. 88; occasional mark is "S. P. Company, Kaolin, S. C." in shield, impressed. (1-12-25)

Knox Hill, Walton County, Florida
  Odom & Turnlee, c.1850-1860; stoneware; no mark. (123)
Lake Butler, Union, County, Florida
  H. F. York, c.1880-1900; redware; no mark. (123)
Leo, White County, Georgia
  Meaders Pottery, c.1890-1900; stoneware; alkaline-glazed ware;
    same family operated pottery at Cleveland, Ga., no mark.
    (10)
Lexington, Fayette County, Kentucky
  John Carty, Sr., c.1796-1845, redware; no mark. (122)
  Ward Mentelle, Sr., c.1796; redware; no mark; came from
    Gallipolis, O., later owned iron foundry. (122)
Lincolntown, Lincoln County, North Carolina
  T. Rhodes, c.1865-1900; stoneware, alkaline-glazed ware; no
    mark. (21)
Lizella, Grawford County, Georgia
  Middle Georgia Pottery, c.1870-1900; stoneware, alkaline
    glazed ware; no mark. (21-121)
Louisville, Jefferson County, Kentucky
  Lewis Pottery Co., 1829-1844; yellow-ware; whiteware; no mark;
    Vodrey and Frost came from Pittsburgh, Penna., as managers;
    Vodrey went to Troy, Ind., in 1830. (1-25-127)
  John and Frederick Hancock, c.1840; stoneware; no mark;
    John Hancock came from East Liverpool, O. (25)
  ——, c.1890; stoneware; no mark. (21)
Lynville, Graves County, Kentucky
  J. W. Pittman, c.1870-1900; brownware; no mark. (106)
Marietta, Cobb County, Georgia
  Franklin Pottery, c.1880-1900; stoneware, alkaline-glazed ware;
    no mark. (81-107-121)
Marshall, Mississippi
  ——, c.1854; stoneware; no mark. (21)
Mayfield, Graves County, Kentucky
  Morris Cooley and Robert A. Hale, c.1890-1900; brownware;
    no mark. (106)

Meansville, Upson County, Georgia
  Rogers Pottery, c.1850-1900; stoneware, alkaline-glazed ware; no mark. (107-121)
  Bishop Pottery, c.1850-1900; same; no mark. (121)
Milledgeville, Baldwin County, Georgia
  J. W. McMillan, 1867-1900; stoneware; no mark. (1-107)
Millville, Pickens County, Alabama
  ——, c.1880; brownware, probably redware; no mark. (21)
Nashville, Davidson County, Tennessee
  Harley Pottery, c.1875-1900; stoneware, brownware; no mark. (100)
  Nashville Art Pottery, c.1886; redware with brown glaze; no mark. (22)
Natchez, Adams County, Mississippi
  ——, c.1854; stoneware; no mark. (22)
New Orleans, Orleans County, Louisiana
  Hernandez & Saloy, Louisiana Porcelain Works, 1881-1890; hard-paste porcelain, small amount made, sold undecorated; imported French workmen and materials; no mark. (128)
Paducah, McCracken County, Kentucky
  A. J. Bauer, Paducah Pottery, c. 1886-1900; redware, brownware; no mark. (106)
Paris, Henry County, Tennessee
  Russell Pottery, c.1855-1900; stoneware, redware; no mark. (21-100)
Pegram, Colbert County, Alabama
  J. W. Williams, c.1890; stoneware, probably alkaline-glazed ware; no mark. (21)
Porter's Station, Henry County, Tennessee
  ——, c.1850-1860; stoneware; no mark. (22)
Pottertown, Calloway County, Kentucky
  ——, c.1888-1900; brownware; no mark. (22)
Richmond (Bybeetown), Madison County, Kentucky
  Bybee Pottery, 1865-1900; stoneware, some with Albany slip; no mark. (106)

Roberta, Crawford County, Georgia (see Dent)

Rodentown, De Kalb County, Alabama

——, c.1890; stoneware; no mark. (21)

Savannah, Chatham County, Georgia

Andrew Duché, c.1732-1750; redware; attempted production of whiteware; no examples known. (55)

Seagrove, Randall County, North Carolina

Cole Pottery, c.1890-1900; stoneware; no mark. (10)

Spring Hill, Hempstead County, Arkansas

——, c.1850-1860; stoneware; no mark. (22)

Steeds, Moore County, North Carolina

Peter Craven, c.1770, (1750?); Staffordshire potter; probably redware, possibly alkaline-glazed ware in approximation of white earthenware; no examples known. (109)

——, Craven, (son) c.1800; same, probably stoneware; no examples known. (109)

——, Craven (son of above), c.1830; same; no mark. (109)

Doris Craven (son of above), c.1866; stoneware, some alkaline-glazed ware; no mark. (10-35-54-109-112)

——, Craven (son of above), c.1900; same; no mark. (10-35-54-109)

James Fox, c.1860; same; no marks; later, with others of his family, joined the Cravens in the Jugtown Pottery. (10-35-54-109-112)

Stevens Pottery, Baldwin County, Georgia

Henry Stevens, 1861-c.1865; stoneware; no mark. (1-25-121)

W. C. and J. H. Stevens (sons), c.1865-1900; same, some brownware, flower-pots, ornamental pieces; no mark. (1-25-116-121)

* Strasburg, Shenandoah County, Virginia

Samuel Bell, 1843-1852, with brother Solomon; redware, slip covered, with bright mottled glazes. (20)

Samuel and Solomon Bell (son), 1852-1882; same, also stoneware; frequent mark is "S. Bell" or "Solomon Bell," with or without "Strasburg," impressed. (20)

S. Bell & Sons, 1882-1900; same; mark is "S. Bell & Sons" or "Bell" impressed. (20-127)

Samuel H. Sonner, 1870-1883; stoneware; mark is name impressed. (20)

J. S. Eberley, 1880-1900; redware as above, some unglazed, covered with rough cream slip; stoneware; mark is name and address, or, on stoneware, "Star Pottery" impressed. (20-127)

Lehew & Co., 1885-1900; stoneware; mark is name and address, impressed. (20)

L. D. Funkhouser, 1889-1900; same; mark is name and address, impressed. (20)

W. H. Christman, c.1890; same; no mark. (20)

W. B. Kenner, c.1890; same; no mark. (20)

Sulphur Fork, on Beaver Dam, Hardeman County, Tennessee

Adam Cable, 1869-1875; salt-glazed redware; no mark. (100)

Toone, Hardeman County, Tennessee

——, c.1880-1900; stoneware; no mark. (21)

Tuscaloosa, Tuscaloosa County, Alabama

Daniel Cribbs, c.1829-1860; stoneware; no mark; brother at Bedford, Ala. (22)

—— Cribbs (son), c.1860-1900; same, some over Albany slip; no mark. (22)

Waco, Madison County, Kentucky

D. Zittel & Son, c.1870-1900; stoneware, brownware; no mark. (106)

Wickliffe, Ballard County, Kentucky

Augustus Keppner, c.1880-1900; brownware; no mark. (106)

Wilmington Landing, Union County, Arkansas

——, c.1850-1860; stoneware; no mark. (22)

Winchester, Frederick County, Virginia

Peter Bell, 1824-1845; redware, stoneware after 1833; no mark; moved from Hagerstown, Md. (20)

Anthony W. Baecher, 1860-1889; redware, some with marbled glazes; no mark. (20)

Wilson's Landing, Dinwiddie County, Virginia

Moro Phillips, 1850-1858; stoneware; no mark; moved to Philadelphia. (1-25)

Winston-Salem, Forsythe County, North Carolina

Moravian Pottery, 1766-c.1830; redware, slip-decorated and plain; no mark; see p. 84. (61)

Walkerville, Georgia (see Cleveland)

Water Valley, Graves County, Kentucky

Water Valley Pottery Co., c.1870-1900; brownware; no mark. (106)

Wilkesboro, Wilkes County, North Carolina

Calvin Cowles, c.1880-1900; stoneware, alkaline-glazed ware; no mark. (21)

(Exact Location Unknown)

Dennis White and Morgan Jones, Westmoreland County, Virginia, c.1677; probably redware; no examples known. (71)

W. D. Preston, Autaga County, Alabama, 1820-1836; probably redware. (22)

Bird Bros., Dallas Co., Ark., 1843-1881; also other owners; stoneware; no mark. (22)

——, Dallas Co., Ark., (near Grant Co. line), c.1850-1881; stone-ware; no mark. (22)

Captain Bonner, Calloway County, Kentucky, c.1856; stoneware; no mark. (22)

C. K. Oliver, Tuscaloosa County, Alabama, c.1856-1862; stoneware; no mark. (22)

BIBLIOGRAPHY

1.   Barber, E. A., *Pottery and Porcelain of the United States,* New York, 1893, 1901, 1909

2.   Barber, E. A., *Salt-Glazed Pottery of Germany, Flanders, England and the United States,* New York, 1907

3.   Barber, E. A., *Lead-Glazed Pottery,* New York, 1909

4.   Barber, E. A., *Historical Sketch of the Greenpoint Works of Charles Cartlidge,* pp. 59, Indianapolis, 1895

5.   Barber, E. A. *Tulip-Ware of Pennsylvania,* Philadelphia, 1903

6.   Belknap, Henry W., *Artists and Craftsmen of Essex County, Massachusetts,* Salem, 1931

7.   Bishop, J., *History of American Manufacturers, 1608-1850.* 2 vols. Philadelphia, 1861-64

8.   Browne, C. A., Williams Haynes and L. W. Bass, *Our Chemical Heritage,* New York, American Chemical Society, 1935

9.   Clark, J. M., *The Swiss Influence in the Early Pennsylvania Slip-Decorated Majolica,* Albany, 1908.

10.   Eaton, Allen C., *Handicrafts of the Southern Highlanders,* New York, 1937

11.   Hough, Walter, *Early Pottery at Morgantown, West Virginia,* (in Annual Report of The Smithsonian Institution, Washington, 1899)

12.   Jervis, W. P., *Encyclopaedia of Ceramics,* New York, (1902)

13.   Jervis, W. P., *Rough Notes on Pottery,* New York, 1896

14.   Jervis, W. P., *A Pottery Primer,* New York, 1911

15.   Mason, George C., *The Application of Art to Manufacture,* New York, 1858

16.   Neaton, ... , *On the Origin, Progressive Improve-*

ment and Present State of the Manufacture of Porcelain and Glass, Philadelphia, 1846

17. Nichols, George Ward, *Pottery, How It Is Made,* New York, 1879

18. Pitkin, Albert Hastings, *Early American Folk Pottery,* Hartford, 1918

19. Prime, Alfred Coxe, *The Arts and Crafts in Philadelphia, Maryland and South Carolina, 1721-1775*

20. Rice, A. H. and J. B. Stout, *The Pottery of the Shenandoah,* New York, 1929

21. Ries, Heinrich, *Clays of the United States East of the Mississippi,* Washington, U. S. Geol. Survey, 1903

22. Ries, Heinrich, *History of the American Clay Industries,* New York, 1909.

23. Sherman, F. F., *Early Connecticut Artists and Craftsmen,* New York, 1925

23a. Smith, *Mr. & Mrs. Chetwood,* Rogers Groups, Boston, 1934

24. Spargo, John, *The Potters and Pottery of Bennington,* New York, 1926

25. Spargo, John, *Early American Pottery and China,* New York, 1926

25a. Spargo, John, *The A. B. C. of Bennington Pottery Wares,* Bennington, 1938

26. Stout, W. H., *History of the Clay Industry of Ohio,* (in *Coal Formation Clays of Ohio,* Ohio Geological Survey, Columbus, 1923)

27. Treadwell, John H., *Manual of Pottery and Porcelain for American Collectors.*

28. Weygandt, Cornelius, *The Red Hills,* Philadelphia, 1929

29. Weygandt, Cornelius, *The White Hills,* New York, 1934

30. Young, Jennie G., *The Ceramic Art,* New York, 1873

Periodical Articles

31. Abraham, Evelyn, "The Pottery of Greensboro and New Geneva," *The Antiquarian,* September, 1931

32. Armstrong, H. R., "The Norwich Pottery Works," *Antiques,* October, 1923

33. Bacheler, O. L., and H. B. Camp, "Craftsmen of the Old School," "Omar Khayyam Pottery," *International Studio,* October, 1923

34. Bowles, Ella S., "Pioneer Pottery," *House Beautiful,* December, 1926

35. Breeze, Jessie Martin, "Jugtown, North Carolina," *Country Life,* October, 1922

36. Burbank, Leonard F., "Lyndeboro Pottery," *Antiques,* February, 1928

37. Butler, L. L., "Bennington Pottery," *Mentor,* September, 1927

38. Buxton, Bessie W., "The Making of a Flower-Pot," *Antiques,* August, 1925

39. Camehl, Ada Walker, A. Mehwaldt, "Pioneer Potter," *Antiques,* September, 1922

40. Carrick, Alice Van Leer, "Mugs and Jugs," *Country Life,* June, 1922

41. Carrick, Alice Van Leer, "Orchard Pottery," *Country Life,* January, 1921

42. Carrick, Alice Van Leer, "Bennington Pottery Owned by Mr. Lafountain," *House Beautiful,* January, 1930.

43. Chandler, L. Reginald, "The Methods of the Early American Potters," *Antiques,* April, 1924

44. Connor, John O., "The Keene Pottery," *Antiques,* February, 1924

45. Cook, Albert, "Unmarked Bennington Pitchers," *Antiques,* December, 1924

46. Cook, Chas. D., "Early Rhode Island Pottery," *Antiques,* January, 1931

47. Cooper, N., "Early American Pottery Whistles," *House Beautiful,* January, 1929

48. Cornelius, Charles O., "Early American Household Pottery," *House and Garden,* April, 1921

49. Dyer, W. A., "Stoneware for the Collector," *Arts and Decorations,* July, 1922

50. Dyer, W. A., "Early New England Pottery," *Antiques,* June, 1922

51. Eberlein, H. D., Tucker, "Craftsman in China," *Country Life,* September, 1929

52. Edson, M. B., "Some Significant American Pottery," *Arts and Decoration,* June, 1925

53. Gates, Burton N., "Frederick Mear, Potter," *Antiques,* January, 1924

54. Goldsmith, Margaret M., "Jugtown Pottery," *House Beautiful,* October, 1922

55. Goyle, G. A. R., "The First Porcelain Makers in America," *Chronicle* of the Early American Industries Association, November-December, 1934

56. Green, Charles W., "Some Bennington Pitchers," *Antiques,* May, 1930

57. Green, Charles W., "Pond Lily Pitchers of Bennington," *Antiques,* June, 1932

57a. Green, Charles W., "Color used in Bennington Parian," *The American Collector,* April, 1938

58. Hornor, William S., "The Tucker and Hemphill Porcelain Works," *Antiques,* June, 1928

59. Keyes, Homer Eaton, "Spatter," *Antiques,* April, 1930

60. Keyes, Homer Eaton, "Perplexities in Pottery," *Antiques,* February, 1933

60a. Keyes, Homer Eaton, "Bellarmine or Bartmann Jugs," *Antiques,* June, 1938

61. Kindig, Joe, Jr., "A Note on Early North Carolina Pottery," *Antiques,* June, 1933

62. Knittle, Rhea M., "Henry McQuate, Pennsylvania Potter," *Antiques,* November, 1928

63. Knittle, Rhea M., "Muskingum County, Ohio Potters," *Antiques,* July, 1924

64. Knittle, Rhea M., "Ohio Pottery Jars and Jugs," *Antiques,* October, 1933

65. Moore, R. C. "The Mountain Pottery of North Carolina," *Ceramic Age*, May, 1929

66. Minton, Leroy H., "New Jersey's Part in the Ceramic History of America," *The Ceramist*, Winter, 1922-23

67. Norton, F. H., "The Crafts Pottery at Nashua, N. H.," *Antiques*, Vol. 26

68. Norton, F. H., "The Exeter Pottery," *Antiques*, Vol. 22

69. Norton, F. H., and V. S. Duplin, Jr., "The Osborne Pottery at Gonic, N. H.," *Antiques*, November, 1935,-

70. Ormsbee, Thomas H., "Poughkeepsie Was Also a Jugtown," *The American Collector*, February, 1936

71. Peterson, Chas. F., "Some Recent Discoveries at Jamestown," *Antiques*, May, 1936

72. Ramsay, John, "Early American Pottery, A Resume," *Antiques*, October, 1931

73. Raymond, W. Oakley, "The Remney Family, American Potters," *Antiques*, June, 1937, July, 1938

73a. Raymond, W. Oakley, "Unmarked New York Pottery, Crolius and Remney," *The Antiquarian*, January, 1930

74. Purdy, Ross C., "William H. Bloor," *Bulletin* of the American Ceramic Society, January, 1937

75. Reifstahl, H., "Tucker China," *Country Life*, February, 1922

76. Reinert, Guy F., "The Last Pennsylvania Folk Potter," *The American Collector*, May 2, 1935

77. Reinert, Guy F., "Slip-Decorated Pottery of the Pennsylvania Germans," *The American-German Review*, March, 1936

78. Reinert, Guy F., "Pennsylvania German Potteries of Berks County," *Historical Review* of Berks County, January, 1937

79. Sammas, Mrs. Thomas, "The Pottery at Huntington, Long Island," *Antiques*, April, 1923

80. Smith, H. L., Cortland County, New York, Pottery, *Ceramic Age*, October, 1935

81. Smith, Richard W., "A Visit to Jugtown," *Forestry-Geological Review*, March, 1934

82. Sparge, John, "The Facts About Bennington—1. The Stoneware of the Nortons," *Antiques*, June, 1924

83. Sparge, John, "The Facts About Bennington—II. The Work of C. W. Fenton," *Antiques*, June, 1924

84. Sparge, John, "Burlington Pottery," *Antiques*, November, 1924

85. Stillwell, John E., "Crolius Ware and Its Maker," New York Historical Society *Quarterly Bulletin*, July, 1926

86. Stowe, Charles Messer, "Pennsylvania Slipware," *The Antiquarian*, November, 1929

86a. Stowe, Charles Messer, "The Deacon Potter of Greenwich," *The Antiquarian*, March, 1930

87. Swann, Mabel M., "The Dedham Pottery," *Antiques*, August, 1926

88. Teall, Gardiner, "Irish and American Belleek," *House and Garden*, June, 1925

89. Teall, Gardiner, "Parian Ware," *House and Garden*, November, 1923

90. Varick, Vernon, "The First and Second Potteries at Norwich, Conn., *Hobbies*, May, 1935

91. Vaughn, W., "Crolius and Early American Stoneware," *International Studio*, August, 1927

92. Watkins, Lura Woodside, "The Stoneware of South Ashfield, Massachusetts," *Antiques*, September, 1934

93. Willis, Katherine, "Early New York Pottery," *Country Life*, September, 1928

94. Willis, Katherine, "New Uses for Old Pottery," *Country Life*, September, 1929

94a. Willis, Katherine, "Founders of Early American Pottery," *The Antiquarian*, August, 1928

95. Winchester, Alice, "Footnote to Tucker History," *Antiques*, October, 1936

96. Wolfe. J, W., "Morgantown Pottery," *School Arts*, May, 1928

97. Wood, Ruth, "Home Memories of the Fentons," *Antiques*, September, 1925

98. Woodhouse, Samuel G., Jr., "The First Philadelphia Porcelain," *Antiques*, October, 1933

99. Whitlach, Geo. I., "Ceramics of East Tennessee," *Ceramic Age*, 1936

100. Whitlach, Geo. I., "Ceramic Industries of Middle and West Tennessee," *Ceramic Age*, 1936

Geological Survey Reports

101. Pennsylvania Geologic Survey, *Report* 88, 1911

102. Indiana Geological Survey, *First Annual Report*, 1861, *Second*, 1870, *Twelfth*, 1882, *Tweentieth*, 1895

103. West Virginia Geological Survey, *Report*, 1906

104. Iowa Geological Survey, *Report*, 1892-1895

105. Illinois Geological Survey, Vols. L-Vi, 1866-1875

106. Kentucky Geological Survey, *Bulletin*, No. 6, 1905

107. Georgia Geological Survey, *Bulletin*, 6-A, *Bulletin*, 18, *Bulletin*, 45

108. United States Geological Survey, *Bulletin*, 286

Personal Letters

109. Mr. Jaques Busbee
110. Mrs. Bessie W. Buxby
111. Mr. James Dronenburg
112. Professor A. F. Greaves-Walker
113. Mr. W. T. B. Gordy
114. Mr. Eugene Houghton
115. Mrs. Rea Mansfield Knittle
116. Mr. J. M. Mallory
117. Miss Anna Nixon
118. Professor F. H. Norton
119. Mr. Guy F. Reinert

120. Mr. Walter J. Sparks
121. Mr. Richard W. Smith
122. Mr. C. R. Staples
123. Mr. T. W. Van Huyning
124. Miss Mabel Weber
125. Dr. Cornelius Weygandt
126. Mr. George L. Whitlach
127. Marked or authenticated examples of pottery (known to the writer, not mentioned above, and quoted when no other information is available, or to give markers marks or local types)
128. Local histories, directories, newspapers, etc., (quoted when no other information is available, or to add to that given above)

American Porcelain Co., Gloucester, N. J.
(parian)

A. M. P. Co.
(impressed)

American Pottery Co., Jersey City, N. J.
(white earthenware)

Impressed

Printed

also same with scalloped circle and without circle

American Pottery Manufacturing co.,
    Jersey City
(white earthenware, brown ware)

Printed

Anchor Pottery Co., Trenton
(white granite)

ANCHOR POTTERY
J. E. N.
(printed)

Printed

252

Anna Pottery, —— Lowell, Ill.
(redware-stoneware)

Armstrong & Wentworth, Norwich, Conn.
(stoneware)

A. & W.
or
ARMSTRONG & WENTWORTH
NORWICH, CONN.
(impressed)

Ashfield (see Hastings & Belding)

Baum, J. H., Wellsville, O.
(white granite)

Printed

Bell, John, Waynesboro, Penna.
(redware)

JOHN BELL
or
JOHN BELL
WAYNESBORO, PA.
(impressed)

Bell, John W., Waynesboro, Penna.
(redware)

JOHN W. BELL
or
JOHN W. BELL
WAYNESBORO, PENNA.
(impressed)

Bell, Joseph, Putnam, O.
(stoneware)

JOSEPH BELL
(impressed)

Bell, Samuel, Strasburg, Va.
(redware)

S. BELL
(impressed)

Bell, Samuel and Solomon, Strasburg, Va.
(redware)

S. BELL
STRASBURG, VA.
(or)
SOLOMON BELL
STRASBURG, VA.
(impressed)

Bell, S. & Sons, Strasburg, Va.
(redware)

BELL
(or)
S. BELL & SONS
(impressed)

Bell, Upton, Waynesboro, Penna.
(redware)

UPTON BELL
WAYNESBORO, PENNA.
(impressed)

Beech, Ralph B., Philadelphia, Penna.
(porcelain)

RALPH B. BEECH
Patented Jan. 3, 1851
KENSINGTON, PA.
(impressed)

253

Beerbauer & Co., L. S., Elizabeth, N. J.
(Rockingham, etc.)

see #4

Impressed

Bennett, Edwin, Baltimore, Md.
(Rockingham, Majolica, white earthenware)

E. B.
(impressed)

Printed

Bennett, E. & W., Baltimore, Md.
(same)

E. & W. BENNETT
CANTON AVE.
BALTIMORE, MARYLAND
(impressed)
or above

254

Bennett, James S., Moultonboro, N. H.
(redware)

J. S. BENNETT
(impressed)

Blair, Sylvester, Cortland, N. Y.
(stoneware)

BLAIR
CORTLAND, N. Y.
(impressed)

Bonin & Morris, Philadelphia, Pa.
(white earthenware)

(script, inscribed under glaze)

Boss Bros., Akron, O.
(stoneware)

BOSS BROS.
MIDDLEBURY,
OHIO
(impressed)

Boughner, Alexander, Greensboro, Pa.
(stoneware)

ALEXANDER BOUGHNER
GREENSBORO
PA.
(impressed)

Boughner, A. & W., Greensboro, Pa.
(stoneware)

A. & W. BOUGHNER,
GREENSBORO
PA.
(impressed or stencilled in blue)

Burgess & Campbell, Trenton, N. J.
(white granite)

Printed

Burley & Winters, Crooksville, O.
(brownware)

Impressed

Burroughs & Mountfort, Trenton, N. J.
(white granite)

B & M Co
royal china

Printed

Butler, A. J. & Co., New Brunswick, N. J.
(stoneware)

A. J. BUTLER & CO.
NEW BRUNSWICK,
N. J.
(impressed)

Bullock, W., Roseville, O.
(stoneware)

W. BULLOCK,
ROSEVILLE, O.
(impressed)

Cadmus, A., South Amboy, N. J.
(Rockingham)

A. CADMUS
SO. AMBOY
N. J.
(impressed)

Caire, Jacob, Poughkeepsie, N. Y.
(stoneware)

JACOB CAIRE
(impressed)

Caire, John B., Poughkeepsie, N. Y.
(stoneware)

JOHN B. CAIRE
(impressed)

Carr, James, South Amboy, N. J.
(yellow-ware and Rockingham)

SWAN HILL POTTERY
(impressed)

256

Carr, James, New York
(white granite)

Printed

Carr & Morrison, New York
(white granite)

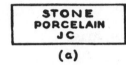

(a)

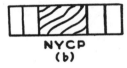

NYCP
(b)

Printed

Camp & Thompson, Akron, O.
(brownware, stoneware)

CAMP & THOMPSON,
(impressed)

Ceramic Art Co., Trenton
(porcelain)

Printed

Chelsea China Co., New Cumberland,
  W. Va.
  (white granite)

WHITE GRANITE

Printed

——, Charlestown, Mass.
(stoneware)

CHARLESTOWN
(impressed)

Chace, L. & B.C., Somerset, Mass.
(redware)

L. & B. C. CHACE
SOMERSET, MASS.
(impressed)

Chollar & Bennett, Homer, N. Y.
(stoneware)

CHOLLAR & BENNETT
HOMER, N. Y.
(impressed)

Chollar & Darby, Homer, N. Y.
(stoneware)

CHOLLAR & DARBY
HOMER, N. Y.
(impressed)

Clark, Nathan, Athens, Lyons and
  Mt. Morris, N. Y.
  (stoneware)

NATHAN CLARK
(or)
NATHAN CLARK
LYONS,
N. Y.
(impressed)

Clark & Fox, Athens, N. Y.
(stoneware)

CLARK & FOX
(impressed)

Commeraw, New York
(stoneware)

COMMERAW
(or)
CORLEARS HOOK
(impressed)

Corlear's Hook, New York

see above

Crafts, Caleb, Portland, Me.
(stoneware)

CALEB CRAFTS
(impressed)

Crafts, Martin, Nashua, N. H.
(stoneware)

MARTIN CRAFTS
NASHUA
(or)
T. CRAFTS & SON
NASHUA
(impressed)

Crafts, Thomas And Elbridge, Whateley, Mass.
(stoneware)

T. CRAFTS & SON
WHATELY
MASS.
(impressed)

Crolius, John, New York
(stoneware)

I. C.
(impressed)

Crolius, Clarkson I, New York
(stoneware)

C. CROLIUS
MANHATTAN WELLS
N. Y.
(impressed)

Crolius, Clarkson II, New York
(stoneware)

C. CROLIUS
MANUFACTURER
NEW YORK

Crown Pottery Co., Evansville, Ind.
(white granite)

Printed

Cushman, Paul, Albany, N. Y.
(stoneware)

PAUL CUSHMAN
(impressed)

Dalton Pottery

see Houghton

Dick, Jacob, Tuscarawas County, O.
(stoneware)

JACOB DICK
TUSCARAWAS CO.
OHIO
(impressed)

Dipple, A. G. Curtin, Lewisburg, Pa.
(stoneware)

A. G. C. DIPPLE
LEWISBURG, PA.
(impressed)

Dry, John, Dryville, Pa.
Dry Bros., Dryville, Pa.
(redware)

D.
or
D. Dry
(inscribed)

Eagle Pottery-

see Hamilton

Eberley, J. S., Strasburg, Va.
(redware and stoneware)

J. S. EBERLEY
STRASBURG,
VA.
(or)

259

(Eberley)

East Lake Pottery

Edmunds, Barnabas & Co., Charlestown, Mass.
(stoneware)

Faience Manufacturing Co., New York
(whiteware)

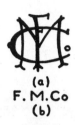

(a)

F. M.Co

(b)

Printed

Fenton, C. W., Bennington, Vt.
(brownware, stoneware)

Printed

Fenton, L. W., St. Johnsbury, Vt.
(stoneware)

Fenton & Hancock, St. Johnsbury, Vt.
(stoneware)

Field, L. F., Utica, N. Y.
(stoneware)

Fisher, J., Hartford, Conn.
(stoneware)

STAR POTTERY
(impressed)

see Hamlyn

BARNABAS EDMUNDS & CO.
CHARLESTOWN, MASS.
(impressed)

L. W. FENTON
ST. JOHNSBURY
VT.
(impressed)

FENTON & HANCOCK
ST. JOHNSBURY
VT.
(impressed)

L. F. FIELD
UTICA
N. Y.
(impressed)

J. FISHER
(impressed)

Figley, Joseph, Newport, O.
(stoneware)

J. FIGLEY
(impressed)

Franklin Pottery, Franklin, O.
(white earthenware, porcelain)

Impressed

Fulper Bros., Flemington, N. J.
(stoneware)

FULPER BROS.
FLEMINGTON, N. J.
(impressed)

Funkhouser, L. D., Strasburg, Va.
(stoneware)

L. D. FUNKHOUSER
STRASBURG
VA.
(impressed)

Gerlach, C., ———, Penna.
(redware)

C. Gerlach
(inscribed)

Goodale, Daniel, Hartford, Conn.
(stoneware)

D. GOODALE
(impressed)

Goodwin Bros., East Liverpool, O.
(white granite)

Printed

Goodwin & Webster, Hartford, Conn.
(stoneware)

GOODWIN & WEBSTER
(impressed)

Greenwood Pottery

see Stephans & Tams

Griffin, Smith & Hill, Phoenixville, Pa.
(majolica)

ETRUSCAN MAJOLICA

Impressed

Hall, E.,   see W. P. Harris

Hamilton, Clem, Tuscarawas, O.   CLEM HAMILTON
(brownware, stoneware)   (impressed)

Hamilton, James, Greensboro, Pa.   JAMES HAMILTON
(stoneware)   GREENSBORO
                                                            PA.
                                                            (or)
                                                   EAGLE POTTERY
                                                   GREENSBORO,
                                                            PA.,
                                               (impressed or stenciled
                                                       in blue)

Hamilton & Jones, Greensboro, Pa.   HAMILTON & JONES
(stoneware)   GREENSBORO,
                                                            PA.
                                               (impressed or stenciled
                                                       in blue)

Hamlyn, George, Bridgeton, N. J.   EAST LAKE POTTERY
(stoneware)   BRIDGETON, N. J.
                                                      (impressed)

Harker Pottery Co., East Liverpool, O.
(white granite)

Printed

262

Harker, Taylor & Co., East Liverpool, O.
(Rockingham)

Raised Relief

Harris, Thomas, Cuyahoga Falls, O.
(stoneware)

THOMAS HARRIS
(impressed)

Harris, W. P., Newton Township, Tuscarawas Co., O.
(stoneware)

E. HALL
NEWTON TOWNSHIP
TUSCARAWAS CO.,
O.

Hastings & Belding, Ashfield, Mass.
(stoneware)

HASTINGS & BELDING
ASHFIELD
MASS.
(or)
ASHFIELD
(impressed)

Haxtun & Co., Fort Edward, N. Y.
(stoneware)

HAXTUN & CO.
FORT EDWARD
N. Y.
(impressed)

Haynes, D. F. & Co., Baltimore, Md.
Haynes, Bennett & Co.,
(majolica, Parian, white earthenware)

Printed

263

Headman, Charles, Rock Hill, Pa.
(redware)

Chas. Headman
(or)
C. H.
(inscribed)

Heighshoe, S. E., Somerset, O.
(brownware)

S. E. HEIGHSHOE
SOMERSET
O.
(impressed)

Hemphill, Joseph, Philadelphia, Pa.
(porcelain)

Jos. Hemphill,
Philadelphia
or
Jos. Hemphill
Philad.
(painted in red, etc.)

Henderson, D. & J., Jersey City, N. J.
(Rockingham, stoneware)

Impressed

Hewett, Isaac, Prices Landing, Pa.
(stoneware)

ISAAC HEWETT
EXCELSIOR WORKS
PRICES LANDING
PENNA.
(stenciled in blue)

Higgins, A. D., Cleveland, O.
(stoneware)

A. D. HIGGINS
CLEVELAND
OHIO
(impressed)

Hopkins, John, Seneca Co., O.
(stoneware)

JOHN HOPKINS
(impressed)

Houghton, E., Dalton, O.
(brownware)

DALTON POTTERY
(impressed)

Huebner, George, Vincent, Pa.
(redware)

C ん

Inscribed

International Pottery- see Burgess & Campbell

Jeffords, W. E. & Co., Philadelphia, Pa.
(white earthenware)

Printed

Jones, Evans B., Pittston, Pa.
(stoneware)

EVAN B. JONES
PITTSTON
PENNA.
(impressed)

Kelly, Peter, Philadelphia, Pa.
(redware)

PETER KELLY
(impressed)

Kline, Phillip, Carversville, Pa.
(redware)

Phillip Kline
(inscribed)

Klinker, Christian, Bucksville, Pa.
(redware)

C. K.
(inscribed)

Knowles, Taylor & Knowles, East Liverpool, O.
(white earthenware, porcelain)

Printed

STONE CHINA
K.T. & K.

Printed

Krumeich, B. J., Newark, N. J.
(stoneware)

B. J. KRUMEICH
NEWARK
N. J.
(impressed)

Lathrop, Charles, Norwich, Conn.
(redware)

NORWICH
(impressed)

Laughlin, Homer
Laughlin Bros., East Liverpool, O.
(white granite)

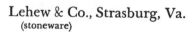

Printed

Lehew & Co., Strasburg, Va.
(stoneware)

LEHEW & CO.
STRASBURG, VA.
(impressed)

Lehman, Lewis, Poughkeepsie, N. Y.
(stoneware)

LEWIS LEHMAN
(impressed)

Lehman & Rudinger, Poughkeepsie, N. Y.
(stoneware)

LEHMAN & RUDINGER
(impressed)

Lewis, Henry, Huntington, L. I.
(redware)

HENRY LEWIS
(impressed)

Lewis & Lewis, Huntington, L. I.
(redware)

LEWIS & LEWIS
(impressed)

Lewis & Gardner, Huntington, L. I.
(redware)

LEWIS & GARDNER
(impressed)

Link, Christian, Stonetown, Pa.
(stoneware)

C. LINK
(or)
C. LINK
EXETER
(or)
CHRISTIAN LINK
STONETOWN
(impressed)

Lyman, Fenton & Co., Bennington, Vt.

Lyman Fenton & Co
Fenton's
ENAMEL
PATENTED 1849
BENNINGTON
VT.

Printed

Madden, J. M., Rondout, N. Y.
(stoneware)

J. M. MADDEN
RONDOUT
N. Y.
(impressed)

Maddock, Thomas & Co., Trenton, N. J.
(white granite)

T.M. & S.

Printed

Mann, John, Rahway, N. Y.
(stoneware)

JOHN MANN
RAHWAY
N. J.
(impressed)

Markell, Immon & Co., Akron, O.
(stoneware)

MARKELL, IMMON & CO.
AKRON
O.
(impressed)

Marteen, W., ——, Penna.
(redware)

W. MARTEEN
(impressed)

Mason & Russel, Cortland, N. Y.
(stoneware)

MASON & RUSSEL
CORTLAND
N. Y.
(impressed)

Mayer Pottery Co., Beaver Falls, Pa.
(white granite)

Printed

Mayers, W. S., Roseville, O.
(stoneware)

W. S. MAYERS
ROSEVILLE
OHIO
(stencilled in blue)

McCarthy Bros., Somerset, Mass.
(stoneware)

McCARTHY BROS.
SOMERSET
MASS.
(impressed)

McNichel, D. E., Pottery Co., East
Liverpool, O.
(white granite)

Printed

Mead, I. M. & Co., Atwater, O.
(stoneware)

I. MEAD
(or)
I. MEAD
PORTAGE CO.
OHIO
(or)
I. M. MEAD & CO.
(or)
I. M. MEAD & CO.
PORTAGE CO.
OHIO
(impressed)

Mear, Frederich, Boston, Mass.
(Rockingham)

FREDERICK MEAR
(impressed)

Medingter, Jacob, Neiffer, Penna.
(redware)

Jacob Medinger
(inscribed)

Mellick, H. H., Roseville, O.
(stoneware)

H. H. MELLICK
ROSEVILLE
OHIO
(impressed)

Mercer Pottery Co., Trenton, N. J.
(white earthenware)

IRON STONE
CHINA

IRON STONE CHINA
MERCER POTTERY Co.

Printed

Mercer, Henry C., Doylestown, Pa.
(tiles, redware)

Impressed

Merrill, Edwin H., Springfield, O.
(stoneware)

E. H. MERRILL
SPRINGFIELD
O.
(impressed)

Miller, Solomon, (John Bell Pottery) Waynesboro, Pa.
(redware)

Solomon Bell
(inscribed)

Millington, Astbury & Poulson, Trenton, N. J.
(white earthenware)

Impressed

Miner, William, Symmes Creek, O.
(stoneware)

MINER
(impressed)

Morris & Willmore, Trenton, N. J.
(porcelain)

Inscribed   Printed

Moses, John & Sons, Trenton, N. J.
(white earthenware)

Printed

Morgan, D., New York, N. Y.
(stoneware)

Myers & Hall, Mogadore, O.
(stoneware)

D. MORGAN
(impressed)

MYERS & HALL
MOGADORE
(impressed)

New England Pottery Co., Boston, Mass.
(whiteware, art ware, porceltain)

RIETI

Printed

Nichols & Boynton, Burlington, Vt. (stoneware)	NICHOLS & BOYNTON (impressed)
Nichols & Alford, Burlington, Vt. (stoneware)	NICHOLS & ALFORD MANUFACTURERS 1854 BURLINGTON, VT
Norton, Luman, Bennington, Vt. (stoneware)	L. NORTON & CO. BENNINGTON VT. (impressed)
Norton, L. & Son, Bennington, Vt. (stoneware)	L. NORTON & SON BENNINGTON VT. (impressed)
Julius Norton, Bennington, Vt. (stoneware)	J. NORTON BENNINGTON VT. (or) J. NORTON EAST BENNINGTON VT. (or)

Norton & Fenton, Bennington, Vt.
(stoneware, Rockingham)

JULIUS NORTON
BENNINGTON
VT.
(or)
JULIUS NORTON
EAST BENNINGTON
VT.
(impressed)

NORTON & FENTON
BENNINGTON
VT.
(or)
NORTON & FENTON
EAST BENNINGTON
VT.
(impressed)

Impressed

Norton, J. & E., Bennington, Vt.
(stoneware)

J. & E. NORTON
BENNINGTON
VT.
(impressed)

Norton, J. & E. & Co., Bennington, Vt.
(stoneware)

J. & E. NORTON & CO.
BENNINGTON
VT.
(impressed)

Norton, E. & L. P., Bennington, Vt.
(stoneware)

E. & L. P. NORTON
BENNINGTON
VT.
(impressed)

Norton, E., Bennington, Vt.
(stoneware)

E. NORTON
BENNINGTON
VT.
(impressed)

Norton, Edward & Co., Bennington, Vt.
(stoneware)

EDWARD NORTON & CO.
BENNINGTON
VT.
(impressed)

Norwich, Conn.

see Lathrop

273

Ohio Valley China Co., Wheeling, W. Va.
(white earthenware)

Printed

Onondaga China Co., Syracuse, N. Y.
(white earthenware)

O.P.Co.
CHINA

O.P.Co.
SYRACUSE
CHINA

IMPERIAL
GEDDO

CHINA
O.P.Co.

Printed

Orcutt, Guilford & Co., Ashfield, Mass.
(stoneware)

ORCUTT, GUILDFORD & CO.
ASHFIELD
MASS.
(or)
ORCUTT, BELDING & CO.
ASHFIELD
MASS.
(or)
WALTER ORCUTT & CO.
ASHFIELD
MASS.
(impressed)

Orcutt, Humiston & Co., Troy, N. Y.
(stoneware)

ORCUTT, HUMISTON & CO.
TROY, N. Y.
(impressed)

Orcutt & Thompson, Poughkeepsie,
N. Y.
(stoneware)

ORCUTT & THOMPSON
POUGHKEEPSIE
N. Y.

Ott & Brewer, Trenton, N. J.
(porcelain)

Printed

Paul, Samuel, ———, Penna.
(redware)

Samuel Paul
(inscribed)

Pauline Pottery, Edgarton, Wisc.
(art ware)

Impressed

Peoria Pottery Co., Peoria, Ill.
(white granite, brownware)

**PEORIA
ILLINOIS**
(impressed)

Printed

275

Pioneer Pottery Co., Wellsville, O.
(white granite)

Printed

Pfaltzgraff Pottery, York, Penna. (stoneware)	PFALTZGRAFF POTTERY (impressed)
Price, Xerxes, Sayreville, N. J. (stoneware)	XERXES PRICE ROUNDABOUT (or) X. P. (impressed)
Purdy, Solomon, Atwater, O. (stoneware)	S. PURDY (or) S. PURDY PORTAGE CO. O. (or) S. PURDY ATWATER (impressed)
Pruden, John, Elizabeth, N. J. (stoneware)	JOHN PRUDEN ELIZABETH N. J. (impressed)
Quigley, S., Cincinnati, O. (brownware)	S. QUIGLEY FRANKLIN FACTORY CINCINNATI O.
Read, Thomas, Newport, O. (stoneware)	T. READ (or) T. READ TUSCARAWAS CO. (impressed)
Remney, John, New York (stoneware)	J. R. (impressed)
Remney, Richard C., Philadelphia, Pa. (stoneware)	R. C. R. (impressed)
Rice, Prosper, Putnam, O. (stoneware)	P. RICE (impressed)

276

Richey & Hamilton, Palatine, W. Va.
(stoneware)

RICHEY & HAMILTON
PALATINE, W. VA.
(stenciled in blue)

Rieti

see New England Pottery

Risley, Sidney, Norwich, Conn.
(stoneware)

SIDNEY RISLEY
NORWICH
CONN.
(impressed)

Robertson, James & Son, Chelsea, Mass.
(art ware)

ROBERTSON & SONS
CHELSEA KERAMIC
ART WORKS
C.K.A.W.
(impressed)

Impressed or Printed

Rogers, John, New York, N.Y.
(redware and Parian figures)

JOHN ROGERS
(impressed)

Rookwood Pottery, Cincinnati, O.
(art ware)

277

Routson, S., Doylestown, O.
(brownware)

S. ROUTSON
(impressed)

Roudebuth, Henry, Montgomery Co.,
Penna.
(redware)

H. R.
(inscribed)

Rouse & Turner, Jersey City, N.J.
(white granite)

R.&T.

Printed

Rudinger & Caire, Poughkeepsie, N. Y.
(stoneware)

RUDINGER & CAIRE
POUGHKEEPSIE, N. Y.
(impressed)

Salamander Works, New York, N. Y.
(Rockingham)

Impressed

Scholl, Michael, Tylersport, Penna.
(redware)

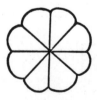

Impressed

278

Sebring Pottery Co., East Liverpool, O.

SEBRING'S
SEMI-VITREOUS
PORCELAIN

Printed

Senefelder, Daniel P., Reading, Penna.
(stoneware)

DANIEL P. SENEFELDER
READING, PENNA.

Impressed

Seymour, Israel, Troy, N. Y. (stoneware)	ISRAEL SEYMOUR (impressed)
Seymour & Stedman, Ravenna, O. (stoneware)	SEYMOUR & STEDMAN RAVENNA O. (impressed)
Shepley & Smith, West Troy, N.Y. (stoneware)	SHEPLEY & SMITH WEST TROY N. Y. (impressed)
Singer, Simon, Haycock, Penna. (redware)	*S. Singer* (inscribed)
Smith, Fife & Co., Philadelphia, Penna. (porcelain)	*Smith, Fife & Co.* (painted in red)
Smith, J. C., Mogadore, O. (stoneware)	SMITH MOGADORE OHIO (impressed)

Smith, Thomas C. & Sons, New York, N. Y.
(porcelain)

Impressed or Printed

```
 _____            _____
(  UNION         )          (  UNION         )
(  PORCELAIN     )          (  PORCELAIN     )
(  WORKS         )          (  WORKS         )
(  GREENPOINT    )          (  N.Y.          )
(  N.Y.          )          (_____)
(_____)
```

```
    _____
   / UNION  \
  / PORCELAIN \
  |  WORKS    |
  |  N.Y.     |
  |_____|
```

Impressed or Printed

Smith, Willoughby, Womelsdorf, Penna.
(stoneware)

W. SMITH
(or)
SMITH
(or)
WOMELSDORF
(impressed)

Somerset Pottery Works, Somerset, Mass.
(stoneware)

SOMERSET
POTTERY WORKS
SOMERSET, MASS.
(impressed)

Southern Porcelain Co., Kaolin, S. C.
(Parian, white earthenware)

```
   _____
  |  SP Co  |
  |  KAOLIN |
  |  S.C.   |
   _____/
```

Impressed

Spinner, David, Melford, Penna.
(redware)

David Spinner
(inscribed)

Stephens & Tams, Trenton, N. J.
(white granite)

GREENWOOD POTTERY
(printed)

Printed

280

Summit China Co., Akron, O.
(white earthenware)

Printed

Swan Hill Pottery

see Carr

Swank, Hiram & Sons, Johnstown, Penna.
(stoneware)

HIRAM SWANK & SONS
JOHNSTOWN
PA.
(impressed)

Taft, J. S. & Co., Keene, N. H.
(art ware)

Printed

Taney, Jacob, Nockamixon, Penna.
(redware)

Jacob Taney
(inscribed)

Tomlinson, Lewis K., Dryville, Penna.
(redware)

L. K. T.
(impressed)
(or)
L. K. T.
(inscribed)

Thompson, C. C., & Co., East Liverpool, O.
(white earthenware)

C.C.T.

Printed

Tucker, W. E., Philadelphia, Penna.
(porcelain)

Wm. E. Tucker
Philadelphia
(or)
Wm. E. Tucker
Philad.
(painted over glaze)

Tucker & Hemphill, Philadelphia, Pa.
(porcelain)

Tucker & Hemphill
Philadelphia
(or)
Tucker & Hemphill
Philad.
(painted over glaze)

Tupper, C., Portage Co., O.
(stoneware)

C. TUPPER
PORTAGE CO.
O.
(impressed)

Turner, William E., West Troy, N. Y.
(Rockingham)

WM. E. TURNER
WEST TROY
N. Y.
(impressed)

Union Porcelain Works

see Smith, Thomas C. & Sons

United States Pottery Co., Bennington, Vt.
(Parian, Rockingham)

Impressed   Raised Relief

Vance Faience Co., Tiltonville, O.
(Rockingham)

Van Horn & Boyden, Ashfield, Mass.
(stoneware)

VAN HORN & BOYDEN
ASHFIELD
MASS.
(impressed)

Vickers, Thomas and John, Caln and
Lionville, Penna.
(redware)

T. V.
(or)
V.
(inscribed)

Vodrey Bros., East Liverpool, O.
(Rockingham, white granite)

Printed

Wagoner Bros., Vanport, Penna.

WAGONER BROS.
VANPORT
PA.
(impressed)

Wands, I. H., Olean, N. Y.
(stoneware)

I. H. WANDS
(impressed)

Wait & Ricketts, Springfield, O.
(stoneware)

WAIT & RICKETTS
SPRINGFIELD
O.
(impressed)

Warwick China Co., Wheeling, W. Va.
(white earthenware)

Printed

Warne & Letts, South Amboy, N. J.
(stoneware)

WARNE & LETTS
(or)
T. W. J. L.
(or)
J. L.
(impressed)

Webster & Seymour, Hartford, Conn.
(stoneware)

WEBSTER & SEYMOUR
(impressed)

Webster, C., & Son., Hartford, Conn.
(stoneware)

C. WEBSTER & SON
(impressed)

Weber, J. A., Barnesville, Penna.
(redware)

J. A. WEBER
(impressed)

Weeks, Cook & Weeks, Akron, O.
(stoneware)

WEEKS, COOK & WEEKS
AKRON, O.
(raised relief)

Wheeling Pottery Co., Wheeling, W. Va.
(white earthenware)

Printed

White & Wood, Binghamton, N. J.
(stoneware)

WHITE & WOOD
(impressed)

Whiteman, T. W., Perth Amboy, N. J.
(stoneware)

T. W. WHITEMAN
(impressed)

Wingender, Chas. & Bro.,
    Haddonfield, N. J.
(stoneware)

HADDONFIELD, N. J.
T. W. & BRO.
(impressed)

Willetts Mfg. Co., Trenton, N. J.

Printed

Williams & Reppert, Greensboro, Penna.
(stoneware)

WILLIAMS & REPPERT
GREENSBORO
PA.
(impressed or stencilled in
blue)

Woodruff, M., Cortland, N. Y.
(stoneware)

M. WOODRUFF
CORTLAND
N. Y.
(impressed)

Wood, Dayton, O.
(brownware)

WOOD
POTTER
DAYTON
O.
(impressed)

Wores, H., Dover, O.
(stoneware)

H. WORES
(impressed)

Works, Laban H., Newport, O.
(stoneware)

L. H. WORKS
(impressed)

Zoar Pottery, Zoar, O.
(brownware)

ZOAR
(or)
S. PURDY
ZOAR
(impressed)

INDEX

287

INDEX

INDEX

INDEX

INDEX

Walker, George 205
Walker, N. U. 216
Wallace, Richard 163
Wallace & Chetwynd 219
Warder, Jeremiah 45, 174
Warne & Letts 47, 180, 283
Warwick China Co. 233, 283
Wands, I. H. 200
Washington, George (on pottery) 45, 104
Washington Pottery 175
Washington Stoneware Co. 233
Water Valley Pottery Co. 243
Watson, J. R. 174
Weaver, J. L. 229
Weaver 170
Weber, J. A. 164, 284
Webster, 201
Webster, C., & Son 193, 284
Webster, Elijah 208, 217
Webster & Seymour 193, 284
Wedgwood, Josiah 85, 97, 98, 152, 154
Weeks, Cook & Weeks 207, 284
Weidle 169
Weigner, Nathan 166
Weise 179
Weise, Henry 168
Weise, James 171
Weise, William 179
Welker, Adam 223
Weller, Samuel 220
Wells, Joseph 232
Wells, S. 232
West, Hardwick & Co. 217
West Virginia China Co. 233
West Virginia Pottery Co. 208
Western Stoneware Co. 224
Wetmore, Samuel J. & Co. 194
Weygandt, Cornelius x, xi, 13, 131
Wheatley, Thomas 212
Wheaton, George 233
Wheeler, L. D. 199
Wheeler & Wood 199
Whieldon 15, 58
Wheeling Pottery Co. 233
White, Dennis 243

White, N. A., & Sons 204
White, Noah 69, 204
White, Noah, & Son 204
White & Wood 189, 285
Whiteman, T. W. 48, 174, 285
Whitman, Robinson & Co. 206
Whittemore, Daniel 200
Whittemore, Joseph 200
Wilbur, Alfred 234
Wiley, Martin 173
Willetts Manufacturing Co. 182
Williams, J. W. 240
Williams & McCoy 229
Williams & Reppert 68, 221, 285
Wilson 197
Wilson, James 202
Wilson, Job 201
Wilson Pottery 55
Wilson, Samuel 222, 232
Winfel, R. 227
Wingender, Charles, & Bro. 168, 285
Winterhalter, Ferdinand 167
Wolfe, William 87, 236
Wood 213, 285
Wood & Brownfield 105
Wood, Enoch 199
Woodman, Samuel 202
Woodruff, M. 191, 285
Woodward, Blakeley & Co. 76, 78, 215
Woodward & Vodrey 215
Woodworth, F., & Co. 190
Wores, H. 213, 285
Works, Iaban H. 225, 285
Worcester, Samuel 218
Wylie Bros. 215
Wylie, John 218, 228

Yates, Bennett & Allen 182
York, H. F. 239
Young, Samuel 223
Young, William, & Sons 49, 113, 182

Zanesville Stoneware Co. 234
Zittel, D. P. 242
Zoar Pottery 234, 285

NAMES OF PLACES

Adams County, Penna. 9, 186
Akron, Ohio (see Springfield, Ohio) 18, 69, 77, 205, 206, 230
Albany, N. Y. 21, 59, 186
Amana, Iowa 71, 122, 207
Allentown, Penna. 162
Amesbury, Mass. 187

Anderson's Landing, Penna. 207
Anna, Ill. (see Lowell)
Ann Arbor, Mich. 207
Annapolis, Ind. 69, 207
Arab, Ala. 235
Ashfield, Mass. 187
Athens, N. Y. 59, 187

298

INDEX

INDEX

INDEX

Pfeiffer's Corner, Penna. 173
Perry, Mo. 227
Philadelphia, Penna. 14, 44, 45, 46, 50, 55, 174, 175, 176, 177
Phoenixville, Penna. 109, 177
Pittsburgh, Penna. 19, 67, 74, 75, 105, 144, 227, 228
Pittston, Penna. 177
Plumstead, Penna. 177
Plymouth, N. H. 201
Porter's Station, Tenn. 240
Portage County, Ohio 235
Portland, Me. 201
Portsmouth, N. H. 201
Pottertown, Ky. 240
Poughkeepsie, N. Y. 201
Poulteney, Vt. 202
Powder Valley, Penna. 44, 177
Price's Landing, W. Va. 228
Providence, R. I. 202
Putnam, Ohio 68, 77, 228

Quakertown, Penna. 177
Quincy, Mass. 100

Rahway, N. J. 177, 178
Ravenna, Ohio 228
Reading, Penna. 178
Red Oak, Ill. 228
Red Wing, Minn. 70, 228
Richmond, Ind. 229
Richmond, Ky. 240
Rich Valley, Penna. 178
Roberta, Ga. 241
Rochester, N. Y. 202
Rock Hill, Penna. 43
Rock House, Ohio 229
Rockland Township, Penna. 178
Rodentown, Ala. 241
Rome, N. Y. 202
Rondout, N. Y. 202
Ronk, Penna. 179
Roscoe, Ohio 229
Roseville, Ohio 229
Rupley, Ill. 69, 229

Salem, Mass. 56, 57, 202
Salem, Ohio 68, 229, 230
Salem Cross Roads, Penna. 230
Salina, Ill. 230
Santa Fe, Ill. 230
Sandyville, O. 230
Sargeant's Bluff, Ia. 69, 230
Savannah, Ga. 96, 97, 241
Sayreville, N. J. 47, 179

Seagrove, N. C. 241
Seidersville, Penna. 179
Seneca County, Ohio 234
Shartlesville, Penna. 179
Shepardstown, W. Va. 179
Sherburne, N. Y. 202
Shoals, Ind. 230
Shoemakersville, Penna. 179
Silvertown, Penna. 179
Somerset, Mass. 202
Somerset, N. J. 179
Somerset, Ohio 230
Somerville, Mass. 202
Soudertown, Penna. 179
South Amboy, N. J. 47, 49, 63, 179, 180
South Ashfield, Mass. (see Ashfield)
South Norwalk, Conn. (see Norwalk)
Springfield, Ohio 230
Spring Hill, Ark. 241
Spring Mills, Penna. 180
St. Clairsville, Ohio 230
St. Johnsbury, Vt. 59, 60, 203
St. Louis, Mo. 230
St. Mary's, Md. 50, 180
Steeds, N. C. 85, 134, 137, 241
Steubenville, Ohio 68, 231
Stevens Pottery, Ga. 241
Stillwater, N. Y. 202
Stonetown, Penna. 180
Stonington, Conn. 59, 203
Strasburg, Va. 16, 35, 86, 122, 134, 137, 140, 241
Sulphur Fork, Tenn. 242
Summit County, Ohio 69
Symmes Creek, Ohio 231
Syracuse, N. Y. 109, 113, 203

Tallmadge, Ohio 231
Thomasville, Ga. (see Jugtown, Ga.)
Thurmont, Md. 50, 180, 181
Tiltonville, Ohio 63, 231
Toone, Tenn. 242
Trenton, N. J. 46, 49, 75, 78, 110, 113, 123, 151, 181, 182, 183
Troy, Ind. 74, 77, 88, 106, 231, 232
Troy, N. Y. 203
Tulpehocken Township, Penna. 183, 184
Tuscaloosa, Ala. 87, 91, 242
Tuscaloosa County, Ala. 242
Tuscarawas County, Ohio 68, 143, 234
Tylersport, Penna. 43, 184

Upper Alton, Ill. 232
Upper Berne Township, Penna. 184
Upper Hanover, Penna. 184

302

INDEX

GENERAL

INDEX

Glaze, lead 6, 11, 13, 41, 42, 58, 128
Glaze mixer 11
Glaze, salt 6, 18, 19, 23, 39, 139
Glaze, smear 25, 110, 133, 157

Harvesters' jug 34, 131
Hotel ware, china (see Semi-porcelain)
Hound-handled pitchers (see Pitchers)

Ironstone 6, 153

Jackfield pottery (see Jet Ware)
Jasper 65, 154, 316
Jars 10, 28-31, 57
Jet ware 14, 44, 51, 58, 132
Jugs 31, 57
Jugs, gray-beard (see Bellarmines)
Jugs, harvesters' (see Harvesters' jug)
Jugs, syrup 31

Kick-wheel 10
Kilns 9, 12, 13, 19, 21, 22, 23, 54, 89, 90

Lamps 35, 72, 131, 140, 147
Lead glaze (see Glaze)
Lotus Ware 114

Majolica 6, 51, 52, 64, 108, 109, 112, 154
Manganese oxide 13, 58, 83, 131
"Marbled Ware" 63, 148
Mica 14, 132
Moulds 11, 17, 20, 21, 25, 26, 60, 133, 134, 143, 147
Mugs 33, 34

Pans 9, 10, 99
Parian 61, 64, 65, 78, 88, 108, 110, 111, 113, 114, 123, 156, 157
Pipe-clay 40
Pitchers 32, 33, 57
Pitchers, hound-handled 21, 26, 46, 48, 51, 52, 63, 76, 87
Porcelain, hard-paste 3, 45, 48, 102, 103, 104, 112, 155, 156, 157
Porcelain, soft-paste 3, 65, 98, 99, 100, 108, 109, 112, 123, 155, 157
Potters' wheel (see Wheel)
Pug-mill 9, 11, 99

Queensware 20, 45, 75, 85, 98, 152

Rebecca teapot 21, 51
Redware 8, 27, 40, 41, 42, 43, 44, 45, 46, 50, 51, 53, 54, 57, 59, 60, 67, 68, 70, 71, 74, 83, 84, 86, 88, 120, 121, 139, 147, 148

Redware, salt-glazed 71, 128
Rib 10
Ring jugs (see Harvesters' jugs)
Ring-pits (see Pans)
Roach traps 34
Rockingham 7, 20, 21, 25, 26, 33, 45, 46, 48, 49, 50, 51, 60, 61, 62, 63, 64, 74, 75, 76, 77, 78, 104, 112, 113, 147
Rogers groups 65

Saggers 12
Salt glaze (see Glaze)
Salt-glazed redware (see Redware)
Salt-glazed tableware 39
Scratched ware 15
Scroddle ware 62, 151
Semi-porcelain 3, 6, 46, 109, 113, 153
Sgraffito 15, 41, 42, 83, 121, 138
Silver lustre 45
Slip clays (see Clays, white-burning)
Slip-coated ware 14, 44, 67, 71, 86, 134
Slip-cup 15
Slip-ware 15, 16, 17, 41, 42, 54, 58, 59, 84, 100, 121, 137
Smalt (see Zaffre)
Smear glaze (see Glaze)
Smoother 10
Staffordshire potters 48, 49, 74, 76, 82
Stoneware 3, 6, 17, 18, 19, 42, 43, 46, 47, 48, 51, 54, 55, 56, 59, 60, 67, 68, 69, 71, 72, 73, 77, 91, 121, 122, 139, 143
Stoneware clays (see Clays)

Terra-cotta (see Art Ware)
Tile, floor and wall 45
Tools, potters' 15

Vases 35, 36

Wet-pans (see Pans)
White Granite 45, 46, 49, 64, 65, 69, 71, 78, 88, 107, 108, 109, 111, 112, 113, 114, 123, 153, 154
Whiteware (white earthenware) 3, 6, 23, 24, 45, 49, 51, 69, 70, 74, 83, 85, 100, 101, 123, 152
Whiteware, transfer printed 49, 51, 105, 107, 123, 153
Wheels, potters' 9, 26

Yellow-ware 7, 23, 25, 48, 61, 64, 69, 74, 76, 77, 78, 88, 102, 104, 113, 151

Zaffre 19, 87, 99

304